The Weekend Real Estate Investor

James O. Parker

Attorney at Law

SPHINX® PUBLISHING
AN IMPRINT OF SOURCEBOOKS, INC.®
NAPERVILLE, ILLINOIS
www.SphinxLegal.com

First Edition: 2006

Published by: **Sphinx® Publishing, An Imprint of Sourcebooks, Inc.®**

Naperville Office
P.O. Box 4410
Naperville, Illinois 60567-4410
630-961-3900
Fax: 630-961-2168
www.sourcebooks.com
www.SphinxLegal.com

This publication is designed to provide accurate and authoritative information in
regard to the subject matter covered. It is sold with the understanding that the pub-
lisher is not engaged in rendering legal, accounting, or other professional service. If
legal advice or other expert assistance is required, the services of a competent professional person should be sought.

*From a Declaration of Principles Jointly Adopted by a Committee of the
American Bar Association and a Committee of Publishers and Associations*

This product is not a substitute for legal advice.

Disclaimer required by Texas statutes.

Library of Congress Cataloging-in-Publication Data

Parker, James O., 1948-
    The weekend real estate investor / by James O. Parker.-- 1st ed.
        p. cm.
    ISBN-13: 978-1-57248-557-0 (pbk. : alk. paper)
    ISBN-10: 1-57248-557-4 (pbk. : alk. paper)
    1. Real estate investment--United States. 2. Real estate business--United
States. 3. Real property tax--United States.   I. Title.
HD255.P374 2006
332.63'240973--dc22
                                    2005037414

Printed and bound in the United States of America.
SB — 10 9 8 7 6 5 4 3 2 1

Contents

Introduction

There are a number of courses or programs promoted over the television, Internet, and elsewhere that promise to reveal the secrets to becoming wealthy—practically overnight—from investing in real estate. Furthermore, they assure us that having no capital to work with and a bad credit rating will not be a problem. The truth is that the people becoming wealthy from these offerings are the people promoting them. There is no doubt that real estate ownership offers an opportunity to accumulate wealth. However, in order to profit from real estate ownership, it is necessary to know enough to wisely select properties, intelligently negotiate to buy them, choose appropriate methods of financing the purchases, properly manage investment properties, and take advantage of the tax laws in order to legally minimize tax liabilities on gains and earnings from real estate.

Since individuals who want to acquire real estate usually must have some money to pay down on property, and perhaps additional funds to do repairs or cover other costs, this book contains some basic advice on how to accumulate savings. There is also a section devoted to the concept of determining a party's wealth by calculating his or her net worth. The concept of net worth is often distorted by the hucksters in their zeal to sell their programs.

Whether real estate is acquired for use as a personal residence, for rental activity, or to repair and resell, there are common characteristics in the acquisition process. A major section of the book is devoted to these basic guidelines for acquiring real estate. Among the topics addressed are performing the due diligence necessary in selecting a property for purchase, negotiating and preparing a purchase contract, and dealing with sellers who breach their real estate contracts.

For many buyers, the purchase of a personal residence is the only involvement that they want in the real estate market. However, a party's personal residence will often prove to be his or her best investment. An entire chapter of this book is devoted to maximizing the investment aspects of a personal residence. There is also a chapter that explains how to finance personal residences, and another chapter on tax laws affecting owners of real estate used for a personal residence.

Buying properties to rent out is what comes to most people's minds when they think of investing in real estate. Major portions of this book relate to selecting, buying, financing, and managing rental properties. There is also a chapter devoted entirely to the federal tax treatment of revenues from rental real estate.

A growing number of investors have become involved in the purchase of property for resale. Chapters in this book discuss buying properties for resale, financing such properties, and the taxation of income received by those who are regarded as real estate dealers.

One of the most appealing aspects of the real estate market is that no matter what level of involvement you are interested in, there is a place for you. However, as with most things, those with superior knowledge usually achieve superior results. What I have tried to accomplish in this book is to share with you the benefit of over twenty-five years of experience as a real estate owner, investor, speculator, and attorney, involved in handling real estate transactions and dealing with tax issues related to real estate. It is my hope that the information you gain from this book will empower you to succeed in securing your financial future by aiding you in formulating a truly workable strategy of real estate investment.

Chapter 1:

The Concept of Wealth

One of the many infomercials recently aired in the wee hours of the morning, aimed at the insomniacs and second shift workers in the process of winding down from their night's work, promised viewers that it would reveal the secrets to wealth accumulation. The announcer offered personal testimony as proof in support of the claim, and enthusiastically proclaimed that John T. of Scranton, Pennsylvania had followed the program's steps and had gone from being broke to becoming a millionaire in a mere four months. An individual identified as John T. then appeared, and after vouching for the fact that he had, in fact, been virtually penniless, proceeded to explain how he had become a millionaire in just four months. John T. explained that by following the procedures set forth in the program being offered for sale by the creators of the infomercial, he had acquired an apartment complex for $400,000, three duplexes worth $200,000, and a group of five houses valued at $450,000, all with no money down through owner financing. John then added up the value of his properties and proudly showed that he was now a millionaire with $50,000 to spare. The program continued with similar testimonials, followed by the particulars of how to purchase the detailed program being offered for sale.

Looking at Real Numbers

It is rare for owners of highly desirable properties to be willing to sell them and finance the sales themselves with no down payment. They simply do not have to resort to owner financing in order to sell good properties at their fair market values. However, owner financing with no down payment may be the only way to sell properties that are in run-down condition or in declining neighborhoods at prices that the sellers would like to get. Even if John's properties are worth what he paid for them, he is not a millionaire by any accepted accounting measure.

In order to get an accurate picture of John's worth, consider his net worth, rather than the gross value of his assets. Consider not only the value of John's assets, but also the amount of indebtedness that he owes on those assets. Taking the net worth approach to John's financial situation results in a vastly different conclusion concerning his financial status. The following balance sheet shows a realistic picture of John's net worth.

ASSETS		LIABILITIES	
Realty	$1,050,000	Mortgages on Realty	$1,050,000
Total Assets	$1,050,000	*Total Liabilities*	$1,050,000

Net Worth   -0-

In reality, John has not generated an increase in his net worth at all by acquiring those various pieces of real estate. In fact, by obligating himself to pay mortgages totaling more than a million dollars, John has subjected himself to considerable risk of default, and if he should fail to make his mortgage payments as agreed, the consequences could be dire.

Most mortgages are *recourse financing*, which means that if the debtor defaults on mortgage payments, the creditor is not limited to merely foreclosing the mortgage and selling the property to raise funds to pay the balance of the mortgage. The creditor may also seek recovery from the debtor for any remaining unpaid deficiency after applying the proceeds from the foreclosure sale to the mortgage balance.

Example: *Sam borrowed $150,000 in order to buy a car wash. He granted the lender a mortgage on the property to secure the loan and signed a promissory note in favor of the creditor in the amount of $150,000. The note provided for full recourse against Sam in the event of default. After about a year, an increase in crime in the area where the car wash was located caused business at the car wash to seriously decline. Sam was unable to make his mortgage payments.*

At a foreclosure sale of the car wash, the property sold for $120,000, of which $5,000 was used to cover the cost of the foreclosure. The remaining $115,000 balance was applied to the unpaid mortgage balance (plus accrued interest), which totaled $149,650, leaving an unpaid deficiency of $34,650. The creditor is entitled to file suit against Sam and obtain a judgment against him for the $34,650 deficiency, plus attorney's fees (if the note that Sam signed provided for attorney's fees, as most notes do). Attorney's fees awarded in such cases are often equal to one-third of the judgment amount. If that were the amount of the fees awarded in Sam's case, the total judgment against him would reach $46,200 plus court costs and additional interest, as provided in the original note or by state law.

It is not uncommon for properties that are sold at foreclosure sales to bring less than their fair market values, since the successful bidder at such sales must generally pay the full amount of the bid in cash soon after the sale, thereby eliminating buyers who must obtain their purchase money through traditional mortgage procedures. In situations in which the debtor overpaid for properties due to the enticement of owner financing, the likelihood of a large deficiency judgment is even greater.

The Impact of Liquidity on Net Worth

Even in situations in which a party has acquired property for its fair market value, there is considerable potential to develop a distorted picture of the individual's net worth. A major source of these distortions is the failure to take into consideration the costs of converting a party's assets into cash, a process known as *liquidating* the assets. The degree of difficulty typically encountered in liquidating assets varies widely among the different categories of assets, as do the costs of liquidation. There may even be considerable variance in the liquidity of various components within a class of assets.

For example, securities, such as stocks and bonds that are traded publicly on an organized exchange, can generally be sold almost immediately during business hours at or near their fair market values, and the commissions associated with such transactions can be less than $10 per transaction when they are conducted by brokerage firms that operate through the Internet. On the other hand, a small holding of stock in a closely held corporation, which is a company with few stockholders that is not publicly traded, may be difficult to sell at all, since the only people likely to be interested in acquiring such stock are those who already own some stock in the company.

Some assets are relatively marketable, but the cost of selling those assets is typically relatively high. The usual commission charged by real estate brokers is 6% or 7%. However, the true impact of the commission in most real estate transactions is much greater than the nominal rate provided for in the listing contract between the real estate broker and the property owner. This is due to the fact that the commission is typically based on the gross sale price of the property rather than the owner's *equity* in the property, which is its net price less indebtedness on the property. Furthermore, sellers of real estate must usually pay attorney's fees in connection with the closing of the sale of their property, and they generally must cover the cost of a *title search*, which is a compilation of the ownership history of the property that proves ownership and absence of tax delinquencies, judgments, and encumbrances, such as mortgages or tax liens. It is also common for sellers of real estate to pay some of the buyer's closing costs, either by negotiations or due to requirements of government agencies, such as the *Federal Housing Administration* (FHA), that insure buyer's mortgages. Typically, the costs associated with the sale of the property are not deducted from the selling price of the property before the commission is calculated.

Example: *John owns a duplex, which he listed for sale with a realtor and agreed to pay a commission of 6% of the sale price in the event of a sale. The realtor presented John with an offer of $180,000 for the duplex and John accepted it. The attorney who closed the transaction for John charged him $500, the title search on the property cost John $200, and the contract called for John to provide the buyer with a survey, which cost $300. The balance on John's mortgage at the time of the sale, which had to be paid from the proceeds of the sale, was $162,000. The realtor's commission of 6% cost John $10,800. The settlement of John's sale is as follows:*

Gross Sales Price of Property	
Less Cost Associated with Sale	*$180,000*
Realtor's Commission	*$10,800*
Attorney's Fees	*$500*
Survey	*$300*
Title Search	*$200*
Total Costs	*$11,800*
Net Sale Price	*$168,200*
Less Payment of Mortgage Balance	*$162,000*
Net Proceeds to John	*$6,200*

Although the realtor's commission was only 6% of the gross sale price of the property, the commission ended up exceeding the owner's net proceeds from the sale by a substantial amount. Furthermore, prior to the sale, if John had been determining his net worth, he would have likely shown the duplex as contributing

$18,000 toward that figure, since it had a value of $180,000 with a mortgage of only $162,000. As a result, John would have substantially overstated his net worth attributable to the duplex, since the net proceeds that he could actually realize from its sale were really only about a third of his $18,000 gross equity in the property. In fact, John might have even been able to find an appraiser willing to value the duplex at more than he eventually sold it for, since properties often sell for less than their appraised values, resulting in an even more inflated value of his net worth. For example, if the property had been appraised for $187,000, John might have believed that his equity in the duplex was $25,000, and the $6,200 that he actually netted from its sale would be less than 25% of that amount.

The transaction costs associated with liquidating an investment are often not the most significant sacrifices that investors must make in converting their investments to cash. The degree to which an investor must reduce the price of an asset in order to sell it quickly varies greatly among the many investments available. Anything that is traded regularly on an organized exchange (stocks and bonds, precious metals, or commodities—such as cotton or grain), can be sold rapidly through those exchanges at their prevailing market prices. However, since the prices of assets sold on such exchanges fluctuate—sometimes wildly—in response to market forces, even those who are holding such investments may not view them as being particularly liquid, since it will be necessary for them to coordinate the sale of those assets with upswings in the market in order to maximize the returns on their investments.

There are options available to investors whereby they can significantly reduce—even eliminate—both the transaction costs and the necessity to discount the price of their investments in order to liquidate them. Deposits in savings accounts will not suffer any decline in nominal value, and may be withdrawn without penalty at any time during banking hours, or perhaps even after banking hours through online banking services. The extremely liquid nature of bank savings accounts is very appealing, but it comes at a dear price. The rate of return currently available on savings accounts is less than 2%, and some do not even pay 1%. Since the current rate of inflation in the U.S. exceeds the rate of return on savings accounts, those who rely on savings accounts as an investment will actually suffer a loss in purchasing power (or *real rate of return,* as it is commonly called).

Generally, in order to boost the potential for return on investments, investors must sacrifice liquidity. Fortunately, there are a variety of combinations of risk and liquidity available to investors. For instance, those who are willing to sacrifice a relatively small amount of liquidity in return for some improvement in yield can put their money in *certificates of deposit* (CDs). They are available with maturity dates ranging from a few months to several years, and generally pay higher yields at the lengthier maturities. The agreements that depositors are required to sign when they put their money in CDs usually provide that the certificates may not be redeemed early unless the bank consents to early redemption, or the depositor dies or needs the money for some emergency purpose, such as medical care. However, in practice, banks permit early withdrawal, but with a penalty equal to some number of months of interest that the CD pays. The penalty for early withdrawal of a CD with less than a year until maturity is typically one month's interest, whereas the penalty for early withdrawal of a CD with a year or more remaining until maturity will generally run from as little as three months' interest up to a year's interest.

Investors who place the potential for high yields at the forefront of their investment objectives generally must be willing to face extreme limitations on their liquidity in order to achieve their desired results. Among such investors would be those who choose to invest in collectibles, like sports cards, antiques, precious stones, or vintage automobiles. Although such investments offer the opportunity to realize sizable returns to those who are knowledgeable enough to distinguish the truly collectible items from those that are merely run-of-the-mill or counterfeits, it is often time-consuming and expensive to find prospects within a limited pool of buyers who are willing and able to pay the full market value for such items. Sales of collectibles that must be effected quickly regardless of price, often referred to as *distress sales,* may yield only a fraction of their true value.

Looking at a True Financial Position

Once a person's net worth is viewed in terms of the liquidity of one's investments, which is simply their ability to be converted into cash at or near their fair market value, the investor's financial position may look dramatically different. This can be readily seen in the following example, involving a comparison of two individuals' net worths, which appear to be equal, but have dramatically different degrees of liquidity.

Example: *George has calculated his net worth to be about $1,500,000. His assets, which are almost entirely real estate, are shown on the following balance sheet.*

ASSETS		LIABILITIES	
Cash	$10,000		
Personal Residence		Mortgage on Personal	
And Contents	$150,000	Residence	$100,000
Apartment Complex	$2,000,000	Mortgage on Apartment	
		Complex	$1,600,000
Shopping Center	$1,500,000	Mortgage on Shopping	
		Center	$1,200,000
Office Building	$900,000	Mortgage on Office	
		Building	$700,000
Duplex on Maple St.	$200,000	Mortgage on Maple St.	
		Duplex	$150,000
Warehouse	$1,300,000	Mortgage on	
		Warehouse	$1,100,000
Convenience Store		Mortgage on Convenience	
Building	$500,000	Store Building	$400,000
Parking Lot	$200,000	Mortgage on Parking Lot	$50,000
Various Single Family		Mortgages on Single Family	
Houses	$800,000	Houses	$650,000
TOTAL ASSETS	$7,560,000	TOTAL LIABILITIES	$6,050,000

NET WORTH = $1,510,000

His brother, Jerry, also has a net worth of about $1,500,000. Jerry's holdings are radically different than his brother's, as shown on the following balance sheet.

ASSETS		LIABILITIES	
Cash	$8,000		
Personal Residence Contents	$150,000		-0-
Certificates of Deposit	$1,000,000		
Treasury Bills	$350,000		
TOTAL ASSETS	$1,508,000	TOTAL LIABILITIES	-0-

NET WORTH = $1,508,000

Although the brothers have almost identical net worths, their financial positions are vastly different in many ways. If, for some reason, George were to need to liquidate a sufficient amount of his holdings to raise a million dollars in cash, he might have to sell virtually his entire real estate holdings. A commission of 6% on sales of $7.5 million worth of real estate would come to $450,000 and his various closing costs could easily amount to another $20,000. Once these combined costs of $470,0000 are subtracted from his $1,510,000 net worth, the remaining $1,040,000 would barely exceed his million dollar target. In fact, it would not be surprising for George to have to agree to sell his properties for somewhat less than their appraised values in order to attract buyers. A discount of even as little as 5% on his properties would reduce his gross receipts from the sales by $375,000, which, even after allowing for the fact that he would pay $22,500 less in real estate commission, would leave him well short of his million-dollar goal. Furthermore, it generally takes several weeks, or even months, to liquidate real estate, and if it is imperative that George raise cash quickly, he would be forced to discount the sale prices of his holdings more deeply, which could result in his netting very little from their sale. In essence, George simply may not be able to liquidate his real estate holdings in a timely manner and realize anything close to the net worth that he is showing on his balance sheet.

If Jerry were to need to liquidate a sufficient amount of his holdings in order to raise a million dollars in cash relatively quickly, he should be able to do so at a cost that is much less than George's. If Jerry's CDs and Treasury Bills are near their maturities, he can simply exchange them for cash upon maturity with no transaction costs whatsoever. If he does not have enough holdings maturing soon enough, he can sell his Treasury Bills for a small commission and redeem CDs at a penalty that could be as little as one month's interest, depending on the number of months remaining until maturity. A wise strategy in placing substantial funds in CDs is to stagger maturities, so that if the need for cash arises, there will always be some CDs that are relatively close to maturity. If Jerry has followed this course of action, he should be able to raise the million dollars that he needs at a modest transaction cost, since he will need to liquidate only about two-thirds of his assets and can hold on to those that would be the most costly to liquidate.

Opportunity Cost of Investments

The analysis of George's and Jerry's efforts to liquidate a million dollars of their assets may make it seem that investing in highly liquid assets is the only sensible investment strategy, and investing in real estate is foolish. This is simply not true. Liquidity is only one of the many factors that should be considered in making investment decisions. The comparison involving George and Jerry started with the assumption that they each needed to liquidate a million dollars of their assets relatively quickly, which would be a relatively uncommon situation. If George was offered an opportunity to participate in an investment that required him to raise a million dollars in cash relatively quickly, he would simply have to face the fact that this would likely not be a wise choice for him, or perhaps not even a possibility, and forgo the opportunity. With the almost infinite investment opportunities available and the limited resources available to investors to participate in the various alternatives, virtually every investment decision carries with it not only the actual cost of the investment, but also the cost of having to forgo the alternatives that were not chosen (a concept generally referred to as *opportunity cost*).

Therefore, George's inability to rapidly convert his real estate holdings into cash in order to take advantage of an alternative investment opportunity should be viewed merely as a normal opportunity cost of real estate investments, rather than a condemnation of such investments. Investors who commonly encounter investment opportunities that require substantial liquidity, and who would like to be in a position to take advantage of those opportunities, would be wise not to invest the bulk of their capital in real estate.

Choosing Your Investment Blend

The concepts of liquidity and opportunity cost are somewhat related. An investor who has chosen to hold assets in cash or in a form that can readily be converted to cash (such as CDs or Treasury Bills, referred to as *near-cash assets*) will have done so at the sacrifice of investments in less liquid assets. However, the opportunity cost of such a choice may be viewed merely as a temporary cost, or perhaps as a postponement of the party's investment decision, since such assets can readily be converted to other forms of investments in the future.

Liquidity, even with all of its virtues, has its shortcomings. Generally, the more liquid that an investment is, the smaller its earning potential. The rate of return on CDs is generally rather modest, and even if the bank that issued the CD earns exceptional profits for the year, it will not share those earnings with CD holders beyond the agreed-upon interest rate. On the other hand, real estate, generally speaking, has appreciated steadily over the long term, and has gone up remarkably in value during some intervals, such as periods of relatively high inflation. There is no ideal blend of liquidity and risk that is perfect for every investor. Choosing a good investment for a given person requires that consideration be given to factors such as the age of the party, whether the investor has the disposition to cope with market fluctuations, time available to devote to management of investments, the investor's expertise and experience in making investment decisions, and the likelihood that the party may need to quickly convert investments to cash in order to meet basic needs or pay obligations. In fact, as a given individual's circumstances change over time, so will the characteristics of what constitutes a wise investment for that person.

•   •   •   •   •

It is one thing to understand how to calculate net worth and to consider the impact of liquidity on the concept of net worth, but figuring out how to acquire net worth to calculate is another issue altogether. Over the course of the next few chapters, attention will be focused on various techniques for wealth accumulation through real estate acquisitions. There are chapters on accumulating start-up capital, investment options that are available, choosing properties, buying properties, financing properties, managing real estate investments, and the taxation of income from real estate.

Chapter 2:

Getting Started

There are a number of promoters who claim to offer a pathway to riches through real estate investments that can be made with no money down. Undoubtedly, there are such opportunities, but they are relatively rare and generally have some serious drawbacks. Few sellers must resort to seller financing with no money down in order to attract a buyer. An investor who has no money to pay down on the purchase of investment assets will not be able to participate in the purchase of any of the choices that require a down payment, and will be limited only to the relatively few that are available without a down payment. However, the investor who has money for a down payment has considerably more choices.

Developing a Savings Plan

There are always going to be those fortunate few who inherit large sums of money, win a lottery, get a nice settlement from a lawsuit, or otherwise come into a sizeable sum of money all at once. However, most simply have to accumulate investment capital through old-fashioned thrift. The person who waits for the big score in order to have money to invest will probably never have any investment capital.

Thrift is a combination of smarts and discipline—but mostly discipline—that leads to a habit of spending less money than you make. Do not get discouraged because you are only able to save small amounts of money on a regular basis instead of large chunks at a time. For those who have been in the habit of spending more than they make and going deeper and deeper into debt, changing their spending habits to allow for even a modest amount of savings is a major accomplishment. Also, once people who have not been savers in the past start to accumulate some savings, they usually feel so good about their accomplishments that they are encouraged to do more. Even a fairly small, but regular, savings plan that is supplemented by windfalls, such as tax refunds or bonuses from employers, can result in a significant accumulation of money over a period of time.

Controlling Spending

Those who have managed to become financially independent through a process of slow accumulation of capital generally work as hard, if not harder, at spending their money as they do at making it. The person who makes an extra $100 may have to pay certain costs associated with earning that money, such as the expense of commuting to and from work an extra day, and will almost certainly have to pay taxes out of the extra earnings. It would not be at all unusual for a worker who earned an additional $100 to net only about $65 after paying taxes and costs related to earning the extra money. On the other hand, if you cut your spending by $100, you will have the full $100 to show for it.

There are a number of ways to cut spending in small increments. Expenditures for food can be cut by using grocery coupons, serving a few meals a week that do not include a meat dish (there may be health benefits from this, as well), buying fewer carry-out or heat-and-serve meals, and preparing grocery lists before you go shopping—and sticking to the list instead of buying on impulse. Those who eat out often can save significantly by cutting back on the number of times they dine out, using discount coupons for meals (these are often available in books sold for modest prices by charitable groups to raise funds), and carrying lunches from home rather than picking something up at a fast food outlet.

Some people buy clothing only when they wear something out and absolutely must replace it. They do not really have any opportunity to increase their savings by cutting their expenses for clothing. Others shop for clothing with such regularity that buying clothes has become a source of entertainment, if not an obsession. Those who have taken clothes buying to an extreme can (and probably must) reallocate much of what they are spending on clothing and generate a significant amount of savings. Most people's clothes buying habits fall somewhere between the two extremes, and therefore, offer varying opportunities for savings. In order to curtail frivolous expenditures for clothing, it is necessary to be able to confine the purchases to fulfilling genuine needs rather than using the purchases to satisfy a whim or to stay entertained.

Spending on entertainment varies widely from household to household. Those who have developed the habit of spending heavily on entertainment and are willing to forgo some of that spending in the interest of their future financial security can often generate significant savings by trimming these expenditures. Often the atmosphere at entertainment facilities causes otherwise conservative spenders to overspend on such things as ridiculously priced souvenirs or refreshments. There are alternatives to consider, such as renting movies rather than going to theaters, or going on day trips to local areas of interest rather than taking elaborate vacations.

Those who are spending money to buy lottery tickets or to gamble in casinos simply must stop altogether. Not only are your chances of winning money in the long run remote, but gambling is addictive. Casino operators and lottery managers know how to entice people to risk money that they cannot afford to gamble. One casino operator, in rebuttal to the contention that gambling was causing financial hardship in the nearby community, stated that the average person that visited his establishment lost only a mere $85, which he contended was a very reasonable price to pay for an evening's entertainment. What he did not point out was that in order to have an average of an $85 loss for each of their patrons, the losers had to lose enough to cover the winnings of those who happened to win, and still produce the $85 average loss. Even if a person gambled at a casino often enough for the law of averages to result in an $85 loss per trip, the individual who goes to a casino just once a week will lose $4,420 a year.

Unfortunately, there are those who go to casinos far more often than once a week, and who feel compelled to gamble larger and larger amounts of money, who will literally gamble themselves into bankruptcy. Most people who develop compulsions to gamble start out gambling only occasionally and wagering only small amounts, but eventually are driven to gamble frequently and are not satisfied unless they wager larger and larger amounts. Casino gambling, playing the lottery, and other forms of gambling, such as gambling online, are simply not compatible with a sensible plan of wealth accumulation.

Financing Purchases

For most people, the purchase of major items, such as furniture, appliances, or automobiles, are made infrequently. Since such items are often financed, the financial impact of such purchases can usually be felt well past the date of the actual transaction. The fact that major purchases are often bought on credit means that buyers are shopping not only for the goods that they want, but also for the credit terms that are best for them. In today's marketplace, there are often a variety of terms available for purchases made on credit, and there may be a lot more to evaluating the options than merely comparing interest rates.

Merchants who sell appliances, furniture, and other relatively costly goods often provide credit to customers who want to finance their purchases. In most instances, the credit is not actually provided by the merchant, but is merely arranged for by the merchant, who secures financing for customers from a bank or finance company. It is not uncommon for the merchant to be compensated by the lender for having arranged the loan. As a result, the lender will need to charge additional interest or fees in connection with the loan in order to be able to afford to pay the merchant a commission for originating the loan and still be able to net its normal rate of return. Therefore, rather than making credit arrangements through a merchant that is selling goods, buyers can often find better rates by dealing directly with banks, credit unions, or finance companies.

More and more retailers are resorting to credit-related gimmicks to market their goods. Some offer deferments that do not require the customer to make payments for several months. However, the terms of some of these arrangements provide for accumulation of interest during the term of deferment, which causes the amount of the indebtedness to steadily increase before payments even begin. Still other merchants offer loans that provide for zero interest for a period of time. The most common pitfall associated with these loans is that they often have provisions stating that if the loan is not fully repaid by the end of the interest-free period, interest will then be imposed back to when the loan was first originated and added to the unpaid loan balance. This eliminates the zero-interest provisions of the loan.

Automobile Purchases

With the average cost of a new car now at about $30,000, the financial impact of buying a new vehicle is of major importance to most consumers. There are abundant choices of vehicles available to consumers, and a wealth of information concerning performance, economy, maintenance history, resale value, and dealer cost of the vehicles. It is not uncommon for manufacturers to offer several versions of the same vehicle, or to even offer essentially the same vehicle, under more than one nameplate. As a result, there may be such a wide range of offerings of a given vehicle that the highest-end version could cost more than twice as much as the most basic version.

Generally, there is a version of most vehicles that offers consumers good value for their money. Manufacturers often offer packages in which several popular options are bundled together and offered at a price that is significantly less than the cost of the options if they were bought individually. Options such as global positioning systems and entertainment systems are appealing, but they are expensive, costly to repair, sometimes require payment of monthly fees to keep them operational, and add little to the resale value of the vehicle. On the other hand, the absence of some of the more basic options, such as power windows and air conditioning, may make ownership of the vehicle much less enjoyable and can seriously reduce its resale value.

The great majority of motor vehicles sold in the U.S. are bought on credit. As a result, it is incumbent upon buyers to devote as much attention to shopping for the credit to make their vehicle purchases with as they do to shopping for the vehicles that they buy. Automobile dealers receive some form of compensation from the lenders on almost all of the loans that they arrange for their customers. Of course, arranging for financing through the selling dealer is more convenient for buyers than shopping for a loan through a bank or credit union, but it is almost certainly going to be more costly. Another aspect of automobile financing, apart from the actual loan itself, is the way in which vehicle sales representatives use the fact that automobile purchases are generally made on credit as a tool in marketing their products. Rather than talk in terms of what the cost of a vehicle or an option on that vehicle would be, they often price the item in terms of its impact on the buyer's monthly payments. Under this approach, a sunroof on a car may be presented as merely costing $24 a month, rather than $1,200, and the sportier version of the car would cost only $99 more a month, rather than an extra $5,000. This marketing approach may make the higher-priced choices seem appealingly cheap, but over the life of the loan, will claim thousands of the buyer's dollars that could have been set aside and used to finance investments or retire other debt.

Interest-Free Financing

New car buyers are now routinely offered discount financing as an enticement to select a particular vehicle. Some manufacturers have even offered interest-free loans on various models. However, interest-free automobile loans may not be as attractive as they appear.

For one thing, it is not uncommon for manufacturers to require very high credit scores in order to qualify for zero-interest loans. This limits the availability of such loans to only those few buyers with unblemished credit histories. Still other interest-free loans are available for only relatively short maximum periods, such as thirty-six months, which results in higher monthly notes than many buyers can pay. For example, a $30,000 loan paid off in thirty-six months would result in a monthly note of $833, even if it were financed at zero interest. In essence, interest-free automobile loans are often offered as a marketing device to get customers into the showrooms, but very few buyers are expected to be able to get the loans or to want them when they become acquainted with the details. However, once a customer who is lured into a dealership by the promise of a zero interest loan sees the various new vehicles and finds one that he or she wants, it is the manufacturer's hope that the customer will want the vehicle badly enough to be willing to finance its purchase with a loan at the prevailing market rate of interest.

Even during promotions that offer buyers interest-free loans for periods of up to sixty months and somewhat relax the credit score requirements, there is still a cost associated with such loans. Generally, zero-interest financing is offered as an option in lieu of a cash rebate. Those who choose the zero-interest loan option often end up paying as much as a few thousand dollars more for their vehicles than those who choose to take the rebate. Buyers who keep their vehicles for a period of time equal to or longer than the duration of their interest-free loans will benefit from their choice, since the interest savings from zero-interest loans virtually always exceed the amount of the rebate that was offered as an alternative. However, those who, either by necessity or choice, attempt to sell or trade their vehicles in a relatively short time will likely owe substantially more on those vehicles than the buyers who chose the rebate over the interest-free loan. Not only will the sellers of automobiles who purchased them recently with interest-free loans in lieu of rebates be unable to compete with the price of new vehicles that have sizeable rebates available, but they will also be at a disadvantage in selling to those who choose to finance their vehicles, since their zero-interest rate loans will not be assumable by subsequent buyers.

Leases

More and more new car shoppers seem to be choosing to lease their vehicles rather than purchase them. It is doubtful that this is a wise choice for most people. Those who lease vehicles must either turn them in at the end of the lease or buy them. The manufacturers have structured most of their leases so that the purchase price of the vehicle at the end of the lease exceeds its fair market value. This discourages the customer from buying the vehicle, and puts them in the market to buy or lease a replacement. Lease agreements allow for a certain number of miles on the vehicle during the term of the lease, with a cents-per-mile penalty imposed on all miles over the allotted amount. Also, charges will generally be assessed against customers who turn in leased cars that have scratches, body damage, chipped or cracked glass, damaged or stained interiors, or anything else wrong with the vehicle that would be considered in excess of ordinary wear and tear.

As an enticement to induce customers to lease another vehicle from them, dealers often allow those faced with mileage penalties or charges for excessive wear or damage to simply add those penalties and charges on to their lease for a replacement vehicle, and pay higher monthly lease payments instead of paying out a lump sum. As a result of the typical practices of manufacturers in structuring their leases, buyers who choose to lease rather than purchase their vehicles will never be without a lease payment. Between increases in the prices of vehicles, mileage penalties, and charges for damage to vehicles that are turned in being added to subsequent leases, those lease payments will increase substantially with each new lease.

The Used Car Option

There are those who say they don't make cars like they used to. They are right. Today's vehicles are far superior to those available to buyers of even a single generation ago. It is not at all unusual to see vehicles with over 200,000 miles that are still dependable and generally serviceable. The improvements in the quality of motor vehicles make the purchase of a used car, rather than a new car, a more attractive option than ever before. Also, with the increased popularity of leasing vehicles, there is an abundance of vehicles available that have been turned in upon the conclusion of leases that are not very old and have relatively low mileages on them. Many lease turn-in vehicles still have factory warranty remaining on them, and many buyers are further comforted by the fact that the vehicle they are considering has become available due to expiration of a lease, instead of the possibility that the vehicle may have been troublesome for the prior owner.

There are a number of publications that report data concerning consumer satisfaction with various models of automobiles, repair histories of different vehicles, and the average market values of most used vehicles. By consulting these publications, buyers can increase the likelihood that they will choose a used car that will give them good value for their money.

Program Cars

A number of the late model used cars offered today are referred to as *program cars*. Dealers who sell program cars usually explain that the vehicles, such as those that were used by the manufacturer's executives, were obtained by the dealer at a manufacturer's auction. In reality, although some program cars were driven by executives, most of them come from the fleets of the companies that rent vehicles on a daily basis. A relatively high number of rental vehicles have suffered physical damage and have been repaired, are often subjected to abuse by customers and rental agency employees, and are not always serviced at the recommended intervals. For these reasons, program cars are often not good choices for used car buyers. However, due to the abundance of the vehicles that are popular with the rental car agencies in the used car market, the price of those models is usually low. As a result, the buyer who can find such a model that was previously owned by an individual, and therefore, better cared for, can often acquire it for less than its true value, since the large supply of used rental units of that model will have depressed the market for the one that was individually owned.

Another group of vehicles that may offer particularly good value to used car buyers are those manufactured in South Korea. Since these vehicles are relative newcomers to the U.S. market, their lack of brand recognition causes them to depreciate much more rapidly than most competing models. However, many of them have drive train warranties of up to 100,000 miles, which is far superior to their competitor's warranties. This combination of relatively low price and superior warranty seems to offer good value for the money for used car buyers. However, since these vehicles depreciate so rapidly, buyers would be ill-advised to even consider purchasing one of them new. Also, since automobile dealers usually offer very low trade-in allowances for these vehicles, they are often available at wholesale prices from individuals who are simply not willing to trade their vehicles in for what they consider to be a ridiculously low allowance.

The Credit Trap

Unfortunately, many Americans have fallen into a pattern of using credit to attempt to obtain a lifestyle that is actually beyond what they can afford. This strategy is doomed to fail, because it generally requires the use of more and more credit to sustain such a strategy, and the debtor will eventually become so deeply in debt that no additional credit is available. Furthermore, by the time creditors cut a debtor off from further credit, the debtor will usually have reached a level of indebtedness that he or she simply cannot pay. This is because creditors, in their zeal to compete to make lucrative consumer loans, will generally extend credit to borrowers beyond their ability to repay their loans. Credit cards pose a source of extreme financial danger to the economic well-being of consumers. Credit card companies begin to bombard consumers with offers of credit cards virtually from the moment that they reach the age of legal consent and continue throughout most people's lives. Credit card companies often offer teaser rates of 0% or some very low rate of interest for an initial period of time. However, after that time is up, the rates elevate to a typical level for credit cards, and if the cardholder fails to make a payment on time, the rates often go up immediately, and commonly are raised to abnormally high rates. It is so easy to get a number of different credit cards with sizable credit limits, and so easy and tempting to use them (since there is no credit application process required before each use once the cards have been issued), that cardholders quickly run up large balances without realizing it until they get their statements.

Once credit card balances have gotten out of hand, cardholders often turn to cash advances on new or existing cards in order to pay monthly payments on other credit card accounts. Credit card balances that have grown beyond the debtors' ability to pay them will then spiral upwardly, even without further charges, due to the accumulation of interest and late charges, and will eventually become totally insurmountable.

Example: *Debbie had been working as a commissioned sales person and had been earning about $65,000 a year. In an apparent move to cut her salary without actually stating that intent, Debbie's employer put her on a salary that was $40,000 with a bonus program. The requirements to earn a bonus were so stringent that she only got about $5,000 in bonus for the year. Rather than scale back her spending to adjust to the $20,000 loss of income, Debbie supplemented her earnings with credit card charges. When she reached her credit limit on a card, she would apply for another card with a different credit card company. When she started having trouble paying her minimum credit card balances, she acquired new cards, got cash advances on those cards, and used the advances to pay other cards.*

After a little over two years, she was unable to pay her credit card minimum payments, and the interest and penalties had pushed her combined balances on her thirty-two credit cards to $103,235. Debbie's debt had reached a level that was so beyond her ability to pay it that she simply had no alternative *but to file bankruptcy. Since Debbie was employed and still earned a reasonably good salary, she was required to file a Chapter 13 bankruptcy, known as a* **wage earner plan***, in which she was to pay $650 per month to the bankruptcy court for a period of sixty months in full satisfaction of her obligations. The total payment of $39,000 was less than the interest that otherwise would have been accumulated on her credit card balances, and offered her an opportunity to start over financially.*

In situations such as Debbie's, it is imperative that debtors act quickly to reduce expenditures in the face of financial adversity. Such adjustments are eventually going to have to be made, and it is clearly in the debtor's best interest to make them before being faced with financial ruin, rather than after. Unquestionably, there are situations, such as medical emergencies, when expenditures simply cannot be avoided. People who find themselves with overwhelming debt, and who want to change their spending habits so they can accumulate savings rather than debt, may find that the fresh start offered by bankruptcy is the only realistic way to begin to accomplish this goal.

Increasing Income

Some people simply do not have sufficient income to permit them to cover their living expenses and still have money to save, or else what they can save by reducing expenditures is just too small to permit them to accumulate a significant amount of savings within a reasonable time. People who find themselves in this position will have to find ways to increase their incomes in order to create an opportunity to generate savings.

Taking a second job in order to generate savings has certain risks to it. For those who take second jobs, there is always the temptation to use the extra income to purchase consumer goods instead of saving it. If this happens, not only will the individual have failed to reach his or her savings goal, but the party will likely have become somewhat dependent on the income from the second job to maintain his or her heightened living standard.

Another problem confronting those who work second jobs is tax-related. Second jobs are usually part-time and earnings from those jobs are generally relatively small. The Internal Revenue Code requires that employers withhold income taxes and the employee's share of FICA taxes, which is composed of Social Security taxes and Medicare taxes, from each employee's earnings. These withholdings may cause workers to feel that their tax liabilities have been taken care of as the earnings were generated. This will be true regarding FICA taxes, but may not be true regarding income taxes. For withholding tax purposes, the employer will treat each worker's earnings as if those were his or her only earnings for the entire year. As a result, a party's income from a second job may be so low that little or no withholding taxes are required. However, earnings from a second job are added to earnings of a primary job for purposes of calculating tax liabilities for the year, and this causes the earnings from the second job to be taxed at the highest marginal tax rate that the worker is in, rather than being taxed as if the earnings from the second job were the worker's only earnings.

Example: *Manoj works at a credit union earning $30,000 a year. He took a weekend job with a local professional sports franchise, from which he earns an additional $8,500 a year. Manoj is single and filing his tax return as single with one dependent. He has reached the 25% marginal tax bracket. The sports franchise has withheld FICA taxes from Manoj's earnings from his second job. However, since the sports franchise has treated Manoj as if he had no income other than the $8,500 that he had earned from it, his personal exemption and standard deduction offset practically all of his $8,500 earning from his second job, and only $120 in withholding taxes were taken out of his earnings to cover his* *income tax liability. The credit union where Manoj works during the week held out the appropriate FICA taxes from his earnings as well as enough withholdings to cover his income tax liability on his $30,000 earnings at the credit union, but nothing in excess of that amount. When Manoj files his tax return for the year, he will have to add together the income from both of his jobs. As a result, the $8,500 that he earned at his second job will be taxed at the marginal rate applicable for income from $30,001 to $38,500 for a taxpayer filing as single. In Manoj's case, that rate will be 25%, which will generate a tax liability of $2,125 (25% x $8,500) on the earnings from his second job. Since the sports franchise withheld only $120 from his earnings from his second job, Manoj will have an income tax deficiency of $2,005.*

If Manoj accumulated his earnings from his second job, the unexpected tax liability will likely be a disappointment, but he will have the funds to cover the tax liability. However, if Manoj has spent or even invested his earnings from his second job, the unexpected tax liability may create an extreme hardship for him. In order to avoid the problem in the first place, Manoj could have instructed the payroll department of the sports franchise to hold out 25% of his earnings from his check to cover his federal income tax liability. This can be accomplished by making such a provision on Form W-4, which all employees are required to fill out to indicate their filing status so that employers will be able to determine how much income tax to withhold from each employee's earnings.

Working as an Independent Contractor

It is common for those looking for a way to supplement their incomes to engage in some sort of activity on their own, rather than taking an additional job as an employee. There are a variety of such options available, such as selling cosmetics as an independent dealer, providing yard maintenance services, or working as a consultant.

Among the problems faced by those who elect to try to earn extra income as an independent contractor is that such activities may jeopardize their primary employment. Some employers simply do not want their employees to get involved in their own enterprises out of fear that they will devote time to such enterprises that should have been devoted to their employer's business affairs. Employers who do not object in general to their employees engaging in enterprises of their own will certainly object to such activities when those activities put the employees in competition with their employers. Even when employees have not signed employment contracts that prohibit them from engaging in activities in competition with their employers, or that otherwise create a conflict of interest, most states recognize an implied duty on the part of employees to serve their employers faithfully.

The typical way in which employees who decide to start doing work as independent contractors after hours run afoul of their duties toward their employers is that they agree to perform work on their own for some of their employer's customers. It really does not matter whether an employer's client solicits an employee to do work on the side or the employee solicits such a relationship—it is improper for the employee to enter into such a relationship, unless the party's employer is informed of the situation and agrees to it.

There are also potential tax problems related to choosing to earn extra income as an independent contractor. People who work as employees are accustomed to having their employers withhold income taxes and FICA taxes from their earnings, and are usually unfamiliar with their responsibilities to pay estimated tax payments to the U.S. Treasury to cover their tax obligations on their earnings from self-employment. As with earnings from a second job, the income from self-employment activities is added to a worker's other earnings as an employee in order to calculate the worker's federal income tax liability, and to calculate most state income tax liabilities, as well. Additionally, unlike those who have taken second jobs where the employers have withheld

FICA taxes from their earnings, those who have self-employment earnings will be required to pay *self-employment taxes* (which are the equivalent of FICA taxes for self-employed workers) in quarterly estimated installments, along with their estimated income tax payments.

Far more burdensome than the administrative chore of calculating the estimated self-employment tax and paying it is the requirement that those who earn self-employed income must pay a nominal tax rate that is the equivalent of both the employer's and the employee's shares of FICA taxes. Although the nominal self-employment tax rate is partially offset, the effective rate of self-employment taxation for most self-employed workers is still over 12%, which is significantly higher than the 7.65% that is the employee's share of FICA taxes.

In calculating the maximum amount of earnings to which self-employment taxes are applied, a taxpayer's earnings as an employee and his or her income from self-employment activities are added together. The statutorily set maximum amount of earnings subject to FICA and self-employment taxes, which was set at $94,200 for 2006, is adjusted annually by a percentage that is the equivalent of the percentage by which the average incomes of U.S. workers changed. Any earnings in excess of the maximum earnings that are subject to FICA and self-employment taxes will be subject only to the Medicare portion of the taxes, which, at a nominal 2.9% rate, should not prove to be particularly burdensome.

Second Jobs in Real Estate

Despite the pitfalls of taking a second job, it can prove to be an especially effective way to accumulate savings for those who are disciplined enough to faithfully save their earnings from their second jobs. There may also be opportunities to gain more than just additional income from a second job. Training of some kind, either formal or on-the-job, is an inherent part of almost every job available. Those who are planning on becoming involved in the acquisition and sale or rental of real estate, as well as those who are considering buying a home to occupy, should consider the feasibility of taking a second job that would enable them to cultivate skills and knowledge useful in real estate ventures.

Working for a construction company, electrical contractor, plumbing company, roofing contractor, carpenter, painting company, or other building contractor, even as a mere trainee or laborer, can prove invaluable to someone who is later confronted with having to evaluate a property in need of repairs. The skills learned in these jobs can then play a role in actually making the repairs. Even jobs at lumber yards and building supply stores offer workers an opportunity to acquaint themselves with products and techniques they may eventually find useful, and may also provide the possibility of developing relationships with suppliers and contractors that would be invaluable on future renovation projects.

Another type of employment that may prove to be an ideal second job for people who aspire to eventually become involved in some aspect of real estate ownership for profit is the job of affiliate real estate broker. Affiliate real estate brokers, who are generally referred to merely as real estate agents, earn commissions by listing properties for sale that are sold and representing buyers who purchase properties that they, or other agents, have listed for sale. In addition to the possibility of earning commissions, real estate agents also benefit by learning of opportunities to buy properties before they are made available on the market. Agents who purchase properties that are listed with realtors will be able to reduce their acquisition costs by the percentage of the commission that they get as the buyer's agent by representing themselves. In order to become an affiliate real estate broker, applicants must generally pass a test and usually must take several hours of continuing education courses related to real estate each year. Real estate agents must also pay fees to regulatory boards in most states. They may also be required to pay dues to local real estate boards in order to be eligible to sell other agents' listings and list properties through a system that makes them known to other agents who are members of the board. These fees can be substantial, as can the cost of the various continuing education courses.

In order to be successful, most real estate agents must be willing to work several hours on weekends, which, although ideal for some people, may be unattractive or even impossible for others. Although working as a real estate agent is not for everyone, the combination of earnings potential, education about aspects of the purchase and sale of real estate, and access to information concerning the availability and pricing of properties make it an option for a second job worth considering. This is especially true for those who plan to get involved in buying real estate in order to accumulate wealth.

Sizeable Results from Small Savings

It is not uncommon for people to feel discouraged because they see no way to reduce their spending enough to rapidly accumulate a large amount of savings. This despair may cause a number of would-be savers to abandon their savings plans before they even begin. In fact, savers can make significant progress toward their financial goals with even modest amounts of savings, as long as savings are accumulated on a regular basis. For example, a person who can reduce expenditures by an average of $10 a day will be able to save about $300 a month or $3,600 a year. Even more importantly, once a saver begins to accumulate funds, those savings will further accumulate funds through earnings, a concept known as *compounding*.

Although interest rates have been quite low in recent years, they will undoubtedly rise to more typical levels in the near future and provide savers with reasonable returns on relatively safe investments. At even a mere 6% compounded rate of return, a dollar will double in twelve years. In another twelve years, that original dollar will become four dollars, and in still another twelve years, it will have become eight dollars. It is this geometric growth rate from compounding that places a premium on savings at the earliest stages of a worker's career.

Since the compounding of returns has such an explosive impact on the future value of investments, if an investor can increase the rate of return on his or her wealth, the results will be dramatic. For example, if the rate of return on investments were increased from 6% to 9%, rather than having to wait twelve years for a dollar to double in value, this would be accomplished in only eight years. More impressively, a single dollar invested at a compounded 9% rate of return would become eight dollars in twenty-four years, rather than the thirty-six years required to accomplish the same amount of growth at a compounded 6% rate of return. Furthermore, at the end of thirty-six years, a dollar invested at a compounded 9% rate of return would be worth almost twenty-three dollars, rather than the eight dollars that it would be worth had that same dollar been invested at only a 6% compounded rate of return.

Leveraging

One way to increase rate of return on investments is by *leveraging*. Leveraging the rate of return on investments involves using credit to obtain part of the investment, and then achieving a rate of earnings on the investment that exceeds the interest paid for the funds used to acquire the part of the asset that was purchased on credit.

Example: *John bought a duplex for $50,000. He paid $10,000 down and financed the remaining $40,000 of the purchase price at 6% interest per annum. Over the course of the next five years, the combination of appreciation in the value of the duplex and the net income realized from rent after paying his mortgage and other expenses totaled $10,000. A gain of $10,000 on a $50,000 investment over a five-year period would not even amount to a 4% compounded rate of return per year. However, since John's actual out-of-pocket investment in the duplex was only $10,000, not the $50,000 purchase price, his $10,000 gain on the duplex actually amounts to a doubling of his $10,000 investment in a mere five years.*

Despite the fact that leveraging investments can greatly increase rates of return, there is a downside to leveraging as well. When an investor leverages an investment, but earns less than the interest rate charged on the borrowed portion of the investment, the earnings on the investor's portion paid into the investment—the party's equity—will have to be used to make up the shortfall in earnings on the borrowed portion of the investment in order to cover the interest payment on it.

Example: *Say an investor paid $100,000 for a piece of land bought as a speculation, borrowing half of the purchase price and using his or her own money to pay the balance. Also say that the investor had to pay 8% interest on what was borrowed, but sold the property in one year at a gain of 6%. The net gain on the equity of $50,000 would be only 4%, since the investor lost two percentage points of the 6% gross gain on his or her equity to cover the 8% interest obligation.*

There are very few investment opportunities that even permit investors to leverage their investments. It is doubtful that lenders would be willing to lend money to investors who wanted to speculate by purchasing collectibles, such as paintings, stamps, coins, or sports cards, since such investments are likely to be viewed as high-risk. These items are considered high-risk because they could be concealed or disposed of without the lender's knowledge, the value of such items is often subject to rapid change, and the markets for collectibles are not usually well-established, since such items usually appeal to only a select group of buyers.

Those who choose to invest in the stock market are permitted to borrow part of the funds they need to purchase securities, and brokerage houses stand ready to make such loans. However, in the U.S., the Federal Reserve regulates the degree to which such purchases can be financed with credit. In recent years, investors have been required to have at least a 50% equity position in their securities, thereby allowing investors to borrow up to 50% of the purchase price on most securities—a practice known as buying *on the margin.* A major pitfall with buying securities on the margin is that if they fall in price to the point that the investor's debt on them exceeds the maximum percentage of their market price allowed, the securities broker is required to send the investor a *margin call.* The margin call is a demand that the investor pay a sufficient amount of additional funds to the broker in order to reduce the debt on the securities that were brought on margin to no more than the maximum percentage allowed at that time by the Federal Reserve. Brokers are required by law to liquidate sufficient holdings to bring investors into compliance when they are unable to make the payments that are required in order to satisfy their margin calls. Therefore, if an investor experiences even a temporary decline in the market value of securities bought on margin, he or she may be forced to sell part of the securities at those lower prices.

Real Estate

The purchase of real estate offers investors a unique opportunity. Not only are buyers expected to use borrowed funds to make real estate purchases, but it is also anticipated that buyers will put very little equity into the transaction and finance 80% or more of the purchase price of any properties that are acquired. Furthermore, there are a host of lenders who actively compete for real estate loans by offering competitive interest rates and charging only modest fees in connection with originating and closing their loans. Even those with less than good credit are often able to find lenders who are willing to give them real estate loans, although interest rates on their loans are usually higher due to the heightened risk of such loans.

In their zeal to compete for real estate loans, lenders have developed a wide array of choices. First mortgages on real estate are generally available for durations of ten, fifteen, twenty, or thirty years, and some lenders may be willing to create loans of special durations for certain customers. Real estate loans have traditionally been made at interest rates that were fixed for the life of the loan, but buyers also have the option to finance their real estate purchases with adjustable-rate mortgages, which offer lower initial interest rates, but include provisions for increased interest, with corresponding increases in mortgage payments, over the life of the loan. There are even loans available in which the interest rate will start at a rate that is below the market, increase annually for the first two or three years, and then remain fixed for the life of the loan. Since lenders will not usually make such loans without being paid a fee that amounts to a prepayment of the forgone interest at the inception of the loan, such arrangements are usually referred to as *buy-down loans*. Buyers are often able to persuade sellers to pay the buy-down fee for them as an enticement to purchase a property.

The fact that buyers of real estate are able to obtain fixed-rate financing on property for very long durations of time offers buyers of real estate one of their greatest opportunities to realize a sizable return on their purchases. When borrowers obtain fixed-rate real estate loans at relatively low interest rates and the economy subsequently experiences price inflation, real estate values will generally go up at a rate that is more than the interest rate and yield a very favorable leveraged rate of return. Although interest rates on new loans will be driven up by inflation, the interest on existing fixed-rate loans will be unaffected, thereby giving borrowers an opportunity to profit at the expense of their lenders. Conversely, if interest rates fall, borrowers who have obtained loans at relatively high interest can refinance their loans at the lower rates and avoid the situation of having to pay interest that exceeds the rate of increase on their real estate holdings. In fact, even in periods of relatively low inflation, the accompanying low interest rates often attract enough home buyers that real estate values still appreciate nicely, despite relatively stable prices in other sections of the economy. Rather than having to refinance just to keep their interest payments from exceeding their annual rate of appreciation, owners of real estate can often actually increase their net rates of return on their property holdings by refinancing.

Owner Financing

In addition to the wide variety of lenders that are in the business of making real estate loans, there are sellers who are willing to finance all or part of the purchase price of the properties that they want to sell. There are sellers who prefer an income stream over a lump sum payment; however, sellers are generally motivated to carry financing themselves because the properties that they are trying to sell are substandard. Banks, mortgage companies, and others involved in the business of making real estate loans usually require appraisals, surveys, determinations as to whether properties are located in a flood hazard area, and possibly some form of inspection for violations of the federal or state Environmental Protection Acts. Of course, sellers who finance the properties that they sell will not require anything that might reveal defects in their properties that would require costly corrective measures. As a result, buyers who believe that they have gotten a bargain in below-market owner financing without having to pay the traditional costs associated with obtaining financing from a mortgage lender may find out the property was not such a bargain. They may eventually come to realize that a major cost of obtaining owner financing is that they must deal with problems that they had not anticipated, but that would have been revealed to them before purchasing the property had they not forgone the various inspections, surveys, and appraisals that professional lenders would have required. There are instances in which owner financing of real estate purchases can be every bit of the bargain that it appears to be, and it should be explored as a possible option. However, it is not nearly as readily available as many of today's real estate investment course hucksters would have us believe.

Second Mortgages

In addition to first mortgage financing options, there are a number of second mortgage choices available to property owners, as well. As the name implies, second mortgages are those acquired by pledging property as collateral when the property is already encumbered with an existing loan. In essence, owners who take out second mortgages on the realty that they own are borrowing against any equity that they may have in the property, although some lenders allow borrowers to obtain loans in excess of the value of their property. Second mortgages are available for various lengths of time. In fact, those seeking second mortgages on realty used as their primary residence may choose a home equity line of credit, which allows them to choose their own rate of payment from month to month, as long as they at least pay the interest for each month. Since lenders do not usually even question borrowers about why they are seeking a home equity line of credit, they can be used as a relatively low interest source of funds for any of a variety of purposes, including the down payment necessary to acquire investment property.

•   •   •   •   •

Given the various attributes of real estate as an investment, it is clear that it is among the investment choices that are most accessible to the largest cross section of our population. The next few chapters will address specific aspects of investing in real estate, including financing, selection strategies, tax considerations, and buying strategies.

Chapter 3:

The Prepurchase Steps

There are a number of degrees to which one can become involved in real estate acquisition. The most basic level of real estate ownership is the purchase of a primary residence. There are even levels of involvement for purchasing a residence. Minimum involvement would entail the purchase of a barely adequate residential property for personal use. Even this basic type of purchase gives the owner a source of wealth accumulation, as equity accumulates from both mortgage reduction and any market appreciation. Those who choose to turn their personal residences into more of an investment vehicle can buy homes larger than what they need, with expandable areas that can be finished off to enhance the value of their properties, or situated on acreage in anticipation of increases in value as the area becomes more developed.

Among the choices for those who wish to become more heavily involved in real estate is the acquisition of property to produce rental income. The spectrum of rental property options is truly vast. It ranges from buying a duplex with the intent to live in one side and rent the other, to acquiring sizable holdings of residential and commercial real estate complexes. Still others choose to acquire properties in need of repairs and fix them up to sell at a profit, and some real estate investors elect to combine rental activities with some buy, repair, and sell ventures. However, regardless of the degree of involvement in real estate acquisition that someone chooses, there are some fundamental concepts that virtually all real estate transactions have in common.

The Need for Due Diligence

When large corporations set out to make major acquisitions, they thoroughly investigate just about every aspect of the company, product, or property that they are interested in acquiring. Such investigations, known as *due diligence*, include verification of any representations made about the asset they are considering acquiring, as well as careful analysis of past trends and anticipated future growth and development. Individuals who are interested in acquiring real estate would do well to mimic the practices of corporations interested in making acquisitions.

Some states have enacted laws that require sellers of residential real estate who have been living in the properties they are selling to prepare written disclosure statements concerning the condition of their properties. These disclosures generally consist of forms that require owners to check off boxes to indicate whether or not they are aware of any problems concerning specific aspects of their homes, such as roofs, electrical systems, appliances, or driveways, as well as questions about whether or not the house has had problems with mold or has any of a number of other shortcomings that may affect its market value or its appeal to a potential buyer. However, those who sell their homes *as is*, or who are selling a house they had not previously occupied, are not generally required to provide such disclosures. Sellers who are required to provide the disclosure statements must merely give their opinions as to the soundness of their properties, thereby making the statements highly subjective. This often leaves disappointed buyers with little recourse when they later discover the defects that challenge the previous owner's evaluation of the property.

Even when a seller's disclosure statements are so specific that it becomes clear when defects are later discovered that the seller has defrauded the buyer, the cost and aggravation of legal action may outweigh the cost of paying to correct the problems that were concealed. Therefore, even when sellers are required to provide disclosure statements regarding the condition of their properties—and especially when such disclosures are not required—it is imperative that buyers conduct thorough investigations of their own on properties that they are considering.

Professional Inspectors

Some buyers have the expertise to thoroughly inspect properties themselves, but even those buyers would probably gain some further insights about the properties that they are considering if they have a good professional property inspector also make an inspection. Engaging the services of a competent professional home inspector is essential for those who lack the skill and experience to uncover defects in properties that could lead to unexpected, costly repairs. Choosing property inspectors with experience and familiarity with the particular type of property being considered is especially important. For example, if the property under consideration is relatively old, it would be preferable to choose an inspector with experience in evaluating properties that were built in the same era as the property being considered. Such an inspector would be much more likely to be familiar with the major problems to look for in such properties, and could more readily discern minor imperfections from major flaws.

Buyers of residential property often buy home warranties to cover the cost of repairs on the homes that they buy. Virtually all of the home warranties that are currently available on the market exclude *preexisting conditions* from their coverage. Therefore, whenever homeowners file claims under their home warranties for repairs to recently acquired houses, they often face the hurdle of having to convince the home warranty representative that the repairs were not necessitated by a preexisting condition. Often, one of the best ways to overcome this problem is by having a home inspection report that indicates that the item that subsequently needs repair was in working order at the time of the inspection. In fact, some of the home warranty companies have programs in which they are affiliated with certain home inspectors and offer a discount when both the home inspection and home warranty are acquired through the same company. Even more importantly, they will not question the accuracy of the home inspector's report that indicated that there had been no preexisting defects in some aspect of the property that later required repair.

It has become a common practice for buyers of real estate to enter into agreements to buy properties with a provision that the properties will subsequently be inspected and that the seller will be required to correct the defects as long as the cost of correction does not exceed a certain dollar amount. If the cost to cure defects discovered by an inspector exceeds the specified dollar limit, the seller will then usually have two options. The seller may either pay the additional cost to complete the repairs, in which case the buyer is required to purchase the property, or refuse to do repairs beyond the specified repair limit, in which case the buyer will then have the choice of either terminating the agreement or accepting the property without the remaining repairs being done. Of course, the parties may always negotiate some compromise to raise the repair limit to a level closer to the amount necessary to do all of the repairs.

Entering into an agreement to buy a property with a provision for a subsequent inspection may not be the best way to buy a property. That approach offers the buyer the advantage that the property would be under a contract that would obligate the seller to sell the property to the buyer, but subject to a favorable inspector's report. However, the price of the property is generally predicated on the assumption that the inspector's report will be favorable.

Furthermore, many of the standard contract forms commonly used by realtors today provide for subsequent inspection of such things as roofs, electrical wiring, plumbing, heating and air conditioning systems, and appliances. By enumerating the specific items that inspectors are to consider, they greatly limit the scope of the inspection. Common problems, such as inoperable windows and doors, cracked glass, cracked walls, damaged floor coverings, peeling paint, and rotted wood, would be outside the realm of the inspection. Even if an inspector were to make mention of such defects, the seller would not be under a duty to correct them, since they were not included among the items listed in the contract that would be subject to a favorable inspector's report. The truth is that realtors, even those representing the buyers, would generally prefer a more limited inspection or none at all, since lengthy repair lists are likely to become obstacles to the completion of a sale and they may lose their commission.

Advantages

At a minimum, a contract to purchase real estate that provides for a subsequent inspection of the property should provide for a comprehensive inspection of all aspects of the property and give the buyers the option of terminating the agreement unless the entire array of defects are corrected to their satisfaction. However, an even better approach is to insist on the opportunity to have a property inspected even before making an offer on it. One advantage to this approach is that the prospective buyer is not under a time constraint to have the inspection done. (This is usually the case with contracts that provide for subsequent inspections that must be performed by a certain date or else the buyer's right to require repair of defects cited by the inspector is forfeited.)

Perhaps the biggest advantage of this approach is the fact that, rather than basing an offer of a purchase price on the assumption that an inspector's report will be favorable and then having to try to persuade the seller to reduce the price due to an unfavorable report, the initial agreement can be based on the actual condition of the property. An inspector's report from a truly comprehensive and thorough inspection of a property can give a buyer a powerful bargaining tool. The fact that home inspection reports are written and generally prepared on a well-organized form usually enhances their impact, as does the fact that they are compiled by a professional, disinterested third party, rather than the buyer, who may be viewed with suspicion and as an adversary of the homeowner during the negotiating process.

Disadvantages

Despite the advantages of engaging the services of a professional home inspector, there are disadvantages to it, as well. If a buyer chooses to have a home inspection done prior to entering into a contract to purchase the property, there is always the chance that someone else will make an offer before he or she does, the seller might accept that offer, and the property will no longer be available. Also, home inspections typically cost at least $200, and can cost substantially more for larger properties. Therefore, the buyer who decides to have an inspection done prior to entering into a contract to buy a property not only risks losing the property to another buyer while waiting on the inspector to look at the property and write up a report, but also risks incurring the cost of the inspection despite having lost the property to another buyer.

Still another negative aspect of using a professional inspector to evaluate a prospective property is that it may release the seller from liability for fraudulent statements he or she may have made about the condition of the property. Typically, when someone makes a misrepresentation in order to induce a party to enter into a contract, and the party who is deceived suffers a loss due to that misrepresentation, the injured party is entitled to recover damages for the loss in a legal action for fraud, provided that the party relied on the misrepresentation. However, when buyers seek the services of a professional inspector to advise them as to the condition of properties they are considering, it is apparent that the buyers were unwilling to rely on the seller's representations and chose to seek the advice of a professional inspector instead.

Make Your Own Inspection

Even when a buyer chooses to have a professional inspector evaluate properties under consideration for purchase, it is still important for the buyer to conduct his or her own inspection. Ideally, the buyer should accompany the professional inspector during the inspection. This gives the buyer an opportunity to evaluate the thoroughness of the inspector, and gives the inspector the opportunity to explain the nature and extent of any defects found.

By making their own inspections, especially prior to entering into a contract to buy a particular property, the buyers will have an opportunity to evaluate features of the property from a subjective point of view that is beyond the basic physical, structural, and mechanical evaluations done by a professional inspector. Buyers looking for a personal residence should measure rooms to see if their furniture will fit and should take along arm covers or cushions from sofas and chairs to see if walls will have to be painted or carpets replaced, not due to defects, but because colors clash with the furnishings. Such inspections also are a good time for buyers to make sure that the expensive curtains that the sellers are willing to leave are a workable color, so that if they are of no value to the buyers, they can be eliminated from the negotiations and perhaps result in a price reduction.

Amazingly, many prospective homebuyers write offers on houses that they intend to occupy after only a cursory walk-through of the property. Buyers often end up agreeing to buy homes for themselves that they only faintly recall in general terms and have no recollection of the details of the property. A follow-up inspection that is more thorough than an initial viewing, and that is done prior to making an offer on the property, gives buyers the opportunity to take notice of both the positive and negative aspects of the house. The follow-up inspection also gives buyers a chance to evaluate what changes they feel will be necessary, and lets them decide whether they really want the property or if it was just the least undesirable property they saw at a time when they had grown tired of looking.

Although a prospective buyer's inspection of a property should include consideration of features and aesthetics beyond the scope of a professional inspector, it should not stop there. Despite the fact that professional inspectors should ferret out basic defects in the property, buyers should look for problems as well. Buyers should look for cracks in walls, ceilings, floors, driveways, and sidewalks. All doors and windows should be opened and closed to verify that their frames are plumb, and buyers should carry a level with them to check floors and walls for undue settlings. Buyers should not hesitate to move things around to inspect under or behind them. It would be better to take the time to move a stack of firewood away from an exterior wall and inspect it, than fail to do so and, after buying the house, discover that the wall behind the wood was rotten or termite infested, but inspectors had failed to discover it because they had been unwilling to take the time to move the wood.

Determine the Costs of Improvements and Repairs

Some prospective real estate buyers are meticulous in having properties inspected by professionals and in conducting their own investigations, but then fail to take advantage of the information that they have so carefully gathered. Often, in their haste to make a deal to buy a property, buyers simply guess at the costs of making improvements and repairs. Sometimes they even fail to carry through with recommended follow-up evaluations, such as having a structural engineer take a look at suspicious cracks in foundations and walls. The right way to use information generated from inspections of properties is to assemble a complete and accurate picture of the actual cost to correct any problems discovered. Of course, it is absolutely essential to fully determine the extent of any defects or damage found in the property in question, and this means that moving forward with further investigations is a must when initial inspections indicate that they are necessary.

Once the full extent of the necessary repairs is known, the potential buyers should get firm estimates of the costs of the repairs from competent contractors. Estimates should be obtained even for repairs that the buyers intend to perform themselves, since they may not have time to do them, or may lack the skill to perform the repairs that they thought they could. Also, written estimates from contractors showing the cost of performing repairs and improvements that were indicated by a professional inspector as being necessary can serve as an invaluable aid in bargaining with the seller over the price of the property, since it then appears that the impetus for a price cut can be traced to inspectors and contractors, rather than to the buyer.

Another advantage of getting estimates from professional contractors for repairs that have been called for as a result of an inspection of a property is that contractors who actually perform repairs are usually more knowledgeable than inspectors who simply discover defects, and they often know of collateral problems to look for that may be more difficult to discover. It is definitely a bad idea to rely on an inspector's guess as to what a repair might cost, since the inspector may have limited knowledge of the scope of the work necessary, and especially since the inspector will not be the one doing the work and will in no way be bound by the figure that he or she quotes.

The purpose of getting these professional estimates is to fully define the extent of the problem, and to then develop a complete, if not worst case, determination of the cost of those repairs. Therefore, this is not the time to seek out the lowest bidders for the various repairs. Buyers should solicit estimates from the area's most reputable and stable providers in order to avoid relying on an estimate from a contractor who is no longer in business or otherwise unavailable when the time comes to have the work done.

If, after the buyers have actually bought the property they were interested in, they want to attempt to cut costs by shopping around for a less-established, but cheaper, contractor, they are free to do so, but their purchase price will not have been predicated on their having to find such an alternative. Furthermore, to the degree that buyers can perform repairs that were cited as a basis for a reduction in the sale price of the property, the savings will accrue to the buyers as payment for their work. Buyers who fail to cite those repairs and provide estimates of their cost, since they plan on doing the repairs themselves, will receive no price concessions for those repairs, and will end up performing them for the financial benefit of the seller.

The Appraisal

Another aspect of a buyer's due diligence in determining the value of a prospective property is the use of an *appraisal* of the property. Taxing authorities appraise properties for the purpose of assessing them and then levying property taxes. Such appraisals are generally public record and are readily available, often on the assessor's website. Since assessors usually appraise properties at intervals several years apart, rather than annually, and generally do not go inside houses when they appraise them, assessor's appraisals tend to be lower than the actual fair market value of the properties. Therefore, it is generally unrealistic to expect to be able to buy properties at the values set by appraisers from the local tax assessor's office. Still, those values can be justifiable starting points for buyers who decide to negotiate with an owner over the price of his or her property. Also, it is generally wise to ascertain the amount of property taxes levied against a property, since these will be ongoing throughout its ownership. This information is usually available from the assessor's office.

Buyers who seek loans to purchase real estate will almost always be required by the lender to have the property appraised by a certified professional real estate appraiser. However, these appraisals are done after the parties have already reached an agreement concerning the sale and purchase of the property, and the appraiser is aware of the contract when doing the appraisal. In doing appraisals of real estate, appraisers consider the recent sale prices of comparable properties and the cost to reproduce the building. If rental property is involved, they capitalize the expected rent that the property will generate. This involves determining a price for the property at which the annual anticipated rental income will yield a competitive rate of return. For example, if a property were expected to generate net annual rental income of $18,000, and it was determined that a 6% rate of return would be appropriate for the property, the capitalized value of the property, which is determined by dividing the net rental income ($18,000) by the rate of return (6%), would be $300,000.

Virtually all appraisers use these three basic approaches to determining appraised values for real estate. However, since they have access to the contract for the purchase and sale of a particular property, it is only reasonable to assume that they cannot help but be influenced to some degree by their awareness of the fact that there is a ready, willing, and able buyer prepared to pay the price agreed on in the contract for the property. Therefore, buyers may find that they can get more conservative appraisals, and use those appraisals to help negotiate lower purchase prices, if they get properties appraised before actually entering into a contract to buy the properties.

Another advantage of having an appraisal done before entering into a contract to buy a property is that the buyer is free to choose an appraiser with a reputation for evaluating properties conservatively, whereas appraisals done as part of the loan process will be done by appraisers chosen either by the lender or at random. Those chosen by lenders often appraise properties liberally so that the lenders can justify making loans to applicants, thereby increasing their loan volume.

If properties do not appraise for the sale price agreed to in the contract, lenders will then usually refuse to lend the buyer sufficient funds to complete the purchase. Since most real estate contracts are contingent on the buyer being able to obtain the maximum loan allowed based on the contract price of the property, the buyer will then be relieved of his or her duty to buy the property. Some real estate contracts even specifically spell out that they are contingent on the property appraising for at least as much as the agreed-upon price.

Most sellers realize that if their property fails to appraise for at least as much as the price agreed on in the contract, it is unlikely that they will eventually find a buyer who is willing to pay more for their property than its appraised value. They will usually amend the sales contract to lower the price of the property to the appraised value. However, if properties appraise for more than the price agreed on by the buyer and seller, the sale price is virtually never raised to the higher price, since provisions for such changes are practically unheard of in real estate contracts. Since appraisals can often help buyers get the purchase price of the properties they are trying to buy lowered, but do not cause the price to go up, even buyers who are not required to have properties that they want to buy appraised should do so anyway, and should put a provision in their contracts to the effect that the contract is contingent on the appraised value of the property being equal to or greater than the contract price. Such a provision will prevent those who buy properties under circumstances in which appraisals are not otherwise required, such as when the buyer is paying cash for the property or the seller is financing the purchase, from paying more for the property than it is worth.

When buyers are paying a substantial amount down on a property, lenders will sometimes offer to waive the requirement of an appraisal or suggest that a cheaper, *drive by* appraisal would be sufficient. In either case, the buyer will lose the potential protection and possible bargaining tool offered by a standard appraisal. Also, appraisers sometimes cite items that must be repaired by the seller as a condition of the sale, which offers still further protection for the buyer, although an evaluation by an appraiser is certainly no substitute for an inspection by a reliable professional home inspector.

Other Inspections

There are a number of other forms of investigation that lenders routinely require before they will lend money on a property. The object of these inspections is to make sure that the property that is pledged as collateral for a loan is not threatened by some peril that could cause it to decline substantially in value or even become unmarketable. Buyers who pay cash for properties or who obtain properties by owner financing will not have a lender who insists on the various precautionary inspections. Even buyers who do get loans from lending institutions to finance real estate purchases may not be required to get any of the various inspections if they are paying a substantial amount down. Instead, the lender will figure that even if there is a problem with the property that hurts its value, as long as the property will still sell for as much as is owed on it, the lender will not suffer a loss, even if the loan goes into default and the property must be sold at a foreclosure sale. In essence, lenders are simply not at all concerned with safeguarding buyers' equities in their properties. Therefore, it is imperative that buyers take steps of their own to protect their interests in the real estate that they own.

One of the more common inspections that lenders require before they will make loans on real estate is a termite report on the properties that are to serve as collateral for loans. These inspections and subsequent reports, which are done by licensed pest control technicians, are commonly referred to as *termite letters*. The inspections include a search of the premises for evidence of wood damaging insects of all kinds, as well as rot or other damage to the structure—or the potential for damage—due to standing water under or around the structure or high moisture content in parts of the structure.

The reports are generally made on a form that provides boxes for the technician to check that indicate that either there are no visible signs of pest damage, there is evidence of damage but no active infestation, or there is active infestation. If prior damage is found, the technician should indicate whether repairs are recommended, and if there is active infestation, a course of treatment should be recommended.

The inspections for wood damaging insects are not infallible. The damage is often so well concealed, especially in structures built on a concrete slab (as most houses today are), that the evidence of insect infestation simply cannot be detected by a visual inspection. However, since these inspections generally cost a modest $50 to $150, which is usually paid by the seller, and have the potential to reveal serious flaws in a property, buyers should insist on such inspections and should make the purchase of the property contingent on the property being free of problems from both wood damaging insects and moisture.

Radon Testing

Another type of precautionary requirement that is common in some parts of the U.S. is the testing of properties for the presence of radon gas. Particularly in mountainous areas, it is not uncommon to find radon gas present in quantities large enough to pose a health hazard for the occupants of some structures. Although measures to prevent seepage of radon gas into buildings can prove costly, failure to take such remedial action in the face of dangerously high levels of the gas will render the property uninhabitable and largely unsellable. Even when remedial action is taken, some future prospective buyers will be unwilling to consider such a property. Therefore, requiring a relatively inexpensive radon gas test before buying a property that is located in an area where the gas is common could prevent a buyer from being confronted with unexpected costly remedial action, and if the results are bad enough, may give the buyer good reason to avoid the purchase altogether.

Flood Testing

Still another common type of test relied on by lenders in determining whether or not to make a loan on a particular piece of real estate is the flood determination. For a fee of about $20, there are companies who will consult maps that have been prepared by the U.S. Corps of Engineers and determine whether or not a particular property is located in an area that has experienced flooding within the last hundred years. If the property lies within the *hundred-year flood plain*, lenders will generally still lend money on the property, but will usually require the borrowers to buy flood insurance.

Flood insurance is available on even highly flood-prone properties. Coverage is offered by most insurance agents who write regular property and casualty policies on real estate, but the actual coverage is provided by the federal government. Many buyers will be so frightened by the prospect of having to endure the trauma of having their property flooded that they will not even consider buying property in a flood zone. Even those who do not believe that the likelihood of flooding of a property they are considering is sufficient to warrant concern, buying the property will still result in a certain loss in the form of the premium that will be paid on the flood insurance that will undoubtedly be required by the buyer's lender. The premiums on flood insurance are not inconsequential, as they often rival the cost of standard property and casualty policies, such as homeowners insurance on personal residences and fire coverage policies on commercial buildings.

Even buyers who pay cash for properties and are not faced with a lender who requires flood insurance must be mindful of the fact that, when they get ready to sell the property, their buyers are likely to need financing to make the purchase and they will likely be required by their lender to buy flood insurance. This will probably affect the price they are willing to pay for the property. Property located in a flood plain should probably be avoided, or at a minimum, should be bought at an appropriate discount. The only way to make an intelligent decision concerning property that is located in a flood plain is to first determine that it is located in one. Therefore, the pittance spent for a flood determination is clearly good insurance at a bargain price.

Environmental Testing

One of the most serious threats to property values that real estate buyers had to face over the past few decades is contamination from hazardous chemicals. Lenders do not usually concern themselves with soil contamination of residential properties, but are very concerned about contamination of commercial property. Such common substances as gasoline, diesel fuel, creosote, motor oil, and dry cleaning fluid, as well as a host of less common substances, have been identified by the U.S. Environmental Protection Agency (EPA) as posing a threat to public safety when they are dumped or allowed to escape into the soil at a site that has not been approved for dumping such substances.

In years prior to passage of environmental regulations laws in the U.S., manufacturers, chemical companies, and operators of various other companies routinely dumped their waste in landfills, holding ponds, streams, and rivers. Many of the underground tanks that were used by farmers to store fuel, or by dealers to hold their fuel inventories, have developed leaks that have contaminated the soil around them. Under current U.S. law, a buyer who acquires contaminated property becomes liable for the cost of cleaning up that property, right along with other previous owners who owned the property dating back to the time it became contaminated. It does not matter that a buyer did nothing to cause the contamination, or that he or she was not even aware of the contamination at the time of the purchase of the property. The buyer will still become responsible for the cost of cleaning up the contamination on the property—and the cost can be staggering. In fact, it is not terribly unusual for the cost of cleaning up hazardous waste on a property to exceed the value of the property once it is cleaned up.

In order to avoid the potentially disastrous results of making loans secured by real estate that is contaminated with hazardous waste, lenders routinely require an *EPA Phase I Inspection*, which must be conducted by an environmental engineer. These inspections generally involve a visual inspection of the property and an investigation of previous uses of the property, including possible interviews of former employees of businesses that are currently operating, or had previously operated, on the site. If the investigation gives the inspector reason to believe that there may be underground tanks on the property, equipment will be brought in that is designed to locate the tanks. Despite the rather superficial nature of the EPA Phase I inspections, they generally are relatively expensive, depending on the size of the property involved.

If the inspector discovers evidence of possible contamination, he or she will recommend a *Phase II inspection*, which involves drilling in spots throughout the property to obtain soil samples for laboratory analysis. Phase II inspections are usually substantially more costly than Phase I inspections. If contamination is found, a plan is developed to clean up the site.

It is amazing how many buyers of commercial property elect not to do an EPA Phase I Inspection when they are not forced to do so by a lender. They usually elect not to do environmental testing on the basis that it costs too much, but in reality, they cannot afford not to do the tests, unless they are familiar with the history of the property and are certain that it is free of contamination. Some buyers subscribe to the theory that ignorance is bliss and figure that, although they suspect there may be some contamination, as long as they do not actually confirm their suspicions by having environmental tests done, they can go ahead and buy the property and rent it out or use it without ever having to remedy any contamination on the property. However, if environmental tests were to later be performed on adjacent properties, it is possible that the contamination found on those properties could be traced back to the property that the buyer bought without doing any environmental testing, and the EPA would likely order that remedial action be taken on all of the properties. Also, when an owner who unknowingly bought contaminated property decides to sell the property, there is a very good chance that prospective buyers will insist on being allowed to conduct environmental inspections and tests. If contamination is found, the owner will face the expense of cleanup, or at a minimum, will have to sell the property at a deep discount, if it can be sold at all.

In addition to inspections for soil contamination, environmental inspectors also look for hazardous materials, such as asbestos, in the structures that are erected on the property. This makes environmental inspections all the more valuable to prospective real estate buyers, since elimination of these hazardous materials is also very expensive and their presence diminishes the value of the properties when they are present.

• • • • •

Engaging the services of a professional inspector, conducting an extensive inspection of your own, getting firm estimates for anticipated repairs, getting an appraisal, and obtaining termite reports, flood determinations, and EPA tests will require both time and money. However, these forms of due diligence should be viewed as a form of insurance, and a basic adage in determining which hazards to insure against is, "Don't risk a lot for a little." Furthermore, what may seem like a lot of money to spend for tests and inspections probably is not when it is compared to the tens of thousands, if not hundreds of thousands, of dollars that the property under consideration will cost.

Chapter 4:

Negotiating the Real Estate Contract

Regardless of whether a buyer is trying to acquire a small strip of land valued at only a few hundred dollars or is interested in buying a skyscraper worth hundreds of millions of dollars, the transactions are accomplished by the buyer and seller negotiating a contract between them, which then controls the actual closing of the transaction. A *contract* is an agreement between two or more parties that meets the criteria necessary for a court of appropriate jurisdiction to be willing to enforce it in the event that there is a breach of the agreement and a lawsuit is filed due to the breach.

The Writing Requirement

For agreements to buy and sell real estate to be considered enforceable contracts, they must be written and signed. Most realtors use preprinted forms that merely require them to fill in the names of the buyer and seller and the details of the agreement. However, it is not necessary that a contract for the purchase and sale of real estate take a specific form, as long as it provides enough details of the transaction that it can be determined what the parties have agreed to do. There are actual cases in which buyers and sellers have written up their real estate sales agreements on napkins, on the backs of envelopes, or on other scraps of paper, and courts have upheld their validity. Generally, any mark or symbol that a party to an agreement makes on the written contract with the intent to authenticate the writing will be considered to be the party's signature. Therefore, merely making an "X," putting one's initials, using a rubber stamp to add one's signatures on a contract, and even typing one's name on the agreement have all been held to constitute signatures, when they are placed on the document with the intent to authenticate it.

The Agreement

At the heart of virtually every contract is the actual agreement between the parties. Agreements are reached through a procedure known as *offer* and *acceptance*. It sounds easy, but the process can become very involved. Offers are usually written up by the buyer or the buyer's agent, and submitted to the seller for his or her consideration. They empower the seller to cause a contract to be formed between the parties by a single indication of affirmation—a signature on the offer indicating acceptance. However, if a seller were to alter even the most insignificant of terms in the buyer's offer, and then indicate acceptance of the offer with the modification, the seller's actions would not constitute an acceptance at all, but would be considered to be a *counteroffer*. This would then allow the buyer to decide whether or not to create a contract by accepting the counteroffer.

One aspect of contract law that surprises some inexperienced buyers and sellers is that once a party responds to an offer by making a counteroffer, the original offer is considered to have been terminated. *Rejection* of an offer terminates it, and when a party to whom an offer is made, known as the *offeree*, chooses to make a counteroffer, it is implied that the offeree's counteroffer was preceded by a rejection. When an offeree alters any of the terms of the sale provided in the original offer, the changes are interpreted as if the offeree had replied to the offer, "No, I will not accept your offer, but I now offer you an opportunity to buy the property on the following conditions."

Because counteroffers terminate prior offers, there is some risk involved in making a counteroffer.

Example: *Sydney and Mary put their house on the market at an asking price of $209,000. It was their hope that they could get $200,000 for the property, so they priced it higher in order to give themselves room to negotiate. Jeff and Carol made a written offer of $200,000 on Sydney and Mary's house, but rather than accept the offer, the sellers decided to try for $205,000, and made a counteroffer to Jeff and Carol at that price. As they discussed the counteroffer, Jeff and Carol each began to point out things about the house that they had not liked and eventually concluded that perhaps they had been hasty in making the offer and decided to keep looking. Carol called Sydney and told him that they had decided not to accept the counteroffer.*

The next day, Sydney and Mary sent a courier to Carol's place of employment with a signed statement that they were accepting the original $200,000 offer that Jeff and Carol had made on their property. The correspondence sent by Sydney and Mary would not constitute acceptance of the original offer that Jeff and Carol had made, since the seller's counteroffer of $205,000 terminated the original offer, and it was no longer available to be accepted. Even though Sydney and Mary indicated in their follow-up correspondence that they were willing to accept the exact terms of the original $200,000 offer, it will not be considered acceptance of the terminated offer, but will be a further counteroffer (albeit with the exact terms of the original offer) that Jeff and Carol will be free to accept or reject.

If Sydney and Mary in the previous example had accepted the $200,000 offer to buy their house, Jeff and Carol would be contractually obligated to complete the transaction, even if they had later changed their minds. This is another aspect of contract law that seems to be troublesome for a number of people. There seems to be a popular misconception that, despite having entered into a valid contract, any of the parties to the agreement will be free to change their minds as long as the transaction has not been completed. This is simply not true. It is true that there must be *consideration* between the parties to an agreement in order for it to constitute a valid, binding contract. Simply put, a commitment to do something that a party is not already legally obligated to do or to refrain from doing something that he or she has a legal right to do can constitute consideration. Therefore, the mere promises to sell and buy property can constitute consideration, just as the actual delivery of a good and payment of money can.

Modifying an Offer

One of the things that has probably fostered the popularity of the mistaken belief that a party can change the terms of a contract or even terminate it prior to completion of the agreed-upon transaction is that people have blurred the distinction between offers and agreements. As a general rule, a party who makes an offer, known as the *offeror*, can modify the offer, or even terminate it, prior to the acceptance. On the other hand, the offeree is always free to alter the terms of the original offer and send it back to the offeror as a counteroffer, which can precipitate a similar response from the original offeror. As a matter of fact, it is typical for buyers and sellers of real estate to go back and forth with modifications of each other's terms in the negotiation process before they finally reach an agreement. Perhaps it is this constant change of terms during the negotiating process prior to reaching an agreement that leads the parties to believe that they can still make changes after the agreement is reached. Failure to understand that the negotiations are over once buyers and sellers have entered into a contract can lead to disappointment.

Example: *Mario submitted an offer to buy Kevin's house for $125,000. His offer required Kevin to pay $2,000 of his closing costs on the loan that he would need to acquire the property, and also required Kevin to include his lawn equipment, washer, dryer, refrigerator, curtains, area rugs, and dining room furniture in the transfer, without additional payment. Kevin responded with a counteroffer of $135,000 for the house with him paying $1,500 of Mario's closing costs and including the area rugs and curtains in the sale, but none of the other things that Mario had listed in his offer. Mario countered with an offer of $130,000 with Kevin paying $2,000 of his closing costs and including the curtains, area rugs, lawn equipment, and dining room furniture in the sale. Kevin accepted that offer.*

In anticipation of his moving into the house, but before the transaction had actually been completed, Mario went shopping for appliances. He discovered that, in order to get appliances similar to the ones in Kevin's house, he would have to pay about $4,000, and he simply could not afford them. Mario then called the realtor who had been representing him and told the realtor to inform Kevin's realtor that Kevin would have to include the appliances in the sale, with no additional payment for them, or he would not buy the house. When he was informed of Mario's demand, Kevin refused to include the appliances. Mario will still be obligated to buy Kevin's house as agreed, since he entered into a binding contract to do so. The time for Mario to stand his ground concerning inclusion of the appliances was during the contract negotiations. Any change in the terms of their contract after its formation requires Kevin's consent.

Right of Rescission

Still another common misconception concerning contract formation that leads to conflicts between the parties is that once a contract is formed, the parties have three days in which either of them may choose to terminate the agreement. U.S. law does provide for a three day *right of rescission* of contracts to buy goods bought from a door-to-door salesperson when the goods cost $25 or more. Clearly, this law does not apply to contracts for the sale of real estate. There is also a federal law that allows borrowers to rescind agreements to borrow money when they are required to mortgage their primary residence as collateral to secure the loans. The lender must inform the borrowers of their right to rescind such loan agreements within three business days of executing the final papers necessary to get the loan. Although this provision does pertain to real estate, it is limited strictly to loans on primary residences that the borrowers already own, and does not apply at all to contracts to buy houses or even to loans that are obtained to enable purchasers to acquire properties that they do not already own, even when such properties are to be used as primary residences of the purchasers. There simply is no guaranteed right of rescission of any period for contracts on the sale and purchase of real estate.

The Requirement of Genuine Assent

It has long been established that, in order to have a contract between parties, they must intend to be bound by their agreement. However, it is just as well established that if a party gives the appearance of genuine assent in reaching an agreement, he or she will be considered to have been serious, whether the individual had actually intended to be bound or not. In making the determination of whether or not a person appeared to be serious when he or she either made an offer or accepted an offer, courts have generally approached the questions from the standpoint of whether a reasonable person who had observed the transaction would have believed that the parties who appeared to reach an agreement were serious or not. A person who is not serious about buying or selling a property should not take steps to appear to enter into a contract for the sale and purchase of real estate just to see what price someone would be willing to pay for a property or sell it for, or that person may end up bound to carry out an obligation that he or she never intended to have to fulfill.

Option Contracts

The fact that offers may be terminated prior to acceptance can prove to be extremely troublesome in the process of attempting to negotiate a contract for the purchase and sale of real estate. When parties who make an offer to purchase or sell property do not specify how long an offer will remain open, it is implied that it will be open for a *reasonable time*. Since everyone's perspective of what constitutes a reasonable time is not the same, it is best to specify how long an offer will remain open within the terms of the offer itself. However, even when an offer states that it will be open for some specific period of time, the offeror may still terminate the offer prior to that time, as long as it has not been accepted, and the termination of the offer will also effectively terminate the provision within the offer that had specified how long it would be open. As long as the offeror does not terminate an offer prior to the date that the offer states that it will be open, it will be open for the specified time. Therefore, soliciting a specific time to keep an offer open from the offeror is of some value, but there is always the possibility of the offer being prematurely terminated.

An offeree can avoid the possibility of an offeror choosing to prematurely terminate an offer by quickly accepting the offer, since the right to terminate an offer is no longer available once it has been accepted. However, this is not always an advisable, or even feasible, course of action.

People who are interested in acquiring commercial property are often in the position where they need to know that a certain property will be available to them at a specific price, and to then have time to explore development possibilities, put together a group of investors, and identify and enter into agreements with buyers or tenants of the completed development. The device for avoiding the possibility that an offeror may terminate an offer prior to acceptance, even if the offer had specified that it would be open for a period of time beyond the date that it was terminated, is the *option contract*. Entering into an option contract is as simple as merely giving the offeror some kind of consideration for his or her promise to keep an offer open for some specified duration. The amount of consideration is immaterial. It can be, and often is, some token amount, such as one dollar, although some offerors demand a relatively substantial amount of money to surrender their right to terminate certain offers prior to some specified time. The parties to an option contract are free to negotiate the terms of the agreement so that the payment for the option will be applied toward the purchase price, if the offeree ultimately accepts the offer, or it can be regarded as a payment that is separate from the purchase price of the property.

An offer and the option contract to keep that offer open for a specific period of time often stem from the same document. However, rather than offering a seller a certain amount of money under certain terms and conditions for a specific piece of property, as is typical in an offer to buy property, a party wishing to enter into an option contract will solicit an *offer* to sell property at a certain price, and under specific terms and conditions, from the seller in exchange for some specified consideration. If the seller agrees to the buyer's terms, then, rather than having an agreement to transfer the property for a specified price, the seller has simply agreed to offer the property for sale to the buyer at a certain price for a specified period of time, and the seller has no right to terminate the offer before that time has expired. If a seller who had entered into an option contract to keep an offer to sell property open for a specific time were to prematurely terminate the offer, he or she would be in breach of the option contract. The result of that breach would be that the buyer would have been deprived of his or her right to accept the offer. Therefore, the breaching owner would be liable for essentially the same damages that the party would have been liable for if he or she had actually entered into a contract to sell the property and then breached the contract.

As with other contracts that deal with the buying and selling of real estate, option contracts involving real estate transactions must be written and signed in order to be valid. Another fine point concerning option contracts is that an offer may be rejected despite the fact that the offer is to remain open for a specified time. If the party who has the option of accepting the offer were to let the other party know that he or she had chosen not to exercise the option and accept the offer, but had instead chosen to reject the offer, the offer would be terminated at the moment of rejection. This can happen even if there is still time left for acceptance under the terms of the option contract.

Option contracts can be a valuable tool for those who see potential in developing a property, but need time in which to determine the feasibility of possible projects and work out the details for carrying out the project chosen. However, they are not always the best choice, nor are they without their cost. Sellers who have properties that they had a hard time selling or that have obvious shortcomings may be willing to obligate themselves to offer to sell their properties exclusively to one buyer for a period of time. They may even be willing to keep the offer open in exchange for just a token amount of payment, in hopes of finally being able to get the property sold. However, owners of more appealing properties may be altogether unwilling to enter into option contracts on their properties, since such contracts require them to essentially take their properties off the market for the period of time covered by the option. If they are willing to enter into option contracts on their properties, they will probably insist on being well-compensated for having done so.

Also, buyers who seek option contracts on properties are in a weaker bargaining position then those who are willing to buy properties outright. Most sellers are looking for a buyer who is ready, willing, and able to do business immediately. The further away from that ideal transaction that a buyer's offer is, the less appealing it is, and the more likely that the buyer will have to overcome the uncertainty of the transaction with some incentive, such as being willing to pay the seller's asking price or close to it, if the transaction is ultimately completed. Buyers who know what they want to do with properties they are interested in, are already convinced that their plans are feasible, and simply need to address a few remaining issues before they obligate themselves to buy the properties, will probably be better served by simply writing an offer that will not bind the buyer to complete the purchase unless certain conditions are met. In real estate contract law, these conditions are known as *contingencies*, and contracts that contain them are referred to as *contingent contracts*. Offers for such contracts are still not viewed by sellers as ideal, but they are closer to the ideal offer than are offers for option contracts.

The Contingent Contract

The advantage offered by contingent contracts is they permit a buyer to enter into an agreement that obligates the seller to sell a piece of property for a set price and under certain terms, but does not obligate the buyer to purchase the property unless certain contingencies are met. However, unlike option contracts, which give a buyer the right to decide to accept an offer and buy a property, or elect to decline to buy the property without even having to give a reason, contingent contracts for the purchase of real estate bind the buyer to complete the purchase of the property if all of the contingencies are met.

Contingencies, which in legal terms are known as *conditions precedent*, are nothing more than certain specified things that must be established as existing, must be changed, or must happen before a party will be bound to perform on a contract that he or she has entered into. The most common contingency in real estate contracts is when the buyers agree to purchase a property on the condition that they are able to secure a loan of an amount necessary for them to complete the purchase. These financing contingencies often specify the maximum rate of interest at which the loan must be available, and some even specify the lender that the loan must be available through.

When contracts contain contingencies, the law implies that if a party to a contract must take action to cause the contingency to be met, he or she will make a good faith effort to cause the contingency to be met. Say a buyer who entered into a contract to purchase realty with a financing contingency in the agreement changed his or her mind about buying the property and decided to avoid having to make the purchase. The buyer may attempt to avoid by simply not applying for a loan, or by applying for a loan but providing incomplete or inaccurate information to the lender in a deliberate effort to get the lender to refuse to make the loan. However, the buyer would still be in breach of contract as surely as if he or she had just outright refused to perform.

Buyers are free to place any number of contingencies in their offers, and it is not uncommon for an offer to provide for more than one. Individuals who are attempting to move from one home to another often make the purchase of a replacement home contingent upon their being able to sell the home that they already own. This permits them to avoid owning two personal residences at the same time, with two mortgages.

Offers to buy houses that are contingent on the offeror being able to sell the house that he or she already owns are generally unappealing to sellers. They often put a contingency of their own in the agreement to clarify what happens if, during the period of time allowed to the offeror to sell his or her house, another buyer makes an offer to buy the property. The new contingency usually gives the first buyer some specified time, typically forty-eight hours, in which to drop the contingency concerning the sale of property already owned and take the necessary steps to close the transaction, or else the contract with that party will become null and void, and the seller will be free to accept the second buyer's offer.

Buyers interested in acquiring property for commercial purposes should, and usually do, put contingencies in their offers to ensure that the property will be suitable for their purposes or they will not be obligated to buy it. The contingencies used to accomplish this result include:

- provisions that the property is properly zoned for the intended use or that it can be successfully rezoned to permit the use;
- provisions that plans for development must be approved by necessary governmental agencies, such as land use and control boards;

- ◆ stipulations that the buyer must be able to obtain the necessary permits from such agencies as the health department or fire department in order to conduct business on the premises; and,
- ◆ the usual conditions, such as that the property is not in a flood-prone area or contaminated with hazardous substances.

Buyers of commercial properties also commonly put financing contingencies in the offers that they make. As with buyers of residential property who have financing contingencies in their contracts, anytime that a buyer of either residential or commercial property has contingencies in a real estate contract that require some action on the part of either the buyer or the seller, it is implied that the party will make a good faith effort, and otherwise fully cooperate, to see to it that the contingency is met.

Chapter 5:

Preparing the Contract

Most buyers make offers on properties that they are interested in by filling in the blanks on a preprinted contract form. The advantage to this practice is that most forms have preprinted provisions requiring the seller to provide proof to the buyer that the property is free from damage and infestation by wood damaging insects, and some even make provisions for inspections by professional inspectors. However, the disadvantage of using preprinted forms is that they may lull the buyer into a false sense that the offer they write on such forms will be comprehensive enough to cover all of the issues that they need to address within the preprinted provisions. In fact, although many of the preprinted forms leave blank spaces where offerors can add in their contingencies, many of them do not provide actual contingencies, since the need for them varies so widely from buyer to buyer. Therefore, it is extremely important that buyers carefully complete the forms that they use to make offers to purchase real estate, so that they do not leave out important aspects of their offers.

In addition to writing in contingencies in fill-in-the-blank contract forms, buyers must also be careful to specifically list any items that they expect to be included with the property that they are offering to buy. Buyers often want, or even expect, the sellers to include such items as curtains, appliances, rugs, and swing sets with the property that they are buying. However, unless an item has been incorporated into a structure to the degree that it is considered to be a *fixture*, such as a built-in stove or dishwasher, which makes the item become part of the structure itself, it will not be included in the sale unless it is specifically agreed to by the parties. The way to get these additional items included in the transaction is to enumerate them in the offer, since acceptance of the offer will result in a contract, and once a contract is formed, neither party is then allowed to make additions or other changes to it without the consent of the other party to the contract.

Avoiding Ambiguities

One of the most common problems that arises with real estate contracts is that, as the parties negotiate back and forth with one another, the final agreement may contain some inconsistent provisions. These are generally referred to as *ambiguities* in contract law. When the preprinted provisions that are already contained in the contract form, before any blanks are filled in, conflict with what the parties write in, there is a rule of interpretation in contract law that provides that anything written in will prevail over the preprinted provisions. Also, if some of what is written in is typed and some of it is handwritten, and there is a conflict between the handwritten and the typed terms, courts will give the handwritten terms preference over the typed terms.

Some contracts are now prepared on computer-generated forms that permit the preparer of the contract to complete the blanks by typing in provisions on the computer, and then printing out a completed contract. Although there has not been enough time for cases involving conflicts between the provisions of the basic computer-generated form and the typed-in terms to make their way into the various states' appellate court systems, it is reasonable to conclude that the provisions that were added in would take precedence over the generic terms of the form. This is despite the fact that the contract was printed as a completed document, rather than a printed form with blanks that had to then be manually completed.

In resolving conflicts between provisions in a contract, courts attempt to ascertain the intent of the parties. It should be evident that the provisions put in a contract by one of its drafters would more nearly reflect that party's intent than would the generic terms of the contract form, whether it was a form that had been printed up with blanks left to be filled in or was computer-generated with blanks to be filled in before printing it.

The most troublesome cases involving ambiguous terms in contracts are those in which the conflicting terms are either all typed in or all written in by hand. In such cases, the rules favoring typed-in terms over those that were preprinted and handwritten terms over typed-in terms are of no help to the court. Inconsistent provisions in contracts are generally the result of an oversight by one or more of the parties to the agreement, and are usually caused by the haste of the parties to complete their negotiations, or due to their inexperience in writing contracts, or both.

Example: *John made an offer to buy Clayton's house for $150,000. In his offer, John indicated the he would pay $20,000 to Clayton upon the closing of the transaction, and required Clayton to finance the balance of the purchase price of $130,000, which John would pay in notes over a period of fifteen years. Clayton scratched through John's price of $150,000 and wrote $200,000 just above it, and then scratched out the $20,000 down payment and raised it to $70,000. John responded by crossing out Clayton's $200,000 figure and writing in $175,000 above it, but forgot to change the downpayment figure, for the combination of $70,000 down payment and $130,000 in owner-financing that still totaled $200,000. Clayton accepted John's offer. In preparing paperwork to close the transaction, the closing attorney saw the inconsistency and called the parties to see what was agreed to by them. John contends that the agreement was for $175,000, with $20,000 to be paid down at the time* *of the closing and $155,000 to be financed by Clayton. However, Clayton contends that he is to receive $70,000 at the time of the closing and a note from John for $130,000, for a total price of $200,000, or, if the price is to be $175,000, he is to get $70,000 at the time of closing and carry financing for John for only $105,000.*

In an effort to resolve conflicts such as the one between John and Clayton in the previous example, courts allow the parties to explain their positions by the introduction of oral testimony, known in legal terms as *parol evidence*. However, in an effort to show respect to legitimate contracts, courts will not allow oral testimony to contradict terms of contracts that are not ambiguous, nor will they allow parties to orally supplement the terms of written contracts with new terms. Even with these restrictions, parties to contracts containing ambiguous terms run the risk that their opponent may simply be more persuasive in court and lead the judge or jury to conclude that they had agreed to something different than they actually had.

In order to prevent shady operators from deliberately preparing unclear contracts and then using the lack of clarity to their advantage, courts have adopted the rule that contracts are to be interpreted in a way that is least favorable to the party that wrote them when the contracts are open to more than one interpretation. Therefore, the drafter of a contract who innocently made the unintentional mistake of including some ambiguous terms in the agreement may be subjected to an adverse ruling as a result of this rule of interpretation. When courts simply cannot determine what the parties intended to agree to, or conclude that, due to mistakes contained in the written contract, the parties never actually reached an agreement, they will rule that there is no contract between them. Therefore, in order to avoid having to incur the expense and inconvenience of having to go to court over a contract, only to get a determination that there is no contract, or even worse, that the terms are far less favorable than the litigant had intended, it is essential to carefully review offers and contracts for mistakes and ambiguities.

Keeping the Agreement Legal

Apart from the requirements that must be met in order to cause an agreement for the purchase and sale of real estate to qualify as a contract, such as putting the agreement into writing and having both parties sign it, there is also the issue of whether it is legal for the parties to agree to the terms that are in the contract. Since the vast majority of real estate transactions involve the purchaser obtaining a loan in order to be able to make the purchase, the buyer and seller must conduct themselves in a manner that respects the rights of the lender, and in particular, the laws that protect lenders. A number of years ago, many savings and loan associations, which were a type of bank specializing in making mortgages to homebuyers, went bankrupt due in part to an unusually high rate of defaults on mortgages by homeowners. At that time, many loans were *non-qualifying*, which means that subsequent buyers of properties with such loans on them could buy those properties without having to produce any financial data that would evidence their ability to pay a loan or their history of loan repayment, but could assume those loans as a method of paying for the property.

Without having to go through the process of proving creditworthiness, a procedure known as *qualifying* for a loan, many buyers with poor credit histories and insufficient incomes bought houses by assuming the non-qualifying loans on them, only to eventually default on those loans. Also, it had become a rather common practice for sellers to give buyers *decorator allowances*, *repair allowances*, or other cash incentives for buying their properties, which were, in essence, a way for the seller to give the buyer the necessary down payment money with which to buy the property. Sellers with the least appealing properties were the ones most likely to give such cash allowances to buyers, since their properties were the hardest to sell. Predictably, buyers who had acquired properties by obtaining loans for most of the purchase price and had gotten the balance of the money needed to complete the purchase from the sellers were not inclined to struggle to make their payments when they encountered financial hardships. They had absolutely none of their own money invested in the property, and therefore, had nothing of their own to protect.

In response to these problems that were partly responsible for the wholesale collapse of the U.S. savings and loan associations, which resulted in a costly governmental bailout, federal regulations and laws governing real estate loans were made more stringent. Non-qualifying loans are simply no longer available, and sellers are not allowed to effectively pay buyers' down payments for them, regardless of how the payments might be labeled.

On the other hand, sellers are certainly allowed to pay for legitimate repairs to the properties they sell, and in some cases, are even required to pay for repairs to the properties they sell. Also, sellers are still allowed to pay *closing costs*, which are expenses associated with obtaining a mortgage and completing the transfer of real estate, on behalf of the buyers. However, any payments made by sellers for the benefit of buyers must be made known to any lenders involved and must be shown on the written, signed summary of the financial aspects of the transaction, referred to as a *settlement sheet*.

Unfortunately, there are still a number of people involved in real estate transactions who are willing to break the law in order to complete a real estate deal. Buyers who lack the necessary money to make the required down payment necessary to get a mortgage for the balance of the purchase price of a property sometimes suggest to sellers that they give them the money needed for the down payment without disclosing that fact on the settlement sheet, since such a disclosure would surely cause the lender to refuse to grant the mortgage. Still other buyers ask sellers to write the contract for their real estate transactions so that the agreement shows a sale price that is larger than the actual price agreed on, but with an understanding between them that is not a part of their formal contract and that the seller must give the money in excess of the actual sale price back to the buyer.

Sellers who are having a hard time selling their properties may also suggest that they are willing to give the buyers *gifts* in amounts necessary for them to cover their down payments and other costs that they must pay in order to purchase those properties, but with the understanding that those gifts will not appear on the settlement sheet. Even some loan originators, who are often working on commission for brokers who are in the business of matching up borrowers with the parties actually supplying funds with which to make the loans, will suggest that sellers surreptitiously provide funds to buyers and offer advice on how to accomplish it.

These and any other real estate transactions in which sellers provide funds to buyers without showing those payments on the settlement sheet are crimes. In fact, when buyers must obtain a mortgage in order to purchase real estate, both the buyer and seller must sign affidavits to the effect that the settlement sheet for the transaction accurately reflects the entire transaction between them. If the parties execute such affidavits when money has changed or will change hands between them, and it is not reflected on the settlement sheet, the parties are guilty of fraud that is punishable by stiff fines, imprisonment, or both.

Some lenders specialize in unusual loans and will permit sellers to give or loan funds to buyers as long as they are given a mortgage on the property that takes precedence over any mortgage that is given to the seller. The determining factor in whether or not transfers from a seller to a buyer are illegal is whether the transfers are shown on the settlement sheet that applies to the transaction. As long as the settlement sheet fully reflects transfers from the seller to the buyer, and the settlement sheet is made available to the lender before the decision to fund the loan is made, there should be no question about the legality of the transfers. However, transfers of funds from sellers to buyers that are inaccurately reflected on pertinent settlement sheets are likely to constitute fraud, regardless of whether the transaction involved residential property obtained for personal use, commercial property obtained for use by the buyer, or residential or nonresidential property acquired for speculation or to hold as rental property.

Chapter 6:

Remedies for a Bad Deal

It is not uncommon for either a buyer or a seller in a real estate transaction to decide that he or she acted unwisely by entering into a real estate contract. Since there is usually a significant amount of time between the time that buyers and sellers enter into real estate contracts and when the transactions are actually closed, the parties have a while to reflect on what they have done. Sometimes sellers conclude that they have simply agreed to sell their properties too cheaply, perhaps having become aware of other transactions involving similar properties that sold for higher prices or receiving an appraisal that is somewhat higher than the agreed-upon sale price. After agreeing to buy a specific property, buyers sometimes learn of the availability of similar properties at significantly lower prices.

In either event, once a party has freely entered into a contract to buy or sell property, he or she will generally be obligated to complete the transaction even if, upon reflection, it appears that the party made a *bad deal*. Rarely are properties sold for exactly what they are worth, and as long as the parties to a real estate sales contract reached the legal age of consent, and were not mentally incompetent or intoxicated at the time that the contract was made, a court will generally enforce the contract, despite the fact that one of the parties has profited from the agreement at the expense of the other.

If a buyer is enticed to agree to purchase a piece of property due to the seller's material misrepresentations of facts concerning that property, this constitutes fraud. Courts will not enforce fraudulent contracts. Also, if a contract is so extremely one-sided that it *shocks the conscience of the court*, then a court will generally declare the contract to be unconscionable and refuse to enforce it. However, courts are hesitant to get involved in the policing of contracts, and will not usually find them to be unconscionable unless the disadvantaged party to the contract was illiterate, elderly, or otherwise suffering from some limitation that made him or her vulnerable to being exploited.

When one of the parties to a real estate contract refuses to carry out the agreement, this is referred to in legal terms as a *breach* of the contract. The most common type of breach of realty contracts is refusal by one of the parties to close the transaction, but any type of noncompliance with the terms of the contract, such as failure to perform promised repairs, will constitute a breach.

Late Performance

One of the most troublesome aspects of real estate contracts concerning the question of whether or not the agreement has been breached is the issue of whether late performances constitute a breach of contract. Real estate contracts usually provide a date by which the transaction is to close. However, it is common for one or both of the parties to be unable to close by that date. Buyers often run into delays in obtaining the loans that they need to complete their transactions. Sellers are sometimes confronted with lists of unanticipated repairs that they cannot get done in time to close on the agreed-upon date, or they have to track down lenders who were paid off but failed to file releases that prove that mortgages showing up in public records have been satisfied.

Most of the time when the closing of a real estate transaction is delayed beyond the specified closing date, the parties to the contract simply wait it out and close as soon as they can. However, there are instances when one of the parties to a real estate contract is unable to close on the date specified in the agreement, and the other party attempts to declare the contract null and void due to the other party's inability to perform when agreed. This is particularly likely to be the response to a delay in closing when the party who is ready to perform would like to get out of the contract for some reason other than the delay in closing, such as when there is an alternative buyer willing to pay more for the property.

A party to a real estate contract who chooses to void the agreement because the other party is unable to perform on the exact day specified in the contract is running a serious risk of being held in breach of contract. Courts have generally held that as long as a party to a real estate contract can perform his or her obligation under the terms of the agreement within a time reasonably close to the specified time for closing, he or she will be considered to have performed in a timely manner, even though performance came later than specified in the contract. There is no precise rule as to what constitutes a *reasonable time*. That will be determined on a case-by-case basis, depending on the particular facts in question.

There is an exception to the rule that permits parties to real estate contracts to be considered to have performed in a timely manner if performing late, which is if *time is of the essence* to the contract. By definition, time is considered to be of the essence in a contract when time is vital to the contract.

Simply stating in a contract that it is a time of essence contract is probably not sufficient to cause a court to rule that it is. Time must really be a vital element of the contract to cause it to be a *time of the essence contract*. For example, if a distributor had to show that he or she actually acquired property on which to construct a warehouse in order to be awarded a contract for the distribution of a line of goods, and the closing date for the property fell on the deadline for providing proof to the manufacturer that he or she had acquired the required property, time would likely be considered of the essence in that contract, and this should be stated in the contract in order to alert the seller to that fact. However, if the buyers of a personal residence want to close in order to move out of their apartment without paying rent for another month, time would not be of the essence, since the consequence of the delay is merely the payment of another month of rent (which, if appropriate, could be recovered from the seller).

Specific Performance

In the provisions of real estate law, all real estate is considered to be unique. As a result, if a seller were to refuse to convey property to a buyer, despite having entered into a valid contract to do so, the buyer would be entitled to the remedy known as *specific performance*. When a court grants the remedy of specific performance, it compels the breaching party to do what he or she agreed to do. The premise behind the awarding of specific performance is that merely giving buyers money damages against a seller so they can go buy similar property elsewhere is inadequate, since it is recognized in the law that there will be no similar property available due to the uniqueness of real estate.

On the other hand, if a buyer breaches a contract to buy real estate, the result is that the seller fails to receive the agreed-upon money in exchange for the property, and there is nothing unique about the money that the seller would receive. However, it may really be more a matter of the seller losing the sale of the property rather than the money, and that may be essential to avoid a foreclosure or to permit the purchase of another piece of property that would be considered unique.

In any event, courts often award specific performance to sellers when buyers breach real estate contracts on a theory of *reciprocity*. This theory provides that if buyers are entitled to specific performance when sellers breach real estate contracts, it is only fair that sellers should have a reciprocal right of specific performance when buyers breach real estate contracts.

Damages

The most basic type of *damages* awarded in any type of action for breach of contract is *compensatory damages,* which take the form of sufficient monetary payment by a breaching party to a non-breaching party to put the victim of a breach back in the same financial position that he or she would have been in had there been no breach. Compensatory damages in real estate contracts are calculated by determining the difference in the agreed-upon price of the property in the contract and the fair market value of the property.

Example: *Curt and Rhonda entered into a contract with Carol to buy her house for $125,000. Carol had planned on getting married and moving into her new husband's house, and that is what had prompted her to sell her house. The day before Carol was to close the sale of her house, she learned that her fiancé was seeing another woman and called off the wedding. She then refused to close the sale of her house. Curt and Rhonda sued Carol for breach of contract and introduced a real estate appraiser at the trial who testified that the fair market value of Carol's house at the time that the contract was signed by the parties was $137,000. Rather than seek specific performance of the contract, Curt and Rhonda requested compensatory damages in the amount of $12,000, which is the difference in the agreed-upon sale price of $125,000 and the fair market value of $137,000. They won their lawsuit, and the $12,000 award that they sought was awarded.*

In the previous example, had Carol completed the sale, Curt and Rhonda would have ended up owning a house worth $137,000 but would have only had to pay $125,000 to obtain it, and would have realized a $12,000 increase in their net worth, referred to as the *benefit of their bargain.* Since Carol breached the agreement, in order for Curt and Rhonda to be able to acquire a house valued at $137,000 for a payment of $125,000, as they would had Carol not breached the agreement, they are going to need an extra $12,000. That is what the court ordered Carol to pay to them as a consequence of her breach, in order to put Curt and Rhonda in the same position that they would have been in had Carol not breached the agreement.

If Carol's house had been valued in the market at the same $125,000 that Curt and Rhonda had agreed to pay for it, then there would be no difference in the fair market value and the contract price of the property, and the court should not award any compensatory damages for the breach. Likewise, if Curt and Rhonda had breached the contract for the purchase of the property, and it was shown that it had a fair market value of $137,000, Carol would not be entitled to any compensatory damages, since she was actually going to sell the property for $12,000 less than it was worth. In theory, she should now be able to sell it for its fair market value, since she has become aware of the property's worth. However, if Curt and Rhonda had breached the agreement and it was established in an action for breach of contract that the fair market value of the property was only $110,000, Carol would be entitled to compensatory damages of $15,000, since that is the difference in the contract price of $125,000 and the fair market value of $110,000. It is also the amount of damages that would have to be awarded to Carol in order to give her the benefit of her bargain, since the only way for her to realize $125,000 from a subsequent sale of her property at its fair market value of $110,000 is for the breaching buyers to pay her the extra $15,000.

In addition to compensatory damages, parties who breach real estate contracts will also be liable for *incidental damages* the non-breaching parties suffer. These usually consist of costs the non-breaching parties incur that, were it not for the breach, they would not have to incur, or expenditures made in connection with the anticipated purchase or sale that are now of no value due to the breach. For example, if a buyer were to pay $250 for a home inspection in preparation for closing the purchase of a house, and the seller breached the contract and refused to sell, the buyer should be entitled to recover the $250 inspection fee as a form of incidental damages, since the inspection will be of no value to the buyer due to the seller's breach.

Chapter 7:

Acquiring a Personal Residence

There are some people who are better off not owning the homes that they occupy, but they are the exceptions, rather than the rule. For most people, purchasing a personal residence permits them to accumulate wealth as they build equity in their property by means of a combination of debt reduction and market appreciation.

Another advantage to home ownership is that if the owner has financed the purchase with a loan that has a fixed rate of interest, the monthly payments for principal and interest will not go up, while landlords usually increase rents to keep up with increases in the cost of living. Homeowners who pay their property taxes and homeowners insurance as part of their monthly mortgage payment will experience increases in their monthly payments as those components of their payments increase. However, landlords will certainly pass on their increases in property taxes and insurance by increasing rents, thereby causing renters to suffer the same cost-of-living increase from higher taxes and insurance costs that homeowners do.

Workers who are provided housing as a part of their compensation may do well to question whether the option to receive a higher salary is available without housing being provided, since any difference in salary when housing is provided is essentially the rent that they are paying for that housing. In many instances, workers would be better off over the long run to take additional pay in lieu of provided housing and using that money to acquire property of their own. For example, some churches provide their pastors with a residence, known as a parsonage, that is owned by the church and made available to the pastor without charge as a part of the pastor's compensation package. However, pastors will generally fare better if they can persuade their congregation to pay them more and buy a home of their own, especially since U.S. tax law permits ordained ministers to exclude from federal income taxation the portion of their incomes that they pay toward acquisition of their homes.

Viewing Your Personal Residence as an Investment

Unfortunately, Americans are not good savers. The U.S. has one of the lowest rates of savings among industrialized nations. As a result of our low rate of savings, many U.S. citizens have little, if any, reserve funds to rely on during periods of unemployment or to meet emergency needs. There are often stories of people who retire with some modest level of savings, only to have those savings wiped out by a single illness. However, those who have purchased their homes and managed to pay off most (or all) of any indebtedness on them, will have a major asset that will offer them any number of options that can provide some financial relief.

Minimal Investment Benefits

Even people who buy their residences without considering the investment aspects of their purchases will still reap some investment benefits from their decision to become homeowners. Buyers who are unlucky enough to buy residences that underperform the market in price appreciation will still be better off—by far—than those who choose to rent their residences instead of buying them.

Elderly homeowners whose children are grown and on their own will likely no longer need as large a home as they formerly did, and will be in a position to sell their homes, replace them with less costly housing, and use the difference to meet health care costs or other financial needs. Those who need to move to an assisted care facility can sell their homes and use the full proceeds of the sale to help cover the cost of their new living arrangements.

Home Equity Lines of Credit

Some homeowners find themselves in need of money, but do not want to sell their properties. Home equity lines of credit may offer these people the option that they need. Borrowers do not need to have their homes paid for in order to be approved for a home equity credit line, and they do not have to even disclose why they want the credit. Home equity loans are available to borrowers of all ages and are often available in an amount equal to the full value of the homeowner's equity, which is the difference in the value of the homeowner's property and the existing indebtedness against it. Some lenders will even make home equity lines of credit based on up to 110% of the value of the borrower's home.

A major advantage of home equity lines of credit is that they can be applied for and approved before the homeowner actually needs any proceeds from the loan. Still another advantage of obtaining a home equity line of credit is that borrowers can choose to borrow only as much of the approved loan proceeds as they actually need. Furthermore, those who have borrowed on their home equity lines of credit are generally allowed to determine their own rates of payback, as long as they at least pay the interest as it accrues on the outstanding loan balance.

The competition among banks to make home equity loans is so great that they will usually absorb the costs of making such loans, such as appraisals and fees to record proof of the loan in the public records, without requiring the borrower to pay any fees. It is also common for lenders to offer initial periods of reduced interest rates on such loans, and even when that period of time is up, rates are often no higher than the rates that the borrowers are paying on their first mortgages. To the extent that borrowers do not actually take out loans against their home equity lines of credit, they will pay no interest or other charges, since lenders do not normally assess any interest or other fees for simply making the funds available.

The various features and characteristics of home equity lines of credit make them ideal sources of emergency funds. By having qualified for a home equity line of credit in advance of their needs, when they have steady employment, borrowers can still draw funds against their credit lines, even though they may be unemployed or unable to work. Some homeowners may choose to finance expensive items, such as automobiles, on their home equity loans, since they can usually take a tax deduction for the interest that they pay on such loans.

Home equity lines of credit may also provide homeowners with a source of funds to use for business purposes. Borrowers who need funds to start or nurture their small businesses can get money for such purposes through home equity lines of credit without having to convince a lender that they have a truly viable business plan. Likewise, buyers who want to acquire investment real estate may find that a home equity loan will give them the funds that they need to acquire or repair such property.

As with most good things, there is a negative side to home equity credit lines. Because they are so easy to get, some homeowners will be tempted to abuse them by using the credit lines to finance vacations or other relatively frivolous purchases, rather than using them for emergencies or to carry out some sound business purpose. People who constantly borrow against the full equity in their property will never have any equity. In fact, those who have borrowed the maximum amount available on home equity credit lines and who have credit limits that permit debt against the property to exceed 100% of its value will be in a position of not being allowed to sell their properties and fully pay off their loans with the proceeds of the sale.

Reverse Mortgages

One of the most recently developed products offered by lenders is the *reverse mortgage*. Rather than making monthly payments on a mortgage *to* a lender, homeowners who have secured reverse mortgages on their properties receive monthly payments *from* lenders. In many respects, the reverse mortgage resembles a sale of property by the owner, but unlike a sale of the property, the owner will still be allowed to occupy his or her home during the term of the reverse mortgage. Afterward, ownership of the property will transfer to the lender. Although reverse mortgages erode away part of the estate of homeowners who obtain them, perhaps leaving little property for their heirs to inherit, they offer elderly property owners who need additional monthly income a way to secure that income by liquidating their homes and not having to move.

The reverse mortgage can be especially helpful in situations in which a married couple owns their home and one of the parties needs nursing home care, but the other spouse wants to continue living in the couple's residence. In order to qualify for Medicaid to cover the cost of the nursing home for the party living there, referred to as the *institutionalized spouse*, there are stringent limits on the value of the assets that both the institutionalized spouse and the spouse still living in the couple's residence, referred to as the *community spouse*, must meet. Although it varies from state to state, the combined total amount of cash, savings accounts, checking accounts, stocks, bonds, and mutual funds that the couple may own is relatively modest for the institutionalized spouse still to qualify for Medicaid. However, there is no limit on the value of the primary residence that they may own without affecting Medicaid eligibility for the institutionalized spouse. Therefore, a viable strategy to be sure that the community spouse has ample funds to live on is for the couple to invest the bulk of their wealth in a primary residence. It will not be counted as a resource in determining Medicaid eligibility for the institutionalized spouse, but will be available to the community spouse to obtain a reverse mortgage on and secure an income stream for him- or herself.

Were a couple to accumulate their wealth in the form of cash, bank accounts, or securities, they would have to pay the costs of nursing home care for the institutionalized spouse until their wealth was spent down to the maximum that they could have and still be eligible for Medicaid before it would cover the cost of the institutionalized spouse's care. The amount of holdings in cash, bank accounts, and securities that couples are allowed to have and each still qualify for Medicaid coverage from an institutionalized spouse is relatively small. By the time a couple has spent down their cash and other holdings to the maximum level that they are permitted, there will not be sufficient funds left to generate a significant level of earnings for the community spouse. That party will have to begin to consume the remaining funds in order to significantly supplement his or her other income, and must face the prospect of rapidly exhausting them.

Increasing the Investment Aspect of Purchasing a Residence

For those who can afford to take advantage of them, there are opportunities for homeowners to incorporate a larger element of investment into their purchase of a personal residence. One way to accomplish this is for buyers to purchase more of a house for a personal residence than they actually need. The term *more* in this situation would include not only larger size houses, but also houses with more amenities, those in upscale neighborhoods, houses built on waterfront lots or on other costly sites, and properties with three-car garages or other additional structures, such as pool houses, guesthouses, or in-law accommodations. From an appreciation standpoint, buying a large house in a less desirable neighborhood is not advisable. In order to devote more funds to the investment aspect of purchasing a personal residence by moving to a larger home than they really need, buyers should buy the larger home in a neighborhood that is at least as well regarded as the neighborhood they are leaving.

The strategy of buying more personal residence than is necessary will cause the homeowner to have to pay larger amounts of property taxes and insurance premiums on his or her residence than would be due on a more modest home. However, taxpayers are allowed to take a tax deduction for the property taxes that they pay on their personal residences, and the deduction may reduce federal and state income tax liabilities enough to significantly offset some of their property tax obligations. For a discussion of the particulars concerning the deductibility of property taxes on federal and state income tax returns, see the Property Tax Deduction section on page 198 in this book.

Buyers who choose to boost the investment aspects of their personal residences by choosing to buy larger homes rather than nicer homes will also have to contend with the prospect of having to pay higher utility bills to heat and cool those homes. Therefore, the concern over utility costs should be heavily reflected in the process of choosing a property. Many larger homes have zoned heating and air conditioning systems that consist of multiple units that heat and cool separate parts of the house. Such systems permit homeowners to vary the degree to which they heat and cool different sections of their homes, and even allow them to shut off the heat and air conditioning altogether to parts of a house that are serviced by a particular unit. When choosing a home that has spaces that are less likely to be used, such as spare bedrooms upstairs, homeowners who buy larger homes than they need can still keep their utility costs in line with those of smaller homes by using such a system.

For those who are not interested in investing in a larger or more extravagant house to live in, but who want to incorporate an investment element in the house that they choose for a residence, there is the option of buying a house that is situated on some acreage. Although buying a house on a larger than typical lot may enhance its market appeal when it comes time to sell, in order to realize the full investment potential that buying a house accompanied by acreage offers, buyers will need to select properties with enough acreage to give them future development potential. If a property has sufficient acreage, it may be possible to earn some income from the property by raising livestock or growing crops, or renting it to others to graze livestock or to farm. Also, by having a relatively large amount of acreage with his or her house, the owner will have the option of selling off parts of the property when the need for cash arises, but can retain the part with the home on it and not have to move.

Another advantage of choosing a personal residence that is accompanied by acreage as an investment, rather than purchasing a more costly house on a small lot, is that the owner can often significantly reduce the amount of necessary property taxes and insurance premiums. Many jurisdictions have special property tax rates for property that is considered to be farmland or is otherwise categorized as undeveloped. To the degree that owners can qualify their properties that include both acreage and their residences for special rates, they will pay less in property taxes than owners of homes of equal value that are situated on small lots that cannot possibly qualify for the special rates.

Whether owners of houses on acreage will have lower insurance premiums than owners of properties of similar value, but that consist of small lots with relatively expensive homes on them, will depend on a combination of factors. On the one hand, since the land surrounding an owner's home will not be subject to damage from perils, such as fire and storms, that are covered by homeowners insurance policies, it will be necessary for the homeowner to insure only the value of the dwelling on the property. Therefore, the owner who has chosen to invest more money in land and less in the house on it will have less to insure than those who have invested heavily in improvements on small lots. On the other hand, since houses that are situated on sizable amounts of acreage are generally located in more rural areas that are served by volunteer fire departments, if any, the property insurance rate for those houses may be considerably higher than the rates in urban areas with first-class fire departments. As a result, even though the owner of a small home on substantial acreage will need less coverage than someone with a large home on a small lot in a suburban area, the rates may be so much higher for the owner of the small home that he or she will pay just as much, or more, on premiums as the owner of the larger urban home. Therefore, it is especially important for buyers who have decided to purchase property in a somewhat rural area to investigate property insurance rates before buying, just as it would be advisable to inquire about property tax rates before buying.

One unique aspect to choosing to invest in a personal residence that is situated on acreage is that the buyer may be able to add to that investment by acquiring additional adjoining or nearby acreage in the future. However, even though the acreage that accompanies a house when it is initially purchased is considered part of the owner's primary residence and is excluded when determining eligibility for Medicaid, parcels that are acquired later, even if adjoining, are not considered to be part of the owner's primary residence. These would have to be liquidated, and the proceeds exhausted, before the owners would qualify to have Medicaid cover the cost of nursing home care without any obligation to repay Medicaid.

There is no question that homeowners who choose to increase the investment aspects of their residences by buying larger or more elaborate homes than they need, or by purchasing homes that are situated on substantial acreage, will be required to devote a larger portion of their earnings to the purchase of those homes than if they purchased a minimal residence. That is the nature of investments. Those who choose to make investments must be willing to forgo expenditures for other things in order to have money to put in their investments. Homeowners should not take on such large mortgages that they do not have sufficient funds to cover their necessary living expenses, but for buyers who are simply required to reduce their spending on luxury items or frivolous purchases in order to pay their mortgages, it should be viewed as a financially wise redirection of expenditures away from wasteful spending and into a form of forced savings.

In addition to the previously discussed expenses of property taxes, insurance premiums, and possibly increased utility bills associated with the decision to buy a larger or more elaborate home in hopes of realizing a gain from the purchase, buyers who employ this investment strategy will also likely incur additional maintenance costs on their properties. These costs would not be a part of the cost of holding more conventional investment assets, such as stocks and bonds.

However, unlike securities and other traditional investments, the purchase of a residence as an investment provides the buyer with an asset that can provide the owner and his or her family with considerable enjoyment from its use.

Still another advantage of selecting a personal residence to buy that exceeds the purchaser's minimal housing needs is that it allows the buyer, who is convinced that real estate ownership is a good investment, to participate as an investor in realty without having to become involved in renting out properties to tenants. Managing rental property can be time consuming, frustrating, and even somewhat risky. By purchasing properties that they and their families will occupy, owners will be able to avoid having to screen and select tenants, deal with tenants' complaints and arrange for repairs, evict delinquent tenants, and prepare properties to be re-rented when tenants leave. Landlords also face the prospect of having to defend against lawsuits brought by disgruntled applicants who contend that the property owner's refusal to rent to them was due to unlawful discrimination, and against lawsuits brought by the tenants who allege that they have suffered injuries due to defects in conditions of the property that they have rented.

Choosing a Property

Choosing which particular property to buy is the most important aspect of buying a home. The old cliché that the three most important factors to consider in choosing which home to buy are *location, location, and location* may well be true, but there are other aspects to consider. Buyers who view their personal residences as an investment should actually put resale value at the head of their list, and factors including location, the style of the architecture of the house, the size of the lot that the house sits on, and the size of the house relative to the size of most of the other houses in the neighborhood, will be primary determinants of any home's resale value.

Choice of Location

Virtually anyone who is knowledgeable about real estate would quickly agree with the proposition that a buyer would be much better off to purchase a modest home in a desirable location than to purchase a large home in an undesirable neighborhood. The factors that distinguish *good* neighborhoods from *bad* ones include:

- the levels of crime in the vicinity;
- the quality of local schools;
- the availability of places to shop;
- traffic congestion;
- types of properties in close proximity;
- the degree to which owners in the neighborhood maintain their properties;
- quality of local government;
- availability of public services; and,
- the neighborhood's history of price appreciation and its outlook for future appreciation.

Crime statistics are compiled by various law enforcement agencies and are generally available to the public. A great deal of other pertinent information can be gathered by simply spending some time in the vicinity of the property and observing the level at which prospective neighbors maintain their homes, the availability of shopping, and the available recreation facilities. A visit or call to the local school board will provide information concerning what school district a house is located in, as well as perhaps some information about the schools in that district. It would also be advisable to investigate the local governments' histories of property tax increases and their plans for programs that are likely to result in future increases. It is essential to determine the proximity of the property under consideration to the nearest fire station and the quality of fire protection, since these will have a major impact on the insurance rates on that property. In fact, it would be a very good idea to check with an insurance agent and get rate quotes on a property *before* agreeing to buy it.

Information concerning historical price changes of properties in a given neighborhood is available through local assessors' offices, public records of past sales, and trade publications, as well as through real estate agents. The most recent appraisals by local assessors should also be readily available to the general public. This is important information, since it is generally not optimal to buy the most expensive house in a neighborhood. The smaller homes will pull down the average prices in that neighborhood, and for the price of the most expensive house in a given neighborhood, buyers can—and often do—buy one of the smaller homes in a better neighborhood.

Different buyers have different priorities that influence what they are looking for in order for them to consider a property to be in a good location. For example, a person on kidney dialysis would consider a property's proximity to a kidney dialysis clinic very important, whereas most people would be indifferent as to whether a property were located near a kidney dialysis facility. However, some aspects of property location, such as the quality of neighborhood schools, are of such fundamental importance to so many people that they should be given serious consideration, even by buyers who are not personally interested in those facilities, since they are likely to have a serious impact on the property's resale value.

The important point to bear in mind when considering the various factors that determine whether or not a location is good is not so much which, or even how many, factors to consider—rather, it is a matter of *when* the factors will be considered. It is not uncommon for buyers who are looking for a property to buy for use as a personal residence to line up a number of properties to see, and upon finding one that appeals to them, quickly submitting an offer for the property so that no one else will buy it before they do. Only after they have agreed to buy a property, or perhaps have even closed the purchase, do they begin to consider the various factors that determine the desirability of the property's location. It is far better to know before buying a property that the schools in the neighborhood where a property is located are on probation due to students' deficient test scores on achievement tests, that a property is in an area with inadequate fire protection, or that homeowners in the neighborhood are required to pay sizable dues to a homeowners association.

Conduct a reasonable investigation of location-related factors concerning a property before making a commitment to buy it.

In virtually all sizable U.S. cities there is a trend towards revitalization of certain inner-city neighborhoods. The buyer who can anticipate what area in his or her city will soon become a target for widespread revitalization will have an opportunity to outperform the rate of appreciation of real estate in general in that city. However, buyers who guess incorrectly in anticipating which neighborhoods are likely to soon be targeted for widespread revitalization could be saddled with a property in an area where real estate values have stagnated. Knowledgeable, experienced realtors can often provide invaluable information and advice concerning past and future trends in their local real estate market. However, buyers should be careful not to lose sight of the fact that location is unquestionably the most important factor in determining property values, since it is the only factor that absolutely cannot be changed.

Choice of Style of House

The time for choosing a home for a personal residence is not the time to consider the latest fad. The contemporary style of home today will almost undoubtedly seem out-of-date at some point in the future. Also, certain styles of housing are popular in some parts of the country, but not at all popular in other locations. Therefore, those who move to a different region and insist on duplicating a style of architecture that was popular where they formerly lived run the risk that there will be little interest in their house when they choose to sell it.

Issues concerning the choice of style can go beyond the cosmetics of the structure. Floor plans that are unusual for a particular region can make a house hard to sell. Basements are so commonplace in some areas that they are virtually an absolute necessity, even for owners who do not personally care for them, in order to avoid seriously reducing the resale value of the properties. On the other hand, soil conditions in some parts of the U.S. make basements totally impractical, and those who insist on including basements when they build their homes are doomed to face problems with standing water in their basements, mold, and mildew throughout various parts of their house.

Still another troublesome aspect of choosing a relatively new style of house is that they often are constructed with new materials that have no history of durability. For example, in the 1950s, some builders built ranch style homes that had roofs made up of sheets of roofing material with tar and rocks covering them. In a short time, most of those roofs leaked, the rocks came loose (leaving bare spots), and the roofs had to be removed and replaced with traditional shingles.

More recently, many builders in the 1980s constructed houses with exteriors that were finished off in a material that was made to look like stucco. The material was not particularly durable, and a hole could be punched in a wall covered in the material by something as routine as bumping into it with a lawnmower. Even worse, installation of the stucco-like material required adherence to relatively stringent procedures, with which many installers were not familiar. The consequence of improper installation was moisture problems in the walls of the houses constructed with the material, which subsequently caused the rotting of window frames and door frames, as well as dangerous mold formation on the inside of the houses. The problem has become so severe that most sellers of houses constructed with such material must now provide prospective sellers with a *stucco report* that is prepared by a certified inspector who has knowledge of the proper installation of the material. The inspector must examine the property to see if the material was properly installed, must check and record the moisture content of the walls of the house, and must indicate any corrective measures that are recommended. Correcting improper installation of the stucco-like materials can be extremely expensive, and the cost of removing the material and replacing it with brick or even siding is often prohibitively expensive. As a result, houses constructed with stucco-like materials in relatively recent years have declined in value, and have been difficult to sell at even depressed prices.

It is making the choice of architectural style of a residence that is likely to create the most serious dilemma for buyers. There is no question that from an investment perspective, buyers are much more likely to maximize the gains on their properties when they buy homes with very traditional styling. However, a buyer's personal tastes and preferences may cause them to become interested in acquiring a less traditional residence. Smart buyers will consider the benefit of choosing a traditional style of property, and if they do not make their choice entirely with an eye toward resale, they will at least give marketability of the property very serious consideration, and will avoid choosing a radical style of architecture.

Considering Property Condition

Houses are relatively complex structures that typically include electrical systems, plumbing systems, heating and air conditioning systems, built-in appliances, structural aspects from their foundations to their roofs, and a variety of components (such as cabinets, doors, windows, fireplaces, and garage doors) that are subject to failure if they are not properly installed and maintained. Some of the results of faulty construction and lack of maintenance (such as excessive settling of the structure, moisture control problems that lead to mold or drainage problems, termite damage, or rotting of wood) can be so extreme that the cost to correct the problems would exceed what the value of the property would be once it was repaired. The consequences of unknowingly buying a house with major defects are so serious that it is simply foolhardy for buyers to take that risk.

Sellers' Disclosures

Sellers are commonly required to fill out forms disclosing their opinions of the properties that they are selling. Buyers may be tempted to rely on those representations and forgo any formal inspections of the property that they are interested in, since inspectors charge for their services and buyers are usually the ones who must pay their fees. However, it must be remembered that the disclosures made by sellers are merely their *opinions* of various aspects regarding the condition of their houses, and their opinions of what is satisfactory may differ from those of the buyers. Also, some houses may have defects or be developing problems that even the sellers are unaware of, and therefore, are not liable for their failure to disclose them.

Inspections

It is common for buyers to become emotional about the selection of a residence. They can become so excited about the fact that a house has beautiful front doors, a stained glass window, or some other feature, or that it is located near where a good friend lives or close to their workplace, or is otherwise especially appealing in some way, that they are unwilling to consider the shortcomings of the property. In fact, some buyers can become so obsessed about a property that they absolutely do not want to hear anything negative about their choice, and they do not want to hire an inspector to compile a report on the condition of the house, due to fear that the report will be unfavorable. This is a dangerous attitude. Even buyers who have made up their minds that they are going to buy a property despite any defects would be well advised to get an inspection of the property, performed by a qualified inspector, so if major defects are found, they may be able to negotiate price concessions on the strength of the inspector's report in order to help cover the cost of repairs.

A home inspection by a qualified home inspector is the minimum investigation that buyers should do regarding the condition of a house that they are seriously interested in buying. Ideally, the inspection should be done even before making an offer on a house, since the results of the inspection can often be used as a basis to negotiate a price reduction or an adequate repair allowance. Also, by having an inspection done before entering into a contract to buy a house, rather than agreeing to buy the house on the condition that the structure must pass inspection, the inspector will have had a completely free hand in determining the scope of the inspection. Instead, preprinted provisions in standard contract forms often limit inspections to such components of a house as electrical and plumbing work, heating and air conditioning systems, roofs, and appliances. When they are given the opportunity to establish their own parameters of their inspections, home inspectors often expand the scope of their reports to include comments about the appearance of the property, projections about repairs that may be needed in the not-too-distant future, and even suggestions for improvements to the property. However, inspectors are not likely to include such comments when they are asked to make an inspection for defects in a house that is under a real estate sales contract. Still another advantage of having a property inspected before entering into a contract to buy is it provides a good way to avoid a conflict—and possibly even a lawsuit—between a buyer who refuses to purchase a property that he or she had contracted to buy due to the results of an inspector's report, and a seller who insists that the reason cited by the buyer for refusing to complete the transaction pertains to items outside the scope of what was to be covered by the property inspection.

As with most professionals, some inspectors are better qualified and more thorough than others. Asking real estate agents and other homeowners to make recommendations on the basis of their experiences with inspectors is advisable in choosing a home inspector. Also, it is often beneficial to choose an inspector who specializes in inspecting houses of the same architecture and that were built at about the same time as the house you are hiring him or her to inspect.

Put the Inspection to Use

Although there are significant advantages to having a property inspected for defects before making an offer to buy it, the cost of such an inspection, which is usually at least $200 and can run much more, may make it unappealing to prospective buyers. The prospective buyer does not know whether someone else may buy the property before the buyer can get the inspection done, whether the seller will even accept the offer, or whether a mortgage company will approve the loan necessary to making the purchase. Buyers who are reluctant to incur the costs of a home inspection before they enter into a contract to buy a specific house should definitely specify in their offers that their obligations to buy properties are conditioned on the seller correcting any defects found in the property by the inspector. In particular, care should be taken to provide that the inspector shall be free to include every aspect of the property in the home inspection. Of course, sellers will probably insist that they be allowed the option of choosing to repair the defects cited by the inspector, or simply declaring the contract null and void, in order to prevent finding themselves in the situation of having to do more than what they consider to be reasonable. However, even if a seller refuses to do all of the repairs, the buyer and seller will be free to negotiate a compromise, and if they cannot reach a new agreement concerning the repairs, both parties will be free of any further duties toward one another regarding the property.

Surprisingly, a number of buyers who go through the process of having a home inspection done fail to take full advantage of the information revealed in the inspector's report. Home inspectors generally have a relatively broad knowledge of home systems and structures. They are often former employees in some aspect of home construction or maintenance, and may have a more in-depth familiarity of one or more parts of the inspection process due to their past employment, but will likely have only superficial knowledge of other facets of the inspection process. Therefore, it is not unusual for inspector's reports to call attention to some irregularity in a structure, such as cracks in brickwork or sheetrock walls, and then recommend consulting with a structural engineer for an expert evaluation of the source and extent of the problem, and the actions and cost necessary to correct it.

Some buyers simply shrug off their inspector's concerns as either the product of an overly zealous inspector or an attempt to avoid personal liability for defects pertaining to elements of the inspection with which the inspector was less familiar. Still others are simply unwilling to invest money in additional inspections. When the recommendation for further inspection involves potentially serious problems, the cost of addressing these defects can be so enormous that a buyer simply cannot afford to ignore the inspector's recommendation. Those potentially serious problems include:
- structural defects;
- excessive settling;

♦ faulty electrical or plumbing systems;
♦ defective heating and air conditioning systems;
♦ inadequate drainage; and,
♦ problems with mold or other trouble related to excessive moisture.

It is true that the fees charged by some of the experts that the buyers would need to consult can be sizable. However, they can often get follow-up inspections from tradesmen (such as plumbers, electricians, heating and air conditioning technicians, and roofers) for little or no fee, since they are interested in establishing goodwill with potential customers in order to get the job of correcting any existing defects. Another advantage of having tradesmen do follow-up inspections is that they will be willing to give estimates for correcting defects in the property and will usually make a firm commitment to perform the repairs for the estimated price if they are given the job within a reasonable time. On the other hand, inspectors can usually only give an educated guess as to the cost of any repairs, and may not even be willing to do that. The actual cost of repairs can greatly exceed the cost that an inspector or buyer had anticipated. For that reason, it is generally a good idea for buyers to get tradesmen to look at problem areas cited by an inspector and give them firm estimates for the cost to correct them, even when the inspector has not recommended follow-up inspections.

The Termite Inspection

Another type of inspection that is an absolute must for a buyer considering the purchase of a home is a termite and wood-destroying insect inspection. Buyers who must get mortgages on the properties that they have agreed to buy will be required by the lender to get such inspections and produce a clearance letter showing that there is no active infestation and no existing serious insect damage to the property. Buyers who pay cash for their homes or who buy them with proceeds from loans against other properties, and buyers who acquire homes by getting the sellers to finance their purchase, will not be required to get such inspections, but they definitely should insist on that inspection on their own. Any licensed termite control company will generally be qualified to perform such an inspection, but the thoroughness of the inspections varies substantially from company to company. Realtors may know inspectors who are likely to be less detailed in their inspections, and may favor using them in order to facilitate the closing of the transaction. Such termite and pest inspectors are not the best choice from the perspective of the buyer, who will benefit from the most thorough inspection. Ideally, the termite and wood damaging insect inspection should be performed by a company of the buyer's choosing, so that he or she may select an inspector with a reputation for thoroughness. However, since most standard real estate contracts simply require that the seller provide a termite and wood destroying insect clearance letter, unless the buyer puts a provision in the offer as to who is to perform the inspection, the seller will be free to choose the inspector.

Flood Plain Inspection

Still another type of inspection that is essential in many parts of the U.S. is a determination of whether or not a property is in a flood plain. Such determinations, which are made by companies that consult maps of flood plains throughout the U.S., can be done without even having to physically set foot on the property, and usually cost about $20 or less. Lenders insist on flood determinations so they can ascertain whether to require the buyer to carry flood insurance on the property. Those who are buying properties without obtaining a loan from a mortgage company should insist on a flood determination themselves, with a provision that they may declare their obligation to buy the property null and void in the event that it is located in a flood plain.

Other Inspections

Depending on the part of the country that a particular property is located in, there may be other inspections or tests, such as tests for water quality (when the house has its own well) or a radon gas test, that would be advisable. Local real estate boards may be able to offer helpful advice as to inspections and tests that are commonly recommended in this area.

Take a Second Look

Despite all of the expert advice that may be available, there is no substitute for a careful inspection by a buyer. Although the purchase of a home represents the largest expenditure that most people will ever make, buyers often decide to purchase a property after casually spending only a short time walking through it. The real attraction of the property may actually be the seller's furnishings or the cleanliness of the house.

Before making an offer on a property, buyers should go back for a second look with emphasis on any shortcomings in the property, rather than its more appealing attributes. It would be advisable for buyers to do things such as:

◆ measure rooms to make sure that their furniture will fit;
◆ walk over the yard and get a feel for what maintaining it will entail;
◆ go back to houses on busy streets during rush hour to gauge the noise level from the traffic; and,
◆ actually park a vehicle in an awkwardly situated garage or carport.

Buyers who are considering purchasing a home and then adding on to it, or building a garage or other structure, should check with local code enforcement authorities before buying the property to make sure that they will be permitted to make those additions to the property. Also, if a property under consideration is located near vacant land or unfinished roads, it would be advisable for buyers to investigate the usage permitted by zoning laws pertaining to the undeveloped property, and local government's plans for completing the unfinished roads.

Wisely choosing real estate requires time and effort. Remember—it is far better to spend a few hours and dollars evaluating a property than spending far more time and money as a consequence of making a poor choice of which property to buy.

Preparing an Offer

Buyers who decide to move forward with their decision to purchase a property will generally do so by making a written offer to buy it. Buyers who are represented by realtors will usually rely on them to prepare their offers, which are generally written on preprinted contract forms that contain certain standard language, some optional provisions to choose from, some blanks to write in things such as the buyer's name, and some altogether blank spaces in which provisions that are unique to that offer can be added. There is considerable disparity in realtors' skill levels and expertise in preparing offers to purchase real estate. For this and other reasons, it is best for buyers to become sufficiently well acquainted with the process and to have an active role in the preparation of their offers.

One of the most fundamental decisions that anyone who is considering the purchase of real estate must often make is whether to have his or her own real estate agent represent him or her, rather than dealing with the agent that listed the property for sale. As long as both the buyer and seller of a property consent to it, realtors are generally allowed by law to represent both of them in a real estate transaction. However, although the law does not seem to recognize the potential for a conflict of interest in such a relationship, known as a *dual agency*, the potential is most definitely there.

Agents who contract with sellers to represent them in the sale of their properties are known as *listing agents*, since the contracts that they enter into to represent a seller are known are known as *listing contracts*. Upon execution of such contracts, the properties are added to the list of those that are available for sale.

Along with provisions for commission rates and the duration of the relationship, listing agreements also contain language in one form or another that requires the realtor to use his or her best efforts to market the seller's property and otherwise represent the seller. The listing agreement will contain an asking price for the property, but sellers and their agents will often discuss pricing strategies, minimum acceptable prices, possible non-price concessions, and a host of other things that are pertinent to the sale of the property, but are not revealed to prospective buyers in the information that the realtor disseminates to other realtors or the general public.

Likewise, buyers often discuss buying strategies, the maximum price that they will pay, and concessions that they would be willing to make, with their realtors. Buyers also often rely on their realtors to gather information for them regarding the property, such as the sale price of comparable properties, historical price data, the outlook for appreciation, and the name of a good inspector to perform a home inspection of the property.

The negotiation process between a buyer and seller of real estate is somewhat adversarial. When the same agent represents both parties, that agent will have to refrain from attempting to advise either the buyer or the seller, or the realtor will likely end up revealing the secret information of one of the parties to the other. As a result, buyers who choose to allow the sellers' agents to represent both parties will likely lose the valuable counsel available by having their own agents, will run the risk that the agent may represent them in a disadvantageous way by favoring the seller, or may be held liable by the sellers if the agents betray the sellers' confidence and enable the buyers to take unfair advantage of the sellers. However, since a real estate agent who represents both the buyer and seller in a real estate transaction will be entitled to the full commission, such an agent will have a strong incentive to push the buyer to purchase the house that the realtor has listed, even if he or she knows of alternative properties that might suit the buyer better, but which have been listed by other agents who will be entitled to their share of the commission.

Most realtors are willing to sign *cooperative agreements* with other agents who present them with offers to buy properties that they have listed. The agreements provide that the agent representing the buyer, referred to as the *selling agent* (since he or she is the one that ultimately sells the property if the buyer's offer is accepted), will receive part, usually half, of the commission that the seller has agreed to pay to the listing agent if the property is sold. Since the agent representing the buyer can usually get part of the commission that is paid by the seller, buyers generally are not required to pay their real estate agents themselves.

There is another major advantage that a buyer has in having his or her own realtor, apart from eliminating the possibility of a conflict of interest when an agent represents both buyer and seller. When a realtor exclusively represents a buyer, that person will not usually have a motive for favoring any one property over the other, since the commission will likely be about the same regardless of which house the buyer chooses from among a group of houses in about the same price range.

Terms of the Offer

Regardless of whether or not a buyer is represented by a realtor, there are certain provisions that should be considered for inclusion in any offer to buy real estate. Offers give the party to whom the offer is made an opportunity to cause a contract to be formed by merely agreeing to the terms of the offer. Therefore, it is imperative that offers include all of the terms that buyers ultimately want in their contracts. Making an incomplete offer with the intent to fill in the details later on is a dangerous approach, since once an offer is accepted, a contract is formed. Once a contract is formed, any changes in it require the consent of both the buyer and the seller. Offers should definitely include a list of any personal property, such as curtains or appliances, that are to be included in the sale of the property. Provisions for property inspections, termite inspections, or any other tests or inspections, should be included in a buyer's offer. Buyers should not assume that the sale of the property will include any terms or provisions that are not included in their written contracts.

Contingencies

Any conditions that must be met before a buyer intends to be obligated to purchase a piece of property or is able to fulfill the duty to buy it, referred to as *contingencies*, should be spelled out in any offer written by a buyer or prepared on his or her behalf. Deciding what contingencies to put into an offer can be challenging. Sellers prefer offers with absolutely no contingencies, so they can count on their properties being sold when they accept the buyers' offers.

The more contingencies that an offer contains, the less attractive the offer will be to the seller. For this reason, real estate agents—even those representing only the buyer—may encourage buyers to minimize their contingencies in hopes that the offer will be accepted and they can collect their commissions. Therefore, it may seem that a buyer and his or her realtor may be at odds with one another on the issue of what contingencies to include in an offer, and to an extent, this is true. However, if a buyer really wants an offer to be attractive to a seller, it is definitely in the buyer's best interest to minimize contingencies in his or her offer. This is why conducting inspections and making inquiries as to the costs of improvements and repairs, as well as verifying the availability of permits to make changes to a property, are best done before an offer is even made, so those issues will not have to be addressed in the form of a contingency.

Of course, buyers who are going to have to get a loan in order to be able to purchase a property should make their offer to purchase it contingent on their being able to get the necessary loan. This contingency can be made more palatable to a seller if the buyer will apply for loan approval with a lender, and get approved for a loan up to some specified limit, before making an offer to buy a property. However, even buyers who go through this process, known as *preapproval*, should put financing contingencies in their offers, since getting preapproved for a loan does not bind the lenders to actually make loans on specific pieces of property when the buyers eventually make their choices.

One of the least appealing contingencies in any buyer's offer to purchase real estate is a stipulation that the buyer will not be bound to make the purchase unless the buyer is able to sell a property that he or she already owns. However, buyers who are unable to buy an additional property without selling one that they own in order to get money for a down payment, or who do not have sufficient income to qualify for an additional mortgage without paying off the one they already have, will have no choice but to put such a contingency in their offers. The only alternative for such buyers is to sell their homes and close the transactions before making an offer to buy another house. This strategy may put buyers in a position to make more appealing offers on properties they are interested in buying, but it could cause them to buy a replacement home hastily or face the prospect of having to rent a place to live and move into it, only to have to move a second time when they finally find a suitable property to buy.

Ask for What You Want

In writing offers to buy real estate, buyers have the opportunity to propose any number of possible provisions, as long as they do not ask the sellers to do something illegal, such as secretly providing money to the buyers so they can make the necessary down payment. Offers requiring that sellers make improvements to their property before the sale, offers requiring sellers to pay closing costs on behalf of the buyers, and offers that require sellers to include some of their furnishings in the sale, are all examples of perfectly legitimate offers.

Buyers should not be bashful about writing offers at prices significantly less than the sellers' asking prices or that require other concessions on the sellers' part, despite urgings to the contrary by their realtors. Although some realtors are aggressive in trying to help their clients get a bargain, others are timid about presenting what they consider to be low offers, and would rather have the buyer pay too much for the property than be embarrassed by having to present a low offer.

Chapter 8:

Investing in Rental Real Estate

One of the more traditional ways to invest in real estate is to acquire property to rent out. There are several aspects of owning rental property that make it attractive, and there are degrees of involvement that are available to fit almost everyone's financial ability and desire to participate in the real estate rental market.

Choosing a Level of Involvement

Those who have limited funds and little time to manage rental property, but who still want to become involved in rental real estate ownership, can do so at the most basic level by purchasing a duplex to live in one side as a primary residence and rent out the other side. This approach gives the owner an opportunity to maintain a watchful eye on his or her rental property without ever having to leave home. Of course, having a tenant that practically lives in the same house as the landlord will make it especially critical that the landlord wisely choose a tenant, with consideration given to the tenant's compatibility as a neighbor, as well his or her ability to pay the rent. Also, living as close to the landlord as the tenant does in such situations will make it very convenient for the tenant to complain about the slightest problem with his or her side of the duplex. However, it is not unusual for owners of duplexes who live in one side and find a good tenant for the other side to be able to collect enough rent from the tenant to practically pay the entire monthly mortgage. This is especially likely to be the case when the landlord has owned the duplex for a number of years and has been able to raise rents to reflect increases in housing costs while the payments on the mortgage loan have remained fixed.

Have a Plan

Individuals who decide to take the plunge into rental real estate ownership often have little or no business experience, and no experience as a landlord. As a result of this inexperience, they may fail to start their venture off with the most fundamental step to success, which is the development of a business plan. Among the first things that lenders require of business owners who are seeking loans is a business plan. They recognize that careful planning is essential to success. By requiring borrowers to submit their business plans, lenders force loan applicants to plan for various contingencies and prove that they have done so. Those who buy properties with the intention of renting them out will generally need to obtain a loan in order to make those purchases. However, lenders will usually view applicants' requests for loans that they intend to buy rental property with as being strictly real estate loan applications, rather than applications for business loans, despite the fact that selecting, acquiring, and managing rental real estate is, unquestionably, a business. Therefore, despite the fact that lenders will not likely require them, aspiring landlords need to realize the necessity of good planning, and should prepare a business plan on their own initiative.

One of the most basic decisions that those who want to acquire rental property must make in developing their business plans is what type of properties they are going to attempt to acquire. Choices include single-family residences, duplexes, apartment buildings, and a wide variety of commercial buildings, all of which have their own unique advantages and disadvantages. All too often, investors who are looking for rental properties make purchases based on the happenstance of what is offered to them, rather than as a part of a well thought-out master business plan. As a result, they often end up with a scattered conglomeration of properties that are nearly impossible to efficiently manage.

In addition to narrowing down the type of property that the investor intends to buy and rent out, his or her business plan should also address the location where properties will be sought. A good business plan for acquiring and renting out real estate should also include a schedule for acquisition, anticipated capital requirements, plans for managing the properties, and exit strategies.

Choosing the Type of Properties to Acquire

There is no single type of rental property that is an ideal choice for everyone. Among the major factors that determine which type of property is the best choice for a specific person are the amount of capital available for acquisition of rental properties, the time available to devote to rental activity, and the skills and experience that the investor has that are relevant to real estate rental.

Multi-family residential properties, such as apartment buildings, often generate more rental income per dollar of investment than single-family rental houses do, but they will virtually always require more time managing them. Therefore, for a person who has retired from full-time employment and wants to become active in renting out residential real estate, especially if that person has experience in managing apartments and maintaining an apartment complex, acquiring an apartment building or apartment complex would make sense. However, a person with an interest in acquiring rental property who has no prior experience in renting out residential property, and has little time to devote to property management, would be ill advised to acquire apartment buildings.

One of the more attractive aspects of investing in rental real estate is that investors can be involved at any of a wide range of levels.

Furthermore, investors can ease into the rental real estate market with the acquisition of one small single-family house, and expand their holdings as rapidly or slowly as they choose, depending on how comfortable they become with being landlords, and the extent of their time and financial resources that they can devote to the acquisition and management of additional properties. Before buying even one property, those who are interested in acquiring rental properties should do the necessary research to determine the profile of their ideal choice to serve as a guide in making their selections.

Evaluating Features

Properties that would make terrific primary residences for their owners are often horrible choices for use as rental properties. Since renters often abuse the properties that they rent, houses with expensive hardwood flooring, top quality carpeting, high quality cabinetry, and any of a number of other costly amenities are likely to suffer substantial damage at the hands of tenants. The landlord will then be faced with the choice of incurring expensive repairs to restore the property to its former condition or replacing damaged components of the property with cheaper substitutes that will likely lessen the resale value of the property. Although houses with nice amenities in them will have a more appealing appearance that may help them rent faster, they probably will not rent for appreciably more money than the less well-appointed homes of the same size that are located in the same neighborhood.

Most homeowners enjoy having such features as central vacuum cleaners, built-in ice making machines, and trash compactors in their homes, but these are not good features for landlords to have in their rental properties, since they can be costly to maintain or replace, and most tenants do not even expect such things in properties that they are going to rent. In an effort to minimize maintenance costs, landlords should provide as few appliances and accessories as they can, and still be able to rent the property out within a reasonable time. Landlords should even avoid providing their tenants with refrigerators when they can, since not only are they costly to buy and repair, but during periods in which properties are vacant or are rented to tenants with their own refrigerators, landlords must keep the refrigerators running, or they will tend to mold and soon become unusable. Tenants will usually accept the landlord's decision not to provide appliances with their rental homes when the landlord explains that if appliances were provided, the tenant would be expected to pay more rent in order to cover their cost, and rather than buying appliances for the landlord, the tenants will be better off buying the appliances of their own choice for themselves. However, know that in certain areas appliances being included with the rental is expected.

Profiting from Rental Activities

There are three basic ways in which owners of rental properties can profit from their rental activities. Since realizing a profit is the pri-mary—if not the only—reason for becoming a landlord, these three considerations should receive major emphasis in the rental property selection process. Historically, many U.S. taxpayers bought rental real estate because they could use losses that were generated from depre-ciation to offset their taxable earnings from employment and other sources. However, tax deductions for losses from rented real estate have been severely restricted by amendments to the Internal Revenue Code. (see Chapter 15.) Apart from any tax savings that might have formerly been available by taking tax write-offs on rental property, landlords have always had the opportunity to realize profits from rental income and market appreciation of their rental properties, and these are even more important today in light of those unfavorable tax law changes.

Buying for Rental Income

In order to realize rental income, a landlord must be able to collect rent in excess of the costs of ownership of the rental property. In addition to mortgage payments, property taxes, and insurance, landlords must also allow for the following:

- ◆ maintenance;
- ◆ advertising and other costs associated with finding a tenant;

◆ periods of vacancy between tenants; and,

◆ sinking funds for long-term upkeep, such as replacement of the roof, painting the exterior, replacing furnaces and air conditioners, and preparing the property for a new tenant when it becomes vacant.

Even with the tax laws that prohibit some taxpayers from using losses from renting out property to offset other income, landlords are still allowed to take an allowance for the wearing out of their property, referred to as *depreciation*, and use it to offset rental income that they would otherwise have to report. The depreciation deduction is permitted, despite the fact that the value of the property is probably actually appreciating. As a result of the depreciation deduction, landlords often show little or no rental income on their books, and may even show losses, but are actually able to generate a positive cash flow that they can use to make improvements to their properties, acquire more rental units, or spend as they please.

To the extent that landlords are unable to cover their out-of-pocket expenses associated with rental property ownership, they will be forced to cover those expenses with income from other sources. Therefore, it is important for buyers of rental property to carefully analyze the rental potential for every property that they seriously consider buying. Opportunities to buy relatively high-priced properties at attractive prices may become available from time to time, but higher-priced properties are usually difficult to rent out for enough money to generate a positive cash flow. (It is difficult to find tenants who are willing to pay rent that is considerably higher than average rents for a given locale.)

For example, for a house that costs twice as much as the average house available for rent in a particular area to generate the same return on investment as an average house in the area, it would have to rent for twice as much as one that sold for the average price. This is because the mortgage payments, insurance, taxes, and other costs associated with owning that expensive house should be about double those associated with owning the average-priced house. However, most renters cannot afford to pay twice the average rate of rent, and those who can pay that much rent would likely be able to afford to buy their own homes. Even people who are going to be in an area for too short a time to make home ownership practical are still likely to shy away from renting an expensive property, since they will be occupying it for only a relatively short time and will get no long-term advantage from renting the more expensive property.

Buyers who choose the least costly properties to purchase for use as rental property will be able to offer the cheapest rental rates, but still may not be able to attract desirable tenants. Tenants who rent housing in an area's worst locations usually do so because they cannot afford a better place to live. Those who can afford to pay at least the average rate of rent for a residence will usually see enough added value from living in an area with better schools, lower crime, and nicer housing that they are more than willing to pay the difference in rent between a house in an average neighborhood and one in a substandard area. As a result, landlords who offer low rental rates, but in unpopular neighborhoods, will probably attract only those applicants who are likely to have trouble paying even below-average rates of rent.

Investors who have chosen to acquire commercial properties to rent out will usually also find that their best choice of properties for generating a positive cash flow are those that are not rented too far above or too far below average rental rates for that type of property in that general area. Only a limited number of businesses can afford to pay relatively exorbitant rates of rent and still expect to make a profit, and properties in undesirable areas usually attract undercapitalized tenants who would like to be elsewhere, but cannot afford a better location, and may well have trouble paying even modest amounts of rent.

Before You Buy

Choosing rental property is not unlike Goldilock's quest for a chair, some porridge, and a bed. Rather than relying on trial-and-error, and perhaps making a costly mistake, aspiring landlords have the opportunity to enhance their chances for success by making an informed decision based on some prepurchase fact gathering. The same features that make the location of a property attractive to prospective buyers will also make it attractive to prospective tenants. Therefore, before making an offer to buy a property for rental, the buyer should investigate the quality and availability of local schools, neighborhood crime rates, the level of fire and police protection, and the proximity of shopping areas and public facilities. Buyers of prospective rental properties should definitely find out what the property tax rates are for properties that they are considering, the history of rate increases, and whether a different rate will be imposed if the property is converted from an owner-occupied property to one that is rented. A similar inquiry should be made concerning the cost of hazard insurance on a property being considered for purchase as a rental unit.

It would also be advisable, before purchasing properties for use as rental units, to determine the rental income that they would likely generate. This information will not be as readily available as tax and insurance information, unless the property is already being rented. Buyers who already own similar properties in the neighborhood will likely be able to gauge what an additional property in the neighborhood could be expected to generate in rent. (This is one of the reasons why it is advantageous for landlords to acquire relatively homogeneous properties.) However, those who do not have rental histories of similar properties available to them can still get useful information to help them estimate a property's rental value by checking newspaper advertisements for similar rental properties, calling the landlords to inquire about the properties, arranging to see some of the properties, and monitoring the properties to see how long it takes to rent them. This sounds easy, but a buyer who has gotten excited about a property will have a hard time waiting to make an offer on that property in order to thoroughly investigate its rental potential.

Buying for Market Appreciation

Although real estate prices have generally risen over the long-term, some properties have appreciated far more than others, and some have even declined in value. Properties with the greatest potential for appreciation may be too costly or otherwise unsuitable for use as rental property. However, there will be properties available that are viable rental units and offer good potential for appreciation. The successful landlords will be those who buy properties that appreciate faster than the average property, while avoiding those that decline in value or lag behind the market in their rate of appreciation.

Landlords who place a high priority on potential for market appreciation when they are looking for rental property to purchase should focus their attention on factors such as:

- ◆ quality and availability of neighborhood schools;
- ◆ low crime rates;
- ◆ adequate police and fire protection;
- ◆ proximity to shopping areas; and,
- ◆ good local government that maintains stable tax rates while providing adequate services.

These are the same things that the landlord should consider in determining whether or not a property will appeal to prospective tenants. However, unlike the evaluation to determine whether a property will rent well, the determination of a property's potential for future appreciation should be based on the outlook for the future as it pertains to these factors, rather than their current status.

In essence, the landlord should attempt to determine what the area where the property is located will be like at the point in the future when he or she is likely to want to sell it. In making this determination, the types of things that should be considered are whether new businesses move in when old businesses close up, whether properties in the area are being maintained, and whether new development is taking place in the area (and if so, whether the newly developed properties are better or worse than existing developments).

Of course, historical data concerning the rate of appreciation of property in an area will always be available, and it may be of some value in predicting future appreciation potential, unless the character of the neighborhood has changed. Rarely do the shabbiest of areas undergo a transformation and become desirable places to be. However, it is not uncommon for areas that are conveniently located, but have become somewhat run-down, to experience a renewed level of interest that drives up property values. Indications of a rebirth in a neighborhood are such things as rapid sales when properties are put on the market, expensive renovation projects on homes in the neighborhood, and an influx of businesses that tend to cater to more upscale customers. The rejuvenation of a neighborhood will tend to have ripple effects that spread to adjacent neighborhoods. Therefore, the landlord who can recognize which neighborhood has just begun to make a comeback, and then anticipate which neighborhood is likely to benefit next from that area's renaissance, can get ahead of the market and position him- or herself to profit from the future redevelopment.

Buying properties in a neighborhood that is an emerging hot spot requires some boldness. Buyers must decide whether recent price increases that such areas will have already experienced have pushed prices of houses in the area beyond their reasonable value, or if those increases are simply a prelude to larger further advances in prices of properties in the area. However, as with properties bought for a personal residence, a rental property of only mediocre quality and condition in a desirable location is far preferable to a rental property that is of outstanding quality and condition in an undesirable location. The difficult part of the equation for successful property selection is finding properties in good locations without having to pay too much for them.

Think Long-Term

Although it is not impossible to find properties that can produce a positive rental cash flow and still have good potential for market appreciation, there is a degree of a trade-off between the two. Fortunately, properties that were too costly to permit them to initially generate enough rent to produce a positive return can eventually do so, as rental rates rise with inflation and increasing popularity of a neighborhood. Some investors feel strongly about a property's potential for appreciation, and can do without immediate net rental income from the property or can even afford to subsidize a negative cash flow from it for a while. These investors should not rule out the properties in better neighborhoods with above-average appreciation potential, despite the fact that there is no real likelihood that the property will generate a positive cash flow for a while. Even properties that are not appreciating rapidly and are not generating net rental income will, by virtue of the fact that the balances on the mortgages on them will be reduced with each payment, still add to the owner's wealth. This is provided that he or she has not made such poor choices that the value of the properties declines or the properties cannot be rented out for at least enough to cover the costs of owning them.

Preparing Rental Properties

Even well-chosen rental properties will not generate positive cash flow if they are not properly managed. Generating rental income requires being able to quickly rent out a property at a competitive rental rate to a tenant who fulfills his or her rental obligation. Once a landlord has chosen property that is sufficiently appealing and was bought at a price that makes it possible to rent it for enough money to generate a positive cash flow, the work has just begun. No matter how appealing a property may be, even minor, superficial deficiencies in the appearance of the property can discourage potential tenants from agreeing to rent it. A property can be located in a very convenient area, but things such as a dirty bathroom or a hole in the sheetrock wall can make such a bad impression on those who come to see it that they do not seriously consider renting it. Therefore, the first step in generating a positive cash flow from a rental property is to properly prepare it before even offering it for rent.

Preparation of property for rental should start with a thorough cleanup of the exterior of the property. The yard should be cut, bushes should be trimmed, broken windows should be replaced, and, if it needs it, the house should be painted on the outside in order to enhance its appearance and preserve the property. Even if a structure does not need to be painted on the outside, it is often advisable to freshen up the paint on and around the doors, since these highly visible areas are often soiled or the paint is worn from constant handling. If a property does not have an attractive appearance upon approaching it, a characteristic often referred to as *curb appeal*, many prospective tenants will never look inside.

A thorough cleaning of the inside of almost any building is a necessity when readying a property for placement on the rental market. A fresh coat of paint on the inside of most houses and other buildings is a relatively inexpensive way to enhance their appearance, and will usually be a necessity to cover the signs of ordinary wear and tear left when tenants move out. Smart landlords paint all of the rooms in all of their houses the same color and can nicely repaint most of their properties with a single coat of that same paint. Carpets should be professionally cleaned, and if they are too heavily soiled for cleaning to be effective or if they are damaged, they should be replaced. Plumbing, electrical systems, appliances, and heating and air conditioning systems should be serviced, and anything that is inoperable should be repaired. Houses that are in move-in condition will invite tenants to do just that. In short, when a landlord shows a rental property to a prospective tenant, there should be nothing about the condition of the property for which the landlord feels compelled to make excuses or apologies.

Landlords need to bear in mind that not only do they need to thoroughly prepare their properties before offering them for rent, but they should also make the necessary preparations quickly. Owners of rental property often like to clean up and repair their own properties. However, if they do not have ample time to quickly prepare a property to rent it, any money that they save from doing their own cleanup and repair work will be more than offset by the rent that they lose. Also, vacant properties are more likely to be vandalized.

Choosing Residential Tenants

Once a property has been made ready to rent out, it is important to aggressively market it to prospective tenants. Advertisements in the want-ad section of local newspapers will reach the most prospective tenants. The few extra dollars spent running a relatively descriptive advertisement, rather than one with merely the bare essentials, will usually be money well spent. Most landlords find it worth while to have permanent "FOR RENT" signs made up that can be placed on whichever of their properties is vacant. The signs alert neighbors, who may have family or friends looking for a place to live, that the property is available, and may also catch the attention of prospective tenants driving through the neighborhood in search of a place to rent.

Another aspect of aggressively attempting to find a suitable tenant involves understanding the role of the landlord in the process. Successful landlords are those who are able to sell tenants on leasing their properties. This involves being willing to meet with prospective tenants on short notice. It will also require having utilities on at the property so that it can be shown at night, and the property should be kept at a comfortable temperature by running either the heat or air conditioning as needed, so that the property will give the impression of being a comfortable place to live. Telling callers to drive by a property and call back if they like what they see is a lazy way to deal with prospective tenants.

If, after questioning a caller over the telephone, the person seems to be a good prospect, the landlord should push for a complete showing in order to have the opportunity to make a sales pitch to the prospective tenant. The initial conversation with a caller is an opportune time for the landlord to find out where the caller's place of employment is located and his or her interests. By learning various things about the prospective tenant, the landlord can then tailor his or her presentation to address the tenant's concerns. For example, there is no need to mention proximity of schools to a prospect who has no children. However, making mention of a nearby satellite campus of a local college would be important to a person who had indicated an interest in going back to school to complete a degree.

Credit Checks

In addition to using the initial call from a prospective tenant to learn something about the caller's needs in order to better market the property to that person, the landlord should also begin to aggressively screen applicants at that time. Some people are uncomfortable asking callers personal questions about their financial matters on the first occasion that they ever have to speak to them, but it will be absolutely necessary in order to avoid wasting time showing properties to callers who are not viable prospects. Most callers understand that in order to rent a property, the landlord must be willing to extend credit to them by permitting them to pay their rent in monthly installments, rather than paying it in a lump sum for the entire term of the lease at its inception. Therefore, it is reasonable for a landlord to ask callers for information concerning their incomes and credit histories at the earliest stage of the rental process.

Most callers are not offended when property owners tell them that they need some preliminary information before setting up a showing of the property, and then following that statement by asking what the caller's net income is per week. If a prospective tenant does not earn enough to cover the rent, or get close to it, with a week's net pay, he or she will likely struggle to pay the rent.

Questioning callers about whether they have credit cards, car loans, or other credit accounts, and the approximate balances and monthly payments on them, will reveal not only whether they have been deemed creditworthy by various lenders, but also whether or not they are financially overextended. Another effective way to flush out information from callers is to state that credit checks of applicants are required before they will be allowed to lease a property and then ask, "What will yours show?" Most people will be reasonably candid in response, and this will give the landlords a chance to thin out callers with a history of nonpayment or slow payment of their obligation.

Security Deposits

In an effort to deter tenants from damaging the properties that they rent, and in order to provide landlords with funds with which to make repairs in the event that tenants do damage the property, virtually all landlords require their tenants to pay *security deposits* at the inception of their leases. Since tenants will also be required to pay their first month's rent, and in some instances, their last month's rent, at the beginning of their leases, some prospective tenants will invariably ask to be allowed to pay their security deposit on installments with their rent. This rarely works out. Most of the time, they do not add in the monthly payment toward their security deposits along with their rental payments, anticipating that the landlord will not go so far as to evict them over the issue of the security deposit, and they usually are right. As a result, the landlord will have no security deposit to cover damages when the tenant moves out. More importantly, the fact that a tenant is unable to pay both the first month's rent and the security deposit together shows that he or she has no financial reserves, and even the slightest unusual expense or loss of income will leave the tenant unable to pay the rent. Therefore, the fact that a security deposit is required, and the amount involved, should be discussed at the time of a prospective tenant's first contact with the property owner, and it should be made clear that the deposit must be paid in full at the time that the lease is executed.

Discrimination

It is illegal for landlords to discriminate against people on the basis of such factors as race, creed, color, national origin, or gender in choosing a tenant, but it is perfectly legitimate for them to refuse to rent properties to applicants with poor credit histories or inadequate incomes to pay the rent. Also, landlords may refuse to rent to applicants who have pets or who will have more people living in the property than it can reasonably accommodate. In fact, zoning laws often limit the number of occupants that are allowed to live in a single residence. Successful landlords know when to say no to a prospective tenant, despite the fact that their properties will remain vacant for a while longer. One of the toughest lessons for novice landlords to learn is that they are better off with a vacancy than they are with a bad tenant.

The Application

Once a prospective tenant indicates a willingness to rent a property, he or she should fill out an application. Questions pertaining to the applicant's race, creed, national origin, or any other factor that is illegal to consider in deciding whether to accept an applicant as a tenant should not be included in the application. However, it should require applicants to reveal the following:

- ◆ names;
- ◆ addresses and telephone numbers of past landlords;
- ◆ credit references;
- ◆ personal references;
- ◆ past and present employers and how to contact them;
- ◆ a person to contact in emergencies;
- ◆ banks in which they have accounts and the account numbers;
- ◆ drivers' license numbers and the state of issue;
- ◆ the license tag numbers on their automobiles; and,
- ◆ Social Security numbers.

The object of gathering such extensive information from applicants is not only to provide the landlord with sources to verify their propensity and ability to pay their rent, but also to provide the landlord with information to help find them if they enter into a lease and then leave owing money for unpaid rent or damage to the property. Having information concerning a former tenant's bank accounts or automobile registration can also prove useful at a later date when landlords are trying to collect judgments against their former tenants.

Verify the Information

Some property owners may assume that since a rental applicant was willing to reveal credit information and supply references and employment history, the applicant has nothing to hide and that doing a credit check, contacting references, and verifying employment and earnings will be unnecessary. This is a dangerous assumption. The least desirable applicants are often the ones most likely to falsify their rental applications.

Credit checks, which are available for a modest fee and can be passed on to the applicant, are a must. In order to be able to obtain credit histories of applicants, landlords will have to enroll with a credit bureau or affiliate with someone who has already enrolled. Landlords must obtain a written, signed authorization from an applicant before requesting a credit report, and such authorizations can, and should, be incorporated into the rental application. References, especially prior landlords, should be contacted, and current employment and earnings should be verified.

Since some employers and references will want written authorization from the applicant before they will release information about that person, a separate form giving blanket authorization for all parties to release information about the applicant to the landlord should be executed along with the application. If the applicant's employer will not release information regarding the applicant's earnings, the landlord should require the applicant to provide proof of earnings in the form of a pay stub.

The Difficulty of Removing Bad Tenants

Obtaining credit histories and verifying information that prospective tenants provide on their rental applications can prove to be tedious, but failure to properly screen applicants can be disastrous. Bad tenants can be difficult to remove. Those who get behind on their rent and are unwilling to move out voluntarily have to be evicted. This requires the following to be completed:

◆ filing a legal action;
◆ getting the tenant served or otherwise officially notified of the impending legal action;
◆ appearing at a hearing to get an order awarding possession of the property back to the landlord;

- waiting for the lapse of any period for an appeal that is set by statute; and,
- obtaining a writ of possession authorizing the landlord to set the tenant's belongings out of the property and then executing that writ.

Eviction actions take time and require the payment of court costs. If the landlord does not handle his or her own eviction, the landlord has to pay attorney's fees. Also, tenants who are evicted almost always leave properties in poor condition—some even deliberately damage the premises as an act of revenge for having been evicted. Worst of all, if at any time prior to actually being forcibly removed from a property, a tenant files bankruptcy, the bankruptcy court may issue a *stay*, which is an order forbidding any action in connection with a delinquent debt being taken against the party who filed the bankruptcy. Once the stay is issued, the landlord must cease any further actions pertaining to the eviction of the bankrupt tenant and allow the matter to be taken under consideration by the bankruptcy court. This can result in a period of several months in which the tenant continues to occupy the landlord's property without paying any rent, but the tenant cannot be evicted. Furthermore, once the tenant's bankruptcy case is concluded, there is considerable likelihood that the tenant's obligation to the landlord for unpaid rent and damages will be *discharged*, which means that the obligation will be forever extinguished.

No matter how carefully landlords screen their applicants, they are eventually going to get a tenant who fails to pay the rent. When this happens, it is imperative that the landlord take swift action. Most tenants develop a payment pattern, such as paying their rent just before the first of each month or by the fifth of the month. Landlords should monitor their tenant's payments from the perspective of whether they have paid their rent by their usual time, rather than whether they have paid by the latest allowable date without incurring a late charge.

When a tenant has not paid the rent by the usual time, the landlord should call the tenant and express concern that the check may have been lost in the mail, since the tenant's checks in the past had already arrived by that date. Such a call serves as a gentle reminder to the tenant, and also alerts him or her to the fact that the landlord is paying close attention to whether or not rental payments are being made on time. Also, during the course of such a telephone conversation, the tenant may reveal to the landlord the fact that something has happened that has jeopardized the tenant's ability to pay the rent. If a landlord does not receive a rental payment at the usual time of the month and cannot reach the tenant by telephone, he or she should pay a visit to the property to see if it has been abandoned, and avoid wasting time that could be used preparing the property to re-rent it to another tenant.

One of the most troubling aspects of being a landlord is taking a firm stance with delinquent tenants. When they get behind on their rental payments, they generally offer any of a number of excuses and promise to soon begin catching up on the delinquency. It is especially hard not to believe long-term tenants who have a good payment history, but there are developments, such as loss of employment or physical disabilities, that will impair a person's ability to pay his or her rent. Prolonging the inevitable move to a less costly place to live will simply cause the tenant to fall further behind on rental payments, while causing hardship for the landlord who is no longer collecting rental payments with which to pay the mortgage on the property. Once a tenant falls behind on rental payments, it is extremely difficult for him or her to catch up, since catching up requires the tenant who has been unable to pay his or her rent to not only start back to paying the monthly rent, but to pay extra rent as well.

To be successful in managing rental property, landlords must take a firm stance with tenants almost immediately when they are late paying their rent, and start eviction proceedings when delinquencies are not quickly cleared up. Those who are not prepared to take such an approach should not become landlords.

When it becomes apparent that a tenant who has gotten behind on his or her rental payments cannot afford to rent the property as agreed, some landlords, in an attempt to get the delinquent tenant to move without having to go through a costly and time-consuming eviction, will offer such tenants enough money to promptly—and voluntarily—move. However, it is illegal for landlords to forcibly remove tenants and their belongs without having gone through the eviction process, and landlords who do so will expose themselves to legal action and liability for the property of improperly dispossessed tenants.

Choosing Commercial Tenants

Managing commercial property is easier than managing residential rental property in some aspects, but in other ways it is more difficult. In selecting a tenant for commercial property, the landlord should evaluate applicants as if he or she were going into an unofficial partnership with the tenant that is selected, since in most cases, the tenant will be earning the money to pay the rent from whatever business activity is conducted at the property. Therefore, in making the determination as to whether to enter into a commercial lease agreement with an applicant, the landlord should focus considerable attention on the viability of the business that the prospective tenant plans to open on the premises, in addition to the party's credit history.

If the applicant has other locations at which he or she is operating a similar type of business, it would be advisable for the property owner to visit one of those locations in order to evaluate both the appearance of the business and its volume of customers. Landlords should also require financial statements pertaining to both the individual seeking the lease and his or her business, if it is already in operation. Obtaining past tax returns can also prove useful in evaluating the stability of a business.

If the prospective tenant is a small corporation, limited liability company, or limited liability partnership, and the landlord enters into an agreement with such an entity, the owners of the business will not be personally liable on the lease. Therefore, it is essential for landlords who rent properties to small companies, whose organizational structures give their owners limited liability, to require the owners of those companies to agree to be personally liable on those companies' leases. This can be accomplished by having the owners become co-obligors on the lease along with their company. When this is done, the lease should state that the owners will be personally liable on the lease, along with their company. Each owner who is going to assume liability should sign the lease, and it should be noted next to each of their signatures that they are signing *individually*.

In addition to the signatures of the business owners who have agreed to be personally liable, the lease agreement should also be signed by an authorized agent of the business, with a notation to the effect that the party is signing on behalf of, and binding, the business. Therefore, if one of the owners who has agreed to be personally liable is also acting as the agent representing the business, that person will have to sign the lease twice—once to create personal liability and once to bind the business.

Managing Commercial Property

The aspect of managing commercial rental property that is usually easier than managing residential rental property is that tenants, rather than property owners, are often responsible for repairs and routine maintenance of the commercial properties they rent. Commercial rental agreements are commonly referred to as *triple net* leases. This means that the rent payment specified in the lease agreement is what the landlord will net after payment of all property taxes, insurance, maintenance, and repairs. This can be accomplished either by the tenant paying those expenses directly, or by the landlord paying them and getting reimbursed by the tenant. If the tenant is renting only part of a structure, such as a bay in a shopping center, the landlord will generally pay the property taxes, insurance, and maintenance costs associated with common areas, and then prorate the costs among his or her tenants based on the percentage of the square footage of the entire structure that each tenant occupies. In any event, in a triple net lease, the tenant is responsible for property taxes, insurance, and maintenance on the space that he or she has leased. The term *triple* is used in describing such leases because the responsibility for these expenses has been shifted, by agreement, from the landlord to the tenant.

Although triple net provisions are very popular in commercial leases, they will not be assumed to be part of such leases unless they are specifically included, and if a lease agreement does not have a triple net provision, the property owners will be responsible for property taxes, insurance, and upkeep on their property. Also, since property taxes, insurance, and the cost of maintaining common areas of the buildings can be quite high, tenants may have a hard time paying their shares of these costs in a lump sum, even when the lease agreement calls for them to do so. Therefore, it is advisable to estimate each tenant's share of annual property taxes, insurance, and common area maintenance costs for the year under the terms of a triple net lease, and have the party pay one-twelfth of that total each month with his or her rent. Such a provision should be included in the lease agreement, along with the further provision that proper adjustments in the tenant's payments will be made once the actual costs of these items is determined. The costs of repairs and maintenance of a specific space are usually paid directly by tenants as they are incurred.

Chapter 9:

The Lease Agreement

Most of the time, when a landlord and tenant enter into a rental contract, they do so by means of a written lease agreement that is signed by both parties. The parties are largely free to negotiate their own lease agreement, although certain provisions may be required by the state that has jurisdiction over the agreement. Landlords should consult with a local attorney to make sure that their leases comply with the laws of the governing state. In an effort to bring about some consistency from state to state concerning the laws pertaining to rental agreements, many states have adopted at least some of the provisions of the *Uniform Residential Landlord Tenant Act*, which was developed by the Commission on Uniform State Laws. Therefore, there are certain lease provisions, which are based on the Uniform Residential Landlord Tenant Act, that should appear in residential leases in states that have adopted the Act. These provisions would likely also be appropriate in leases in states that have not adopted the Act, unless a given state has laws to the contrary.

Most leases start out by identifying the parties to the lease. The landlord is often referred to as the *lessor* and the tenant is referred to as the *lessee*. The length of the rental period should be set forth in the lease. In the absence of such a provision, most jurisdictions will regard the lease as a month-to-month tenancy. Although it is not required, parties to a lease are free to provide for renewal provisions in the agreement. Otherwise, when tenants remain in possession of leased property after the lease has expired, the tenant usually will be considered to be on a month-to-month tenancy during the holdover period.

There are a couple of approaches to renewal provisions. Some landlords put renewal clauses in their leases providing that if the tenants do not give notice of their intent not to renew their leases at least thirty days before they expire, they will automatically renew for a term equal in length to the original term, and under either the same conditions or some alternative stated conditions.

Whether courts will enforce such provisions will be a matter of state law, and to some extent a matter of local practice, since state statutes governing rental agreements often contain sections that give courts the authority to refuse to enforce *unconscionable* provisions. Such provisions are so one-sided that they *shock the conscience of the court*, and some courts may find the automatic renewal clauses unconscionable.

Another approach to renewal provisions in leases is to provide tenants with the option to renew their leases. Renewal options, which are especially common in commercial leases, often provide for multiple renewal periods, and usually specify rent increases of either a set amount or an amount based on increases in some determinant, such as the *Consumer Price Index*, upon each renewal. In order for a renewal option to take effect, the tenant must usually give the landlord written notice of the intent to renew within thirty days of the expiration of the existing lease term.

Provisions for Security Deposits

The specific provisions regarding a landlord's rights and duties pertaining to security deposits vary from state to state, but there are certain common characteristics shared by most states' laws. Some states place limits on the amount of the security deposits that landlords may require of their tenants. The limits are usually expressed as some multiple of the monthly rental rate, such as twice the monthly rent, and some states' provisions are even sophisticated enough to have higher multiples for furnished properties or for tenants with pets. Most of the states that have limits define what constitutes a security deposit, so that not only payments that are labeled as security deposits are included, but *pet deposits* and payments of advance rent, such as required payments of the last month's rent at the inception of the lease, are also regarded as part of a tenant's security deposit.

Landlords are not required to demand security deposits from their tenants, but are permitted to do so, both as an incentive to their tenants to be careful not to damage the properties that they are renting and as a source of funds from which to pay for repairs when tenants are careless. However, the very name "security deposit" makes it obvious that the funds paid to the landlord for this purpose should not be considered to be the landlord's money, unlike rental payments. In fact, money given to a landlord as a security deposit is actually still the tenant's money that has merely been entrusted to the landlord to ensure the tenant's performance. Once the tenant has fully performed the terms of the rental agreement, the landlord is under a duty to return the security deposit to the tenant. Therefore, most states require landlords to put the security deposits of their tenants in a special escrow account that is established exclusively for that purpose, and to inform their tenants which bank the account is in and the number of the account. A landlord may put all of his or her tenants' security deposits in a single escrow account rather than opening a separate account for each tenant, but the account must be limited only to security deposits and cannot be commingled with any of the landlord's own funds. Some states even require security deposits that are to be held for more than some specified time to be placed in interest-bearing accounts for the benefit of the lessee.

Another common provision pertaining to security deposits is that, if the tenant vacates the premises without owing any unpaid rent, the landlord must either supply the tenant with a list of damages that the landlord contends are the responsibility of the tenant or must refund the security deposit to the tenant. Although not all states prescribe a time limit in which the landlord must provide a list of damages or a refund to the tenant, most states do, and it is commonly either fourteen or thirty days. Some state laws start running the time limit from the day the property is vacated, while other states start it from the time that the tenant provides the landlord with his or her new address.

The laws regarding security deposits, and the requirements for returning them, are so varied from state to state that it is imperative for landlords to check their state and local statutes. Better yet, consult with an attorney in order to make sure that you comply with those laws, as some states allow tenants to recover even more money than they actually lost, known as *punitive damages*, from a noncomplying landlord.

Recovering for Damages to Rental Property

Landlords who want the right to recover for damages to their property that are the responsibility of their tenants should make provisions for such recovery in their leases. State statutes usually establish that tenants will be responsible for damage to leased property in excess of ordinary wear and tear. However, judges are so accustomed to lease provisions for liability of tenants for damages that failure to include such a provision in a lease could cause a judge to be reluctant to award such damages.

In the event that a tenant vacates a property, leaving damages that he or she is responsible for, most states require that the landlord supply the tenant with a list of purported damages. This not only delays the landlord's duty to return the tenant's deposit, as previously discussed, but also preserves the landlord's right to recover a judgment from the tenant for the damages. The list of damages must be sent to the tenant's last known address within a certain time prescribed by state statute, commonly ten days, before any of the damages have been repaired. Most states require the landlord to be willing to meet with the tenant at the property to review the damages, and then note whether the tenant disputes the damages or agrees with the landlord's assertions.

Confrontations between tenants and landlords over damages usually focus on whether or not defects cited by the landlord already existed at the time that the tenant took possession of the property. It is highly recommended that, at the time of the execution of their leases, landlords have their tenants inspect the properties that they are renting, note any preexisting defects, such as stains on carpets or cracked glass, and sign an acknowledgment that the property has no other defects except those noted. This approach should keep the landlord from trying to recover for damages that were preexisting and noted, and should prevent the tenant from being able to successfully argue that defects in the property that he or she formerly occupied were preexisting when no notation of the damages was made.

Payment Provisions

Leases should specify what day of the month rent payments are due, and when payment will be considered late and cause a late charge to be imposed. Some states impose a minimum number of days past the due date that tenants must be given before their rental payments may be regarded as late, and states commonly place legal limits on the amount of late charges that landlords are permitted to assess. Landlords are allowed to require tenants to pay fees when checks that they write are nonnegotiable, but state laws usually impose limits on those charges, as well.

Landlords should specify the place where payments are to be made, since some states provide that in the absence of contrary provisions, rental payments are to be made at the property that the tenant is renting, which will require the landlord to physically collect the rent. It is also advisable to spell out in the lease that the tenant shall have the burden of proving that rental payments have been made, in the event that a dispute as to whether rental payments have been made should arise. Otherwise, it will be very difficult for a landlord to prove that a tenant has failed to pay his or her rent if the landlord's oral testimony to that effect were to be contradicted by testimony from the tenant.

Limitations and Conditions on Use of Rented Property

It is not uncommon for the landlord to suffer some of the consequences of a tenant's unusual use or neglect of rental property. In order to avoid complaints from neighbors, threats of citations from government authorities, or even legal action, landlords need to be able to control their tenants. Limitations on ways in which tenants may use properties, activities that constitute a disturbance in the neighborhood, the number of occupants that can live in a dwelling, and the keeping of pets are the types of lease provisions that give a landlord the right to evict an unruly or uncooperative tenant.

Lease agreements should also include provisions that require tenants to treat the premises to control bugs and rodents, and to keep the yard mowed, free of debris, and reasonably maintained. In order to prevent tenants from making changes to the exterior of a rented property that will be costly for the landlord to correct when the tenant leaves, the lease should provide that the tenant is forbidden from making changes to the property without the landlord's written consent. With such a provision, if the tenant makes changes without the necessary consent, it will constitute a form of *damage* to the property that the landlord can use the security deposit to correct.

Subleasing

Most leases restrict *subleasing* of the rental premises. Subleasing involves an original tenant entering into an agreement to let someone else take over the lease and occupy the property. Rather than absolutely prohibiting subleasing, which may violate the laws of some states, most leases require the tenant to secure the landlord's written permission to enter into a sublease. It is essential that such a restriction be included in a lease due to the fact that most states' laws favor the assignability of contract rights, and without such a provision, the landlord could be stuck with a tenant that he or she does not want. The lease should also clearly state that even if the landlord approves of the tenant subletting the property that he or she has rented, the original tenant would still be liable on the lease if the sublessee defaults. This will make it clear that subleases are not to be construed as *novations*, which are substitutions of one obligor for another, resulting in a release of the original obligor from any further liability on the obligation in question.

Warnings and Acknowledgments

In a residential lease, the landlord almost always secures and pays for insurance that covers damage to the properties he or she rents out, as well as liability insurance that covers losses incurred as a result of tenants or other people being hurt on the property. However, the landlord's insurance policy will not cover damage from fire, theft, or other perils sustained by tenants to their personal property, and the landlord's liability coverage will not protect tenants from liability for injuries sustained by others due to the tenants' negligence or misconduct. Therefore, it is advisable to state in the lease agreement that the landlord is providing no insurance coverage on behalf of the tenant, that the tenant is advised to obtain his or her own insurance, and that the tenant acknowledges having been so advised.

Commercial leases often require tenants to either acquire and pay for certain insurance policies that are obtained for the benefit of the landlord, or to reimburse the landlord for the premiums that he or she must pay for insurance on the leased premises. Since the tenant in such cases is paying the insurance premium, there is considerable potential for the tenant to misunderstand the nature of the policy's coverage, and wrongfully conclude that the policy will cover his or her personal property and liability. However, since the landlord will not suffer a loss if the tenant's property is damaged, the landlord will not have an *insurable interest* in the tenant's property, and will not be entitled to insure it. Therefore, the tenant must buy insurance to cover his or her own property and liability, and the commercial rental agreement should clearly state that the landlord's insurance will not cover any of the tenant's property or personal liability, and should advise the tenant to buy personal coverage. Also, in light of the potential for confusion as to the nature of the insurance that the tenant must pay for, it is imperative that commercial leases contain a statement in bold print that the tenant acknowledges that the insurance required by the landlord will not cover the tenant's property or liability, and that he or she shall be responsible for obtaining his or her own coverage.

It is also advisable to insert provisions in a lease that require the tenant to acknowledge that the landlord has not represented that the neighborhood in which the leased property is located is free of crime, and that the landlord does not assume any responsibility for the tenant's safety and security. It would also be appropriate to state that the tenant shall be responsible for his or her own security. However, many state and local ordinances require landlords to provide smoke detectors in their residential rental units.

Damaged Premises

When property that has been leased suffers damage due to fire, storms, or other perils that are not the fault of the tenant, and the building becomes untenantable as a result, most states' laws allow the tenant to terminate the lease unless the lease provides otherwise. Therefore, even if the property were to become untenantable for even a short time, the tenant would have the option of terminating the lease. In order to avoid this situation, landlords commonly provide for some period of time, such as thirty days, during which they can repair damaged properties, and the tenant's only remedy is *abatement* of the rent during the untenantable period, rather than the termination of the lease.

Eminent Domain

Although it is rare for them to do so, state, local, and federal governments have the power to force landowners to sell them their properties so that they can be used for the common good of society for such projects as construction of roads, parks, or public stadiums. Whenever a governmental entity invokes its authority to force an owner to sell his or her property, a power known as *eminent domain*, the government must fairly compensate the owner for the property. The fact that the property is leased and generating a good cash flow will be a factor that can help increase its appraised value. State laws provide that leases will terminate in the event of eminent domain. Since the existence of the lease may help the landlord get more for the property being taken, and since the tenancy will be disrupted, the tenant may have a legitimate claim to part of the landlord's compensation, unless the lease provides otherwise. Therefore, it is advisable to include a lease provision that, in the event of the leased property being taken by eminent domain, the lease will automatically terminate on the date that the landlord must surrender possession to the governmental entity buying it, and the tenant will have no right to any of the compensation paid to the landlord for the property.

Notice Requirements

Before written statutory provisions governing the relationship between landlords and tenants were enacted, courts required landlords to give written notice to tenants that they were delinquent on their rent and that they were liable for damages to the property. Landlords who failed to give such notices were not awarded any recovery for delinquent rent and damages. Modern statutes have retained the notice requirements, but permit the parties to waive the requirement of notice of unpaid rent in their lease agreement. It is imperative that landlords include a waiver of notice of unpaid rent in their lease agreements. However, state laws virtually universally prohibit waiver of the statutory requirement that the landlord give notice of damages, and a list of those damages, to the tenant.

The lease should specify the acceptable means for giving notice—such as by hand delivery, overnight delivery service (like FedEx), or certified U.S. Mail—and should provide both the tenant's and the landlord's addresses where notice should be delivered. If the address that is given for the tenant is the property that is being rented, the lease should provide that, unless the tenant gives the landlord his or her new address within a specified time (such as ten days of moving), the landlord can continue to send notices to the address of the rental property.

Notices of intent not to renew a lease or to exercise an option to extend a lease, as well as some other notice requirements, are often set at thirty days. However, both tenants and landlords are sometimes surprised to learn that courts construe the thirty days' notice requirement to mean a full month, and do not count any of the days in the month in which notice is given as part of the thirty days.

Example: *Jason owns a house that he leased to Clark for one year. The lease has a provision that, unless either party gives notice to the other at least thirty days prior to expiration of the lease, it will automatically renew for another year under the same terms as the original lease. The original lease was to expire on October 31st. Jason wanted to prevent the lease from renewing and sell the house. He gave notice to Clark on October 1st, that he did not want the lease to automatically renew for another year. Even though when Jason gave notice on October 1st there were still thirty days remaining in October before the end of the lease, he did not comply with the thirty-day notice requirement, since by the laws of his state none of the days in October can count as part of his notice. Since Jason did not give notice before the beginning of the full month that was to be Clark's last month of occupancy, Clark's lease automatically renewed and he has the legal right to remain in possession of the premises for another year, unless he decides to voluntarily give up that right. In order to prevent the lease from renewing, Jason should have given notice of nonrenewal to Clark no later than September 30th.*

Provisions Regarding Breaching Tenants

During the course of a lease, it is common for a tenant to fail to make a rental payment on time or to otherwise breach the lease agreement. Despite the fact that such breaches will give landlords the right to evict the breaching tenant, they usually do not take such action if the tenant will remedy the breach within a reasonable time. However, when a party fails to enforce a provision in a contract, courts will often regard the nonenforcement as an act that waives the provision, unless the contract specifically states that failure to fully enforce any term of the contract shall not constitute a waiver of that term. Therefore, landlords should provide in their lease agreements that failure to enforce any of the terms of the lease shall not constitute a waiver of those terms, so that they can still take action against tenants who persist in repeatedly committing the same breach of the lease agreement.

State law often requires landlords to make a written demand for payment of delinquent rent, unless the requirement has been waived in the lease. It is certainly advisable to waive it. However, even if the demand requirement has been waived, presenting a written demand for payment of delinquent rent may get a response from the former tenant that shows that the landlord is mistaken as to the amount of rent due or that the tenant has a defense to the landlord's claim. It could spare the landlord some embarrassment to become aware of these issues prior to presenting the case in court. Also, such a demand may lead the former tenant to approach the landlord about settling his or her claim. In any event, landlords who have made demands for payment of rents, given proper notice of damages, and given former tenants the opportunity to settle matters between them before filing suit, will generally make a better impression in court than landlords who have not been candid about such matters with their former tenants.

Landlords whose properties have been damaged by tenants should approach the situation from the very beginning as if they were preparing to file suit against their former tenants in order to recover payment for those damages. In addition to providing tenants with a list of damages before any repairs are done, the landlord should take pictures of the damaged property. Ideally, landlords should take pictures of their properties at the time they were turned over to tenants in order to have *before* and *after* photographs to introduce into evidence in suits for recovery for damage to their properties. The laws of practically every state restrict the rights of landlords to recover from tenants for *ordinary wear and tear*. Therefore, as landlords proceed with repairs to their properties, they need to carefully distinguish damage that exceeds ordinary wear and tear, since that is all that the law will allow them to recover. They will have the burden of proving the amount of their recoverable damages.

Example: *Rob leased a house from Jean for two years. At the end of the lease, Rob moved and Jean had to paint every room in the house to freshen it up and had to repair a hole in the sheetrock in one room. The carpet, which was five years old when Rob leased the property, was showing signs of wear in the doorways, and in one of the bedrooms, there were permanent oil stains on the carpet where Rob had worked on his motorcycle.*

Jean should be able to recover for repairing the hole in the sheetrock, but repainting the inside of the house appears to have been necessitated by ordinary wear and tear. The worn spots on the carpet are probably attributable to ordinary wear and tear, but the oil stains are not, and Rob should be liable for the value of the damaged carpet. However, if Rob were to raise the issue of the value of the carpet in court, the value of the carpet should be depreciated to reflect the fact that it was seven years old at the end of Rob's lease, and Jean should be awarded only the value of her seven-year-old carpet, rather than the cost of new carpet to replace it.

In the event that a landlord must file a lawsuit to recover unpaid rent or repair costs from a tenant, virtually all courts will include reimbursement of court costs as part of the landlord's judgment, if he or she wins. However, landlords who successfully sue breaching tenants will not be awarded money to pay their attorneys' fees, unless the lease agreement provides that the tenant shall be liable for those fees. Therefore, it is essential that landlords provide in their leases that tenants will be liable for the costs of collecting delinquent rent and the costs of repairs from the tenants, including reasonable attorney fees, if a landlord must engage the services of an attorney in order to collect what is owed.

Specifying Jurisdiction

Another provision that should be included in every lease agreement is a stipulation as to which state's laws shall govern the agreement. Such a provision is particularly important when parties to the agreement reside in different states, such as when the tenant or landlord is a corporation with locations in various states, or when the agreement is entered into electronically between parties in different states, since there may be some question as to where the agreement was actually finalized.

Chapter 10:

Buying Real Estate for Resale

Still another way in which to profit in the real estate market is to buy properties and resell them. Occasionally, a speculator will have an opportunity to buy a property from someone who is either in a hurry to sell it or who has priced it without doing any market research as to its value, and can then resell it at a profit without having to do much to improve the property. However, most of the time, properties that are bought with a relatively quick resale for a profit in mind are in need of considerable repair work. In fact, many of the properties that are offered to real estate speculators are in especially bad condition and will require extensive repairs. For this reason, those involved in buying, repairing, and reselling real estate will need to be more knowledgeable than those who buy properties to use as their own residences or to use as rental property.

People who buy run-down properties in order to fix them and resell them need to be reasonably certain that they are fully aware of the repairs that will need to be done to the properties they buy, as well as the cost of those repairs. After experiencing some success in buying, repairing, and reselling properties, buyers may become so confident in their ability to evaluate properties that they become overly confident and even careless. The profit from buying, repairing, and reselling properties does not come from being able to sell them at premium prices that are beyond what the typical person can sell them for. The profit from this activity is made by purchasing the properties at low enough prices to permit the buyer to make a profit on them when the repair costs are kept within budget.

It Takes Discipline

Being successful buying and reselling properties requires extreme discipline. It is not easy to find properties that are available at prices that will give the buyer an opportunity to make a profit on them. When speculators have not been able to find a property in a while, they get overly anxious and either pay too much for a property or buy one that is in need of such extensive repairs or is located in such a bad neighborhood that they should not have bought it at all.

Repairs

Every dollar spent for repairs that exceeds the anticipated cost is a dollar that would have been profit had the repairs been done for a cost that was within budget. The most promising of properties can become losses when the buyer must make repairs that were either altogether unanticipated or cost more than expected. Therefore, it is absolutely essential that buyers discover all of the defects in the properties that they buy for resale, and that they accurately determine the full amount of the costs of those repairs. Even experienced buyers would benefit from having an inspector or contractor carefully examine properties that they are interested in making offers on and are in need of extensive repairs. To the extent that properties need repairs that will not be performed by the buyer, it would be highly advisable to get firm estimates from those who will be doing the work. It is foolish to assume that the cost of repairs will be the same for one property as it was for some other property that required similar repairs. Differences in the extent of repairs or the types of materials used, increases in labor and material costs, or the realization by the contractor that he or she simply performed a prior repair too cheaply, can all cause significant differences in the costs of two apparently similar repair jobs.

Buyers of properties that are in need of repairs will not be able to get traditional loans on them from mortgage companies. As a result, not only will such buyers need to have sufficient capital or a nontraditional financing source with which to purchase properties and repair them, but also will be without the usual safeguards of appraisals, termite clearance letters, surveys, radon gas tests, and flood certifications that lenders commonly insist on before they will make mortgage loans. Despite the fact that speculators who buy properties to repair and resell are usually reluctant to spend any money on properties that they do not have to, are often in a hurry to execute contracts for their latest find, and feel that they are experts on evaluating properties, they need to be disciplined enough to get their own termite clearance letters, flood certification, and if appropriate, radon gas tests. These are inexpensive tests and inspections that can be very revealing, and can give the buyer important information that he or she can use as a basis for negotiating a price for the property.

If additions have been made to a property that is under consideration, it is probably worth the few hundred dollars a survey would cost in order to avoid buying a property that has construction encroaching into easements and setbacks. These problems will show up on the buyer's survey when the property is resold and may cause potential buyers to be unable to get a loan on the property. Appraisals on houses in need of extensive repairs are usually too incomplete to be worth what they cost. A report from a competent and thorough inspector would be informative, and a market analysis of prices in the neighborhood by a realtor who is acquainted with the area would be very useful in helping a prospective buyer determine what he or she could realistically resell a property for, once it is repaired.

Contractors and Craftsmen

Ideally, a speculator who is buying property to repair and resell it will have the ability and time to do some of the repairs that are needed.

There will almost always be some aspects of extensive repair projects that are not part of the major contractors' duties and may be hard to find someone to do, but could be performed by an owner who has some basic skills in home repair. Also, there are times when a contractor may be unavailable or fails to complete a job as promised, and by being able to fill in on that part of the repairs, the owner can speed up completion of the project.

A major component necessary in order to be successful in buying properties that are in need of repairs, getting those repairs done, and reselling those properties at a profit is being able to find craftsmen who offer the owner the combination of reasonable pricing for their availability, dependability, and ability to complete work of reasonable quality in a timely manner. It usually does not take long to learn that the lowest bidder is often not the least costly choice. Since speculators who buy and resell property are almost always short on capital, contractors failing to show up as promised or failing to complete their work within the agreed-upon time can create serious financial hardships for the property owner. If the owner had to borrow money to buy and repair a property, the delay in completing repairs will clearly cost the owner additional interest on the loan.

Look at All the Costs

Failure to have a house ready to sell at the time of the year when the real estate market is favorable to sellers, or before mortgage interest rates increase, could cause the sale of the property to take longer. This increases the seller's costs associated with holding the property, which include not only interest, but also taxes, utilities, and insurance on the property. It may also cause the property to sell for less than it would if it had been completed when the market conditions were more favorable for the seller. However, the cost that is associated with delay in completing repairs to a property, which then delays its sale, that most troubles those who are buying properties for resale is the *opportunity cost* of not being able to take advantage of the opportunity to buy other properties because their capital is still tied up in the property that they are unable to sell due to a contractor's failure to perform as promised.

Once a person engaged in buying and reselling properties finds good contractors to perform repair work, it will be essential to cultivate good relations with them. This way, they will be willing to respond quickly to requests to look at properties and give binding estimates to do repairs, despite the fact that the property has not actually been bought by the party requesting the estimate, and may never be bought by him or her. One of the best ways to develop a good relationship with contractors is to pay them as promised. This requires property owners to refrain from becoming overextended to the point that they simply do not have enough capital to fully fund all of the projects that they have undertaken.

There are simply more properties available than any one person will have capital enough to purchase, repair, and resell, or will have time enough to watch over. The limitations on a buyer's time and available capital, which combine to create the party's opportunity cost that is associated with any property that is bought for the purpose of resale, must be at the forefront of the factors being considered when choosing which properties to buy. If a property has suffered damage such that the extent of the repairs necessary will not be fully determinable until the repairs are actually underway and the damaged parts of the structure have been torn away, the buyer should calculate the amount of his or her offer for the property on the assumption that the damage is the absolute worst case. With interest, insurance, taxes, and other costs associated with just holding a property, plus the costs of repairing it, the real estate commission, and other costs associated with reselling the property, buyers have little margin for error in determining the maximum price that they could pay for a property and still be able to realize a profit from its resale. Those who are successful at buying properties for resale have come to realize that they are far better off to have underestimated the value of a property, causing them to offer too little for it and not getting it, than they are to overestimate its value and pay so much for it that it is certain to result in a loss, as well as tie up capital and time that could have been spent on a better choice.

Seasoning Costs

Although getting a property repaired and sold quickly will cut down on holding costs and increase profits on the property, too rapid a resale may cause the subsequent buyer to be unable to get the property financed. Mortgage lenders have become wary of making loans on properties that have recently been bought and are being resold. They suspect that the resale is a sham transaction designed to permit the speculator, with the help of an accomplice who is the "buyer," to borrow money against the property on the basis of a sales price that is much higher than the speculator paid for it. They also fear that the property is being resold at an exorbitant price to a bona fide but naïve buyer, with the help of a cooperative appraiser who is willing to over-value the property. Therefore, it may be necessary to *season* the property by holding it for at least six months before reselling it, and those who are buying properties for resale need to plan for such a holding period. Some properties are in need of such extensive repairs that the time it takes to do them, coupled with delays due to bad weather or lack of availability of contractors, will easily take six months—probably more. There are ways to cope with the need to hold properties for a while, even when they need little or no repairs.

Sometimes people sell their properties hurriedly because they are having financial difficulty, and would be willing to take less for their properties if they are allowed to continue to live there for a while after the sale, since they have no particular alternative place to live. Likewise, there may be sellers who want to sell their homes and use the proceeds they get from the sale to help pay the cost of building new homes, but would like to rent back the original homes that they sold until their new ones are completed. If a property is not in too poor a condition, it can simply be advertised and rented for a while before it is made ready for sale. If a property that is ready for resale needs to be held by the speculator a bit longer, it may be possible to enter into a sales contract in which the seller will rent the property for a while before the sale actually closes. In any event, it is usually best for those who are buying properties for resale to close their purchases quickly, even though they may not get possession immediately, in order to lengthen their holding periods.

Controlling the Scope of Repairs

One of the hardest aspects of buying properties, repairing them, and selling them, is knowing when to stop making improvements to the properties. People who get involved in this activity are often previous employees of the construction industry and are accustomed to doing improvements for homeowners. Still others are drawn to the activity because it gives them an opportunity to be creative in resurrecting dilapidated properties. The result of these influences is that those who buy properties for resale that are in need of repair tend to go beyond mere repair of the properties, and begin to renovate them.

The various types and levels of upgrades that can be made to properties are virtually endless—as are the potential costs. Replacing plain cabinets with new, premium grade cabinetry and installing granite counter tops in place of ones that are made of Formica do make a property more impressive to prospective buyers. However, it is doubtful that an appraiser, whose evaluation on the property will determine how much a buyer can borrow in order to buy the property, will be willing to significantly reflect those improvements in the appraisal. Appraisers tend to focus on recent sales of comparably sized properties in the same neighborhood in determining property values. On the other hand, adding a porch to a property that already needs repairs to siding, trim, and roofing where the porch will go, may make such an improvement in the appearance of the property that the added expense is easily justified.

It is generally more difficult to make a profit from buying and renovating properties than it is from buying and merely repairing them, when the properties are acquired for resale. The successful buyers/sellers of such properties are the ones who have developed the ability to recognize which expenditures for repairs and improvements will increase the market value of the property beyond what they cost, and are disciplined enough to limit expenditures to those repairs and improvements.

Governmental Regulations

Those who are considering buying properties that are in need of repair need to be absolutely sure that they will be free to decide what repairs to make and how to go about making them. The danger that they face is that governmental regulations at some level may dictate what changes they can make to certain properties. For example, it is not uncommon for owners of properties that are in areas designated as historic districts to be required to keep their properties in conformity with the original architecture of those neighborhoods. Therefore, an owner may be required to replace trim work, doors, windows, or other damaged components of a structure with matching replacements that have to be custom made at a cost that is several times what modern versions of those same items would cost at a building supply outlet. Likewise, there may be restrictions on tearing down all or part of the structures located on a property, as well as restrictions on adding on to a building or placing additional structures, such as a garage, on the property.

Even when there are no governmental regulations in place regarding an owner's right to make changes to his or her property, there may be subdivision restrictions that accomplish the same thing. Therefore, it is essential for buyers who are considering purchasing properties that they plan to do extensive work on and resell them, to investigate and make sure they will not run into restrictions that will greatly increase the cost of the work or prevent them from doing it altogether. Although such an investigation is especially important when properties under consideration are relatively old, even some newer properties have subdivision restrictions that make inquiry about them advisable before buying those properties.

Finding Properties

Determining which specific properties to select is certainly challenging, but finding viable choices to select from may be even more difficult. Running advertisements in local newspapers offering to buy homes will probably generate a number of calls, as will advertisements on billboards, but answering the calls and finding out about each caller's property will take a good deal of time. Buyers who are prepared to close properties quickly may do well by letting local realtors know that they are *wholesale* buyers. That way, realtors will call them when they come across properties that the owners need to sell in a hurry, or properties that owners want to sell but that are in need of repairs that they cannot afford to make.

Buying at Foreclosure Sales

Some buyers in search of properties to repair and resell have success buying properties at foreclosure sales. These sales, which are conducted on behalf of creditors when debtors are unable to pay their mortgages as agreed, are advertised in local newspapers in accordance with the laws of the state in which the property is located. In larger cities, there are usually publications that contain very little information other than legal notices, new lawsuits that have been filed, property transfers, issuance of licenses and permits, and other data generated by governmental agencies. These are the types of publications to consult for information on foreclosures in areas that have such publications. Foreclosure notices will describe the property to be sold, identify the owner and unpaid lender, and give the time, place, and terms of the sale. A representative of the lender who has initiated the foreclosure is often the only bidder at the foreclosure sales, and the representative will usually bid up to the amount that is owed to the lender on the property. Therefore, people who expect to make a good buy at a foreclosure sale will need to find sales of properties in which the debtors owe substantially less than the properties are worth. It is absolutely essential that bidders at foreclosure sales review title searches on the properties to be sold at foreclosure sales and make sure that their attorney can get them a title insurance policy on the property.

When properties are bought at foreclosure, the successful bidder gets a deed that conveys the property without any promises (*warranties*), that the buyer is getting a good title to the property, except that the party executing the deed warrants that he or she has not given such a deed to anyone else. In the typical non-foreclosure sale, the seller conveys the property to the buyer by means of a warranty deed, and in doing so, gives the buyer certain *covenants of title*. These covenants are legal assurances from the seller that he or she actually owns the property being conveyed, and that it is free of encumbrances, such as mortgages, liens, or easements, except to the extent that they are noted in the *warranty deed*. One who conveys property by a warranty deed also covenants to defend against any future claims from parties purporting to have an ownership interest in the property, or claim against it, at the time that the seller conveyed it to the buyer. In essence, warranty deeds carry the assurance of the *grantor*, who is the party executing the deed, that the *grantee*, who is the party getting title to the property by means of the deed, is getting *marketable title* to the property. Deeds given as a result of a foreclosure do not assure that the buyer will get marketable title.

Among the disadvantages of buying properties at foreclosure sales is that buyers do not usually have the same opportunities to inspect the properties themselves, or have inspectors to evaluate them, as they do when buying properties from their owners. Also, buyers will not have the benefit of getting disclosure statements from prior owners regarding the condition of the properties that they buy at foreclosure sales. Another serious drawback to buying properties at foreclosure sales is that the buyer must bid on the properties without putting any contingencies in their bids. As a result, they are not free to bid on the property with the provision that they will not be obligated to buy the property if they get an unfavorable inspection result or termite report. Perhaps even more importantly, buyers at foreclosure sales cannot bid with a financing contingency, but rather, must be fully prepared to pay the entire amount that they bid virtually immediately. Therefore, the option of acquiring properties at foreclosure sales is effectively unavailable to all but those who can pay cash for the properties they are buying.

Buyers who are uncomfortable buying properties in the atmosphere of pandemonium that tends to surround foreclosure sales, or who are simply financially unable to participate in such sales, may still be able to benefit from the fact that foreclosed properties often sell for less than what they could be expected to bring in a normal sale. At foreclosure sales, it is quite common for the lender who has initiated the sale to be the high bidder on the property, and the lender will subsequently need

to market that property. Generally, when lenders buy foreclosed properties that were pledged as collateral on loans that they made and had
become delinquent, they then attempt to resell them in *as is* condition
without spending money on the properties for repairs or even cleanup.

Buying from Lenders

After a property has remained on the market for a while at a price
equal to what the seller paid for it at the foreclosure sale, which was
probably also the balance of what the defaulting debtor owed on the
property, the seller will usually realize that the condition of the property
and circumstances of the sale will necessitate a substantial price
adjustment in order to attract buyers. Since there is no mortgage
against the properties to contend with, buyers have a realistic chance
of buying the properties at prices that are well below their initial
listing prices. Furthermore, unlike owners who often have the option
of taking their properties off the market and continuing to live in
them if they do not sell, lenders have no choice but to sell properties
obtained by foreclosure. Whether or not to accept an offer will come
down to a business decision for them. This will be significantly influenced by how long their properties have been on the market.

An advantage to buying properties that have been foreclosed on from
lenders who have bought them at their foreclosure sales, rather than
buying them at the actual foreclosure sale, is that the buyer will have
time to better evaluate the property. There will still be no disclosure
statements regarding a property's condition from a prior owner, but
prospective buyers will have the opportunity to thoroughly inspect the
properties themselves, get a professional inspector to evaluate the property, get a termite inspection done, and conduct any other tests or
inspections that seem appropriate. An offer can even be written so that
the buyer is not obligated to complete the purchase if the test results are
unfavorable, thereby establishing whether the seller will do business at
the buyer's price before the buyer incurs the expense of the inspections.

Financing contingencies can also be put in offers to buy such properties. However, it is often difficult to get loans on properties that

are in need of extensive repairs. A financing contingency may cause the seller to turn the offer down, rather than entering into a contract on the property that limits the seller's right to sell the property to others while the buyer attempts to obtain a loan that is doubtful. Buyers who have collateral (other than the property that they are buying) that they can pledge for a loan would still benefit from having time to arrange for such a loan. A financing contingency under those circumstances would probably not be as distasteful to a seller if the proposed collateral is in good enough condition to collateralize the buyer's loan.

Buying previously foreclosed properties from lenders still usually carries the risk that the buyer is not guaranteed a marketable title to the property by the seller. Those who buy foreclosure properties from lenders, who have acquired them by being the high bidders at their own foreclosure sales, do not get a *trustee's deed*, as they would have if they bought the properties at the actual foreclosure sale. The lenders who buy properties at their foreclosure sales are the ones who get title to those properties by means of a trustee's deed. However, their subsequent conveyance of the property is usually done by means of a *special warranty deed*, which is sometimes referred to as a *limited warranty deed*. This gives the buyer no better warranties than the trustee's deed, which is merely that the seller has not conveyed the property to anyone else by the same kind of deed. Buyers are free to attempt to negotiate for a warranty deed from the seller, but it is doubtful that the seller will agree to it.

Title Problems

Among the problems that can threaten the validity of the title to property that was bought at a foreclosure sale is the possibility that the foreclosure itself was not properly done. If the advertisement of the sale did not accurately describe the property that was being sold, was incomplete in disclosing the terms of the sale, or was not run for the number of times required by law, the foreclosure sale may be invalid. Also, *actual notice*, rather than *notice by publication*, is often required in order to eradicate federal tax liens and state sales and income tax liens, and failure to give the required notice will cause those liens to survive the foreclosure sale and remain as an obligation against the property. Delinquent property taxes cannot be eliminated by means of a foreclosure sale, regardless of what notice is given, but notice of property tax delinquencies will be available in the public records and can be taken into account in making offers to buy foreclosed properties.

Still another potential claim against properties that are bought at foreclosure sales are any debts or obligations that were *liens of record* against the property before the loan that is being foreclosed was a lien of record. For example, if a lender who had given a borrower a second mortgage on a property were to foreclose on it, the foreclosure would not eliminate the first mortgage holder's lien. Likewise, the same would be true of tax liens and judgments that were filed before the lien that the lender is foreclosing on was filed. Giving notice, actual or by publication, to holders of liens and claims that were filed against property prior to the time that a foreclosing lender's lien was filed will not cause the foreclosure to eliminate those liens.

In light of the potential title problems with a buyer's property that is bought at a foreclosure, it is unquestionably advantageous for buyers to obtain properties from lenders who have bought them at their own foreclosure sales, rather than buying them at the foreclosure sales themselves. By waiting a while after lenders have bought foreclosed properties before buying them from the lenders, the subsequent buyer will have a chance to see if anyone steps forward to challenge the sale or asserts a claim against the property. In general, the longer that a subsequent buyer can wait between the time of the foreclosure sale and the time that he or she buys the property, the better off he or she will be. In any case, it is essential that buyers of such properties obtain a title insurance policy on them, which guarantees that they are getting marketable title to the property. Buyers should verify the availability of such policies before agreeing to buy such properties.

Tax Sales

Some buyers attempt to acquire realty at *tax sales* that are conducted by government officials who sell owner's properties to pay delinquent property taxes. The biggest drawback to acquiring properties at tax sales is that state laws provide owners and creditors with liens against the properties the *right to redeem* the properties by paying the buyers back what they paid for the properties, plus interest at the rate set by the statutes of the state involved and expenditures for repairs to the property. The amount of time that eligible parties have in which to redeem properties that have been sold at a tax sale varies from state to state and ranges from as little as thirty days to as much as four years.

Some states conduct tax lien sales at which the high bidder must foreclose on the lien (after any redemption time allowed) in order to acquire ownership of the property. Other states give tax deeds to the high bidders, subject to redemption by eligible parties within the period of time prescribed by state law. Still other states' laws provide for auctions of either tax liens or tax deeds. However, regardless of what form of conveyance is used, the governmental agency that is conducting the sale will not give the buyer any assurances that he or she is getting a marketable title, or that the improvements on the property meet zoning requirements or building codes. Furthermore, the tax sale will not eliminate liens or encumbrances against the property that existed prior to the tax delinquencies that gave rise to the sale. Therefore, before bidding on properties that are up for auction at a tax sale, it is absolutely imperative that a buyer do a thorough title search of the property in order to discover any mortgages, judgments, or tax liens (other than property taxes) that will affect the title to the property. Title searches are available through title companies and attorneys' offices, but they will generally cost around $200, which will make it prohibitively costly for prospective buyers to conduct such investigations of very many properties. Undoubtedly, there are people who acquire properties at bargain prices at tax sales, but most owners will pay their delinquent property taxes before losing good properties at a tax sale, and the few attractive properties that are sold at tax sales are likely to be redeemed. Also, title insurance policies are often not available to buyers who acquire properties at a tax sale.

Developing an Acquisition Plan

Determining which specific properties to buy, while using the criteria previously discussed to make that determination, is clearly an extremely important aspect of any plan to invest in real estate. Another important factor to consider in formulating real estate investment plans is the ultimate degree of involvement in real estate ownership that the investor would eventually like to have. Once a person decides what type of properties to buy and how many of them to buy, he or she can then determine the rate of acquisition that will be necessary to meet that goal. If the goal is realistic, the buyer can formulate a long-term plan for meeting that goal.

For most people, a good starting point for investing in real estate is the acquisition of a personal residence. With few exceptions, people who do not own their own homes will end up paying out enough money in rent to more than pay for a home that would be nicer than the ones that they rent. Also, ownership of a personal residence can help a party acquire investment real estate, since lenders tend to view homeowners more favorably than renters, and homeowners can usually borrow against the equity that they have in their residence, which may prove to be an important source of funds with which to acquire or repair investment properties.

Investors who are considering buying properties to rent out, or to repair and resell, but who have no previous experience in these activities, should start out slowly. Inexperienced real estate investors are virtually bound to make some mistakes in selecting properties or underestimating the costs of repairs, and it is advisable to make these mistakes on a small scale, while developing the judgment necessary for making good real estate investments. Also, not everyone will enjoy being a landlord, or coping with the problems that are typically encountered in repairing and marketing neglected properties. It is best for an investor to discover his or her distaste for the activities before acquiring numerous properties that would need to be disposed of quickly.

Once an investor has determined that he or she would like to continue with the acquisition of additional pieces of real estate, it is time to develop a long-term strategy for the acquisition of properties. A workable strategy for property acquisition must be a synthesis of the investor's desire to own investment property, capital available for acquiring properties, and time available to devote to real estate investments. Once these parameters are established, there are so many levels available for participation in real estate investment that there is unquestionably one that is right for every serious investor.

Those who feel that investments in real estate offer good potential for appreciation and have capital available for investment, but are not interested in taking on the responsibilities of dealing with tenants or repairing and reselling neglected homes, can simply buy unimproved real estate and hold it in anticipation of appreciation. However, unimproved land will not generally produce income, unless it is farmland that can be rented to someone to grow crops on or enrolled in a conservation program that pays the owner a stipend. Therefore, this option is limited to investors who can pay cash for properties or who have sources other than income from their investment property to pay notes on the mortgages on those properties.

Investors who want to own rental property or who want to speculate by buying and selling properties—and who have the capital to do it, but no time—may want to consider taking on a business associate who has time to manage the activities, but lacks the necessary capital to acquire properties on his or her own. These types of arrangements give two parties an opportunity to get involved in real estate investing that could not do so without each other. However, the parties need to anticipate the possibility that they might find it necessary to sever their relationship, or that either of the parties may die or become disabled while they own properties together, and should be prepared to deal with those events.

A good, sensible plan for the average person who wants to acquire wealth in order to be able to retire early or live more comfortably upon retirement is to slowly, but steadily, accumulate quality rental houses over a period of years. An investor who acquires his or her first rental property at age 27 and then acquires just one additional property every three years will own ten rental houses by age 54. The most recently acquired properties will still have unpaid mortgage balances against them, but the properties that were acquired in the earliest years will be paid off or have only small remaining balances. If the properties were worth an average of only $100,000 each and the mortgage balances on them totaled half of their combined values, which is unlikely since properties acquired in earlier years would have undoubtedly cost far less than their later market value and would have required only small mortgages with which to buy them, the investor would have a total equity of $500,000 in the properties. Owners who have acquired properties over a period of years are also likely to be receiving sizable amounts of net rental income from them, since the mortgages on some of the properties will be either fully paid off or so small that the mortgage payments consume very little of the rental income generated by the properties.

The most successful investors who have chosen to slowly acquire rental properties over a substantial period of time are those who are constantly improving their holdings by selling off properties and replacing them with better ones. This amounts to combining the purchase of properties for rental units with the activity of acquiring properties to repair and resell. Buying properties both for resale as well as buying some to retain for rental units are quite compatible activities, provided that the buyer has both the skills and capital to do both. Landlords who are looking for rental properties will inevitably run across properties that are not well suited for rental property, but have good potential for repair and resale—and buyers who acquire properties to resell will occasionally acquire one with excellent potential as a rental unit.

Investors who have experienced success in either buying properties and renting them out, in buying properties for resale, or both, are often tempted to speed up the acquisition process, rather than moving forward at a controlled pace. They may feel that it makes no sense to postpone the benefits of investing in real estate when there are plenty of properties that are readily available. However, this is the kind of attitude that can get the real estate investor in serious financial trouble. It is inevitable that landlords are going to have an occasional deadbeat tenant who does not pay the rent, and may even be difficult to evict if he or she files bankruptcy. Other tenants will vacate properties, leaving them in need of expensive repairs that will take the landlord a long time to recover for, if recovery can be had at all. There will also be times when rental properties remain vacant for a while.

Stick to What You Know

In the event of any one of these occurrences, the landlord will be faced with having to pay not only the cost of any repairs that are needed, but also the mortgage payments and other routine costs of owning the property. Therefore, the landlord who has used most of his or her capital to acquire properties and has little in reserve to meet contingencies faces the risk of defaulting on mortgage payments, which could lead to foreclosures, judgments against him or her, and a credit rating that is in shambles. At the same time that landlords are depleting their capital by acquiring more properties than they should, they are also multiplying the likelihood that they will have problems, since they will have more properties to keep rented and more tenants to breach their leases.

Similar problems arise when investors who buy properties to repair and resell overextend themselves. Mortgage payments must be made when loans were obtained to buy properties for resale, and these payments, along with insurance premiums and other costs associated with holding the properties, will continue from the time that the properties are acquired until the sale of them is completed. Repair costs and costs associated with the sale of a property can also exceed expectations. Investors who have left themselves with insufficient capital to allow for these contingencies will face the same possibilities of foreclosure, judgments, and ruined credit that defaulting landlords face.

Acquiring too many properties too quickly is not the only way in which real estate investors overextend themselves. Some investors expand their real estate holdings into areas in which they have no experience, and either make bad choices or fail to fully grasp the amount of time and capital that their new endeavors will require. For instance, a landlord who had success in renting out residential property may find the lure of owning commercial property irresistible. Acquiring land and developing a shopping center may seem especially appealing in light of the fact that contractors can erect strip centers that are metal buildings with brick or stone facades for under $50 a square foot, including exterior lighting and a paved parking area.

However, what the uninitiated investor may not be aware of is that the structure will be merely a shell with concrete floors and no interior walls, no restrooms, no finished electrical work, and no heating and cooling systems. Tenants will have to finish the construction on the spaces that they rent to suit their needs, but the landlord will have to contribute toward the cost of the completion in order to attract tenants. The landlord's payment toward finishing off spaces for his or her initial tenants will usually run $25 or more per square foot. Therefore, even at only the $25 per square foot rate, the landlord would have to pay $37,500 toward finishing out a 1,500 square foot bay for the first tenant to occupy that space. Furthermore, it is common for landlords to grant tenants a period of occupancy without charging rent in order to give them time to complete the building out of the space. Also, it generally takes longer to rent out commercial spaces, and the landlord will have all of them empty at the same time when the center is first built. Obviously, a landlord of a newly built shopping center, who does not have adequate capital to cover his or her share of the cost of building out the initial tenants' spaces, cover mortgage payments, and pay for other costs associated with ownership of the property prior to finding tenants, can end up in a dire financial situation.

·   ·   ·   ·   ·

Developing a workable plan regarding the type of properties to acquire and a schedule for acquiring them is an excellent starting point for those who have decided to invest in real estate. However, developing the discipline to resist the temptations to deviate from a sound plan is essential for successful real estate investing.

Chapter 11:

General Information Regarding Real Estate Loans

Due to the size of the typical real estate purchase, it is rare for buyers to be able to acquire properties without having to borrow money to do so. Buyers attempting to acquire a property as a primary residence, as well as landlords, investors, and real estate dealers, all have a variety of financing options to consider. Some of those options are available to all buyers, regardless of whether they intend to occupy the property as their primary residence, but some types of financing are limited to buyers who intend to occupy the property that they are trying to finance.

Choosing a Mortgage Term

Regardless of whether someone is acquiring a personal residence or real estate investment property, one of the fundamental decisions that a buyer must make is what *length of loan* is best when the acquisition of the property requires financing. Loans are commonly available *amortized* over a period of thirty years. Most of the various types of loans that are available are offered with a fifteen-year amortization as an option, and some are available at virtually any interval. Shorter amortization periods result in higher monthly notes, but also generate much more rapid equity accumulation in route to their earlier payoffs.

The difference in the monthly mortgage note payments between mortgages of equal amounts but with substantially different periods of amortizations can be surprisingly small. For example, the monthly principal and interest payments on a $100,000 loan at 6% that is amortized over a thirty-year period would be $599.56, whereas the same loan amortized over a fifteen-year period would require a monthly payment of $843.86. Therefore, by paying only $244.30 more per month—an increase of 40%—the borrower can pay off the loan in half the time. While it is true that most buyers do not keep properties long enough to pay off even fifteen-year mortgages, this is no reason to shun the shorter-term loans. In fact, it may be even more important for borrowers who intend to sell their properties in a few years to opt for the fifteen-year mortgage over the thirty-year loan. A borrower who gets a thirty-year mortgage for $100,000 at 6% interest per annum will have paid off only $6,045.64 at the end of five years, but had he or she chosen a fifteen-year term, $23,900.90 of the loan would have been repaid. This difference of $16,955.26 would be realized as additional equity by the owner upon sale of the property. The results are even more dramatic at the end of ten years, when the thirty-year loan would have been reduced by only $16,314.28 and the fifteen-year loan balance could have been reduced by $56,350.03, resulting in over $40,000 in additional equity for the seller who chooses the fifteen-year loan. Buyers should definitely consider fifteen-year mortgages, even if it means buying a little less house in order to be able to make the higher payments.

In determining whether or not the payments on a fifteen-year loan are manageable, buyers must consider that most lenders require borrowers who are buying primary residences to pay one-twelfth of their annual property taxes and insurance premiums with each monthly note. Those payments are set aside in an *escrow fund*, and are used to pay the taxes and the insurance on the mortgaged property when they come due. This practice prevents the situation of borrowers being unable to pay these expenses when they have not budgeted for them, but it also raises their monthly mortgage payments.

Adjustable-Rate Mortgages vs. Fixed-Rate Mortgages

The amount of the monthly note that borrowers must pay in order to amortize a given amount of debt will be determined not only by the term of the loan, but also by the *rate of interest* charged by the lender. Rates on a loan of a particular term for a borrower with good credit will not vary a great deal, if at all, from lender to lender. By shopping among lenders for a mortgage, borrowers may be able to find a company that charges less in costs associated with originating the loan, but it is doubtful that rates on identical loans will differ more than a quarter, or even an eighth, of a percentage point. In order to significantly reduce the interest rates on their mortgages, borrowers will have to take an *adjustable-rate mortgage*. Lenders are willing to charge lower interest rates in the initial years of mortgages if borrowers will agree to rate adjustments periodically in the future. The right to adjust interest rates on mortgages protects lenders from the risk of holding mortgages at low fixed interest rates, and then facing subsequent increases in the market rate of interest that they must pay in order to attract funds. Rates that do not adjust are considered *fixed-rate mortgages.*

There are a variety of adjustable-rate mortgages available, but they all have the common characteristic of starting out at an interest rate that is lower than the rate available on a loan similar in size and duration, but with a fixed rate of interest. Adjustable-rate mortgages are often identified by such references as "3/1" or "5/1" loans, and are usually referred to by the acronym *ARMs*. A 3/1 ARM is an adjustable-rate mortgage that will not be adjusted for three years, and the 5/1 ARM rate will not be adjusted for five years. The rates will be tied to some form of *interest index*, such as the composite yield on some group of federal securities, that will be specified in the borrower's loan documents. The loan documents will also specify the frequency of adjustments and the maximum increase, known as a *cap*, in the interest rate that is allowed per adjustment and over the life of the loan, if the loan documents provide for such caps.

Reduced initial interest rates are offered on ARMs as an enticement to borrowers to choose them. However, the rates after the period of low initial interest are usually structured so that even if market rates of interest do not rise, the interest on a typical ARM will increase, because lenders will no longer give borrowers the same rate discounts that they had given them as an inducement to choose an ARM. If market interest rates rise, borrowers can anticipate even larger initial and subsequent interest rate increases that are limited only by the cap on the adjustments.

Whether an ARM is a good choice for a borrower will depend largely on how long he or she intends to own the property that is being financed. Buyers who are practically certain that they will move either before or soon after the initial rate adjustment can significantly reduce their mortgage payments without having to suffer the detriment of rate adjustments. Also, if mortgage interest rates are quite high, and considered likely to significantly fall before the rates will be adjusted, an ARM may be a good choice even for buyers who expect to own the properties that they are purchasing for a very long time. However, when interest rates are comparatively low, buyers who acquire properties that they intend to hold well past the time at which rates on an ARM would be adjusted should stick to fixed-rate mortgages. Borrowers should be especially leery of ARMs when they anticipate that the economy is about to experience a period of inflation, since borrowers with fixed-rate mortgages reap the benefit of increased property values during inflationary periods, without suffering any increase in the size of their mortgage interest payments.

Graduated Payment Mortgages

Somewhat similar to the ARM is the *graduated payment mortgage*, which starts out at a reduced initial payment level with definite increases provided for certain times. These mortgages are designed for buyers whose incomes are not high enough to qualify for the fixed-rate loans that they need. The ideal candidates for such loans are borrowers who are anticipating increases in their incomes by the time that their notes increase. While this type of loan may be useful to buyers such as recent college graduates who have just begun their careers, it is not uncommon for lenders to structure these loans in a way that the reduction of the initial payments causes those payments to fall short of paying even the interest on the loan, a situation known as *negative amortization.*

In such situations, a borrower will actually owe more on a loan at the end of a year of payments than he or she did at the beginning of a year. As a result, borrowers who take out graduated payment mortgages will have to pay enough of an additional amount in subsequent mortgage payments to compensate for the amount of their negative amortization, plus interest on that amount. Also, if a borrower who chose a graduated payment mortgage that generated negative amortization were to decide to sell the property before being able to overcome the deficiency with higher payments, he or she may owe more on the property than it is worth, unless the property had appreciated enough to make up for the negative amortization.

Costs of Completing Real Estate Transactions

There are more costs associated with acquiring real estate than merely paying the purchase price of the property. Some of those costs must be paid in order to effect the transfer of the ownership of a piece of real estate from one party to another. Other costs are associated with obtaining a mortgage with which to buy a piece of real estate, and some costs are for items that are part of the transfer of ownership and part of the cost of obtaining a mortgage. Together, these costs are usually referred to as *closing costs.*

The Costs of Transferring Ownership

In order to place a transfer of ownership in the *chain of title*, which is the record of ownership of a piece of real property, a document must be recorded in the public record that establishes who the party is that has become the new owner. In a sale of a property, the instrument used to convey ownership is a *deed*, and it is placed in the public record by recording it in the office of the official who has been designated to maintain land records by the laws of the state in which the property is located. Virtually every state charges some fee for recording deeds, and many of them charge transfer taxes based on the price for which the property is sold. These transfer taxes are a significant component of the cost of transferring ownership of real estate in some states.

The party who drafts the necessary documents and closes a real estate transaction is known as a *settlement agent*. Some states require that real estate transactions be closed by licensed attorney. The buyer and seller can both use the same attorney to close their transaction, or they can use separate attorneys. The buyer's attorney will represent the lender in seeing to it that the loan is closed in accordance with the lender's instructions when the buyer takes out a mortgage on the property. The fees charged by settlement agents vary depending on local custom in the area where the settlement agent is located. The fees are often divided into a *closing fee* and a *document preparation fee*, and some settlement agents charge additional small fees for notarizing documents or storing records of the closing.

The Costs of Obtaining a Loan

Some lenders charge a *loan origination fee*, which is commonly 1% of the loan amount. The justification of this fee is that it gives the lender funds to cover the costs of processing the loan without having to break down the charges and assess them separately. This is a charge that is negotiable, and borrowers can often shop around for a lender and find one that will make the loan that they need without charging a loan origination fee. However, lenders who do not charge origination fees often charge a variety of other specific fees, such as an *underwriting fee, automation fee, tax service fee, administrative fee*, and *processing fee*, which can add up to as much as, or more than, the typical loan origination fee. Therefore, a buyer who is comparing loan options needs to be sure to question a lender concerning the various fees that will be charged in connection with a loan, so that he or she can determine whether the lender who offers a loan without charging an origination fee is simply collecting the origination fee in the form of other charges.

Lenders sometimes charge interest at the inception of a loan. Such interest charges, known as *loan discounts* or *discount points*, are especially common when the borrower gets a loan at an interest rate that is below the market rate they should be charged. The discount points represent the cost of a *buy down* of the interest rate on a loan. They are used by borrowers with good credit to get a rate that is below the prevailing market rate, and are used by buyers with poor credit histories to bring their rates down to a level that is closer to what they would have been charged if their credit histories had been good. When a lender quotes an interest rate at *par*, this means that no discount points will be charged in order for a borrower to get that rate. Some loan originators refer to loans as *zero, zero loans*, which means that neither a loan origination fee nor any discount points will be charged by the lender on the loan.

Borrowers will be required to authorize their lenders to obtain a credit report, and they will be required to pay for the cost of the report, which is usually around $25. Lenders also usually require appraisals, surveys, flood determinations, and in some areas, additional evaluations (such as radon gas tests), all of which must be paid for by the buyer, unless the seller has agreed to cover these costs. Although these various evaluations and tests are required by lenders to help establish that the proposed collateral for a loan is sound, they will also help buyers avoid making costly mistakes, and should be obtained even if no lender is involved or the lender does not require them. Termite clearance letters are also required by most lenders and should be required in every real estate buyer's contract, but they are usually provided by the seller at his or her expense.

Another item that lenders require in order to safeguard their interest in the property that they take liens on as collateral is *title insurance*. Sellers must usually provide a *title search* of their property, which shows who has ownership of the property, who holds a mortgage or other lien on the property, and whether the property taxes on the property have been paid. Title searches are usually done by title companies or attorneys who will offer buyers a title insurance policy on the property, provided that the seller can convey *good title* to the property, as evidenced by the search.

Title insurance protects both buyers and lenders from claimants who assert an ownership interest in the property, as well as from parties with previously undiscovered liens. A one-time premium, based on property values for owner's policies and the amount of a mortgage for a lender's policy, is charged for title policies. Policies bought for the benefit of lenders will offer no coverage for the owner's equity in a property. However, owners who are required to buy lender's title insurance policies can add an owner's policy by merely paying a small administrative fee, plus the premium on the difference between the amount of the mortgage on a property and the price for which it sold. Buyers who are paying cash for the properties that they buy would be well advised to buy title insurance, since such policies not only offer them protection, but also establish that they have gotten good title to their properties, and can, therefore, convey good title upon sale of them, unless they have done something to raise doubts about the titles.

In order to protect their collateral against future destruction, lenders require borrowers to place *hazard insurance policies* on the properties that they mortgage, and they must also obtain *flood insurance coverage* on mortgaged properties that are located in a flood plain. Buyers are free to choose their own insurance companies, but they must pay a year's premium on required policies at the time of the closing. If a borrower must carry mortgage insurance on his or her loan, a lump sum payment toward that premium is often required at closing. The borrower will have no input in determining the mortgage insurance provided. An explanation of mortgage insurance is provided in the sections on FHA loans and conventional loans in Chapters 12 and 13.

As previously mentioned, in addition to the initial premium payments for the various types of insurance that borrowers must carry, lenders often require borrowers to make monthly payments of one-twelfth of their annual insurance premiums and property taxes into an *escrow account,* from which the future insurance premiums and property taxes on the mortgaged property can be paid when they come due. These payments are made as part of the borrower's monthly mortgage note. However, in order to have sufficient funds in the escrow account to be able to pay the property taxes and interest the first time that they come due after the property is closed, adequate initial deposits (based on the time remaining before tax and insurance payments are due) must be placed in the escrow account at the time of the closing.

Example: *Bartholomew purchased a house on January 15ᵗʰ that was located in an area where property taxes for the year are due on the first of each June. His property taxes are to be paid through an escrow account at the time of the closing, so that the lender will have sufficient funds to fully pay the taxes when they come due in June. His annual property taxes of $1,200 will require a payment of $100 per month by him into his escrow fund to cover his taxes. Interest on loans is paid in arrears, so Bartholomew's first payment will not be due until the end of the first full calendar month after he had taken out the loan. Therefore, Bartholomew's payments, which will start on March 1ˢᵗ, will result in an escrow contribution of only $400 toward property taxes before they are due. As a result, a payment of at least $800 needs to be collected at the time of closing and placed in escrow in order for the lender to have the $1,200 needed on June 1ˢᵗ to fully pay Bartholomew's property taxes.*

Since insurance premiums are paid for a full year at the time that loans close, there is little deficiency for a borrower to make up at closing in order for the lender to have sufficient funds to pay the next year's premiums when they come due. The only real deficiency is created by the fact that at least a month will go by before a borrower makes his or her first mortgage payment. However, since the premium payment on insurance policies must be made on or before the due date in order to prevent lapse of coverage, lenders figure in an extra couple of months of initial escrow deposits at closing to provide a cushion in the escrow account. Historically, lenders' practices regarding escrow accounts generated surpluses that were at their disposal without accruing any interest. In response to criticism over this practice, federal legislation was passed that restricts the amount that lenders can require borrowers to place in their escrow accounts. However, payments that borrowers are required to make at closing in order to establish escrow accounts can still be a sizable expense associated with obtaining a real estate mortgage.

When buyers close mortgage loans on the first of a month, their first mortgage payments will be due in exactly one month, and it will fully cover that month's interest charge. However, when buyers close their loans on some other day of the month, they would be overcharged if they were required to pay a full note on the first of the very next month, and they would be undercharged if they waited until the first of the month following a full month after they obtained their loan and then paid no more than their regular note. Lenders solve this problem by requiring borrowers, at closing, to pay interest for each day, starting with the day on which the loan closes and running to the last day of the month. The payments are referred to by lenders as *per diem interest charges*. By charging per diem interest at closing, when borrowers make their first full mortgage payments on the first of the month following the first full month after their loans are closed, the interest component of that payment will be accurate.

Financing the Costs

Payments that borrowers must make at closing to cover insurance premiums, establish an escrow account, and pay per diem interest, are collectively referred to as *prepaid items* or simply *prepays*. Together, they comprise a substantial part of the cost that borrowers must pay when they obtain mortgages on real estate. Borrowers are allowed to add most of the closing costs that they must pay, except for prepays, to the cost of the properties that they are mortgaging, and borrow against that total. Therefore, borrowers who are attempting to minimize the amount they must pay out at closing would be better off negotiating with sellers and getting the sellers to pay the prepays for them, since the prepays cannot be financed, rather than getting sellers to pay other closing costs or come down on the price of the properties, since those outlays can be financed.

• • • • •

Most of the various expenses discussed will be part of a buyer's closing costs, regardless of which type of real estate mortgage loan he or she may choose. However, each of the various types of real estate mortgages that are available have their own unique characteristics and requirements. Therefore, it is necessary for each borrower to consider the various alternatives and find the type of loan that best fits his or her needs. The help of a mortgage lender with a good reputation can be invaluable in making the best choice among loan alternatives. However, borrowers should assume ultimate responsibility in making their own choices of loans. In order to make that choice wisely, it is necessary that they have some understanding of the basic types of loans that are available to them. The following two chapters provide a basic explanation of the most popular types of mortgage alternatives that are currently available to borrowers in need of a real estate mortgage.

Chapter 12:

Financing the Purchase of a Personal Residence

There is a variety of different financing options available for financing a personal residence. This is due, in part, to the fact that there is no ideal loan that would be best for every buyer. The loan options available to buyers with large amounts of money available for a down payment will be considerably different than those available to buyers who can make only small down payments, just as buyers with good credit ratings will have more options than those with poor credit histories. The following segments discuss a few of the more popular mortgage options available to buyers to finance their principal residences. However, there are less common ways that may be available to some homebuyers, such as loans from family members, that will not be discussed.

Seller Financing

Buyers and sellers are always free to enter into sales agreements that provide for the seller to provide the financing of the buyer's purchases. From the buyer's perspective, seller financing (also called *owner financing*) will generally save him or her a substantial amount of money that would otherwise be paid to lenders and others in connection with securing a loan. Owner financing may also provide a buyer with a poor credit history an opportunity to purchase a home, provided the seller is willing to overlook the buyer's past payment performance. However, just as sellers take the risk that buyers may default on their owner-financed mortgages, buyers also take some risks when they buy homes that are financed by the sellers.

Banks, mortgage companies, and other lenders who make loans to buyers so that they can acquire personal residences protect themselves from default by borrowers by requiring them to pledge the homes they buy as collateral for the loans they get to be able to buy them. Since lenders want to be sure that their collateral will be marketable in the event that they must foreclose on the property, they insist that property that is pledged as collateral for a loan be appraised by a competent appraiser, and that proof be provided from professionals showing that the property is not located in a flood zone and that it has not suffered damage from termites or other insects. Lenders often require surveys as well, in order to verify that the structures on the property have not been built where they encroach on easements or on the property of adjacent landowners. If a property does not appraise for enough to justify the amount of the loan sought by the borrower, the lender will refuse to make the loan, and the seller will most likely have to lower the price of the property to the appraised value in order for the sale to be completed. Likewise, if flaws in the property are revealed by inspections, tests, appraisals, or surveys, lenders will likely require that some appropriate action be taken, or the loan will be denied.

Although lenders impose the requirements that they do for their own benefit, those same requirements also help prevent buyers from paying more than they should for the properties they buy and from buying houses with serious problems. Buyers who purchase properties by means of owner financing will not have a lender requiring proof that the houses they are buying are reasonably priced and in sound condition. It will be especially important for such buyers to protect themselves by including provisions in their purchase agreements that require the properties to appraise for at least as much as the purchase price and to have favorable results from surveys, inspections, and reports.

By no means are all properties that are offered for sale with owner financing overpriced or suffering from hidden defects that the seller wants to keep concealed. Some sellers are willing to offer financing in order to increase the attractiveness of their properties to prospective buyers, and may even offer interest rates that are below those offered by lending institutions. Still other sellers may be willing to carry loans on the properties that they have for sale because they like the idea of collecting interest on loans that are secured by real estate.

One of the biggest drawbacks to relying on owner financing to acquire a residence is that, in most cases, it is simply not available. Most people who are selling their homes will have a mortgage on their properties that they must pay off with at least part of the proceeds from the sale, and they will need the equity from their sales in order to buy a replacement residence. Landlords who are selling off some of their rental properties, heirs who are selling properties that they have inherited, and homeowners who have decided to sell their houses and move into retirement rental properties are good candidates to approach for owner financing. These properties are more likely to be debt free and the owners are less likely to need the money to acquire replacement property.

Sweat Equity
Even when a seller cannot afford to give a buyer the financing that he or she needs on a property, owner financing may offer some partial financing alternatives. Some properties are in such run-down condition that lenders will not make loans on them until they are repaired, but the owners have no money with which to repair them. Such situations frequently offer prospective buyers, who have the skill to do the needed repairs themselves, an opportunity to acquire homes cheaply and create what is known as *sweat equity* in the properties when the repair work that they do increases the value of their homes to a level substantially higher than what they paid for them.

Balloon Notes

Since lenders usually will not make loans on certain types of properties, such as those needing repairs, sellers who are not interested in carrying long-term loans on their properties may be able to sell what seems to be an unsellable property by financing the property only for a sufficient length of time for the buyer to repair it, with the buyer then being required to pay it off at the end of that time. This can be accomplished by a loan with payment terms set as if it were to be paid off over an extended period of time, such as thirty years, but with a provision that the unpaid balance will be fully due and payable at the end of some short period of time, such as two years. Such loans are made by the use of what is known as a *balloon note* that causes the monthly payments, other than the final *balloon payment*, to be as low as they would be for a long-term loan, but results in the lender being fully paid in a short period of time. The object of this approach is to give the buyer a way to acquire the property, and then have enough time to repair it, so that a lender will then refinance the property for the new owner to make the balloon payment on the loan from the seller.

Second Mortgages

Still another form of partial owner financing is the *second mortgage.* If the buyer can assume the seller's first mortgage on the property being sold, but does not have enough money to fully pay the seller for his or her equity in the property, a second mortgage from the seller offers a solution. This puts the seller in a financial position to receive some of the proceeds from the sale on installments, and the buyer can afford to make payments on both a first and second mortgage. Even in situations in which the buyer gets a new loan in order to purchase a property, it may be necessary to get a second mortgage from the seller for part of the purchase price in order for the buyer to be able to get the new first mortgage. Some lenders will loan a certain percentage of the appraised value of a property that a buyer borrows against without regard to where the buyer gets the remaining part of the purchase price. When such a loan is involved, it is permissible for the seller to give the buyer a second mortgage for the difference between what the first mortgage lender will loan on the property and the amount of money needed to purchase the property. Owners with properties that are so slow in selling that they would be willing to drastically cut the price in order to sell them are often amenable to giving buyers the second mortgages that they need in such cases. The amount of those mortgages is often no more than the amount that they would have been willing to cut the price of the property, and even if the buyer defaults on the second mortgage, the sellers are no worse off than if they had discounted the properties and sold them without taking a second mortgage on them.

Example: *Ivan wanted to sell his house, but news stories about how crime in his neighborhood had increased last year had caused sales of houses in the area to slow down. Ivan had purchased the house many years ago and had paid off his mortgage. He realizes that, although the house will appraise for $60,000, he must cut the price substantially in order to get it sold quickly, and is contemplating reducing his initial asking price of $60,000 to $50,000, or even a little less. Juan is interested in buying Ivan's house, but has only about $3,000 and his credit rating is weak. He has found a lender that will loan 80% of the appraised value of the house, to give Juan an interest rate that is about 2% higher than the rate charged on loans to buyers with good credit. It does not matter to the lender where Juan gets the other 20% of the purchase price of the property. If Ivan will give Juan a second mortgage for the 20% of the purchase price that is not covered by Juan's first mortgage, and Juan pays his closing costs with the $3,000 that he has, Ivan will net $48,000 in cash from the sale, which is about what he was thinking of offering to sell the property for, and will hold a second mortgage for $12,000. If Juan does not pay the second mortgage, it is doubtful that Ivan would want to foreclose on the property, since the first mortgage would still be a claim against the property.*

However, Juan may actually pay the second mort-gage, or if he does not make monthly payments, Ivan will still have a claim, which must be satisfied if Juan sells the property. Even if Ivan never receives any payment on the second mortgage, he would be no worse off than if he had sold the property for $48,000, which he was prepared to do.

FHA Loans

The *Federal Housing Administration* (FHA) was created during the Great Depression in order to help make loans available to homebuyers. The agency is now a part of the federal *Department of Housing and Urban Development* (HUD). However, the government does not make FHA loans. They are loans that are *insured* by the Federal Housing Administration.

Mortgage companies, banks, and other private lenders who make home mortgages can originate FHA loans for borrowers who qualify for them. In order to qualify for an FHA loan, a borrower must have sufficient income to meet FHA guidelines to be considered likely to be able to make the monthly payments on the loans being sought, must have sufficient funds available for the required down payment, and must be considered creditworthy. The creditworthiness of applicants is judged by length of employment, credit history, and the amount of outstanding obligations that the party already has. As long as an applicant has been employed for a year or more, that should be sufficient. Borrowers who have a significant amount of prior credit transactions and have repaid their loans in a timely manner, for the most part, should have an adequate credit history to qualify for an FHA loan.

Prospective home buyers can determine about what size FHA loan they would qualify for, assuming that they are creditworthy, by going to the HUD website at **www.hud.gov**, which contains a section entitled "Information by State" on the main page. By clicking on the box set up for state selection, the various states will appear. Upon choosing a state and clicking the "Go" circle, general information about specific programs for the state that was selected will appear, as well as a list to the left of the text material that includes the topic "homeownership." Clicking on it will produce another list of topics under the heading "More from HUD," which is highlighted by a green background. Among the topics under that heading is "How Much Home Can I Afford?" By clicking on that choice, a "Homeownership Guide and Calculator" will appear, which requires the entry of income data, monthly debt, and other obligations, such as child support and alimony. By entering the requested information and clicking on "Get Estimate," a calculation will appear that shows:

- ◆ the maximum sale price of the house that the buyer could purchase with an FHA loan;
- ◆ the maximum loan amount allowed and the monthly principal and interest payments on the loan;
- ◆ other monthly costs associated with owning the property, such as taxes, insurance, and repairs;
- ◆ the required down payment for the purchase;
- ◆ the total closing costs for the purchase; and,
- ◆ total cash that the borrower must have in order to close the purchase.

The same information will also be provided for other types of loans and displayed alongside the FHA loan figures.

These figures are based on national averages and are for a married couple with two dependent children. The figures can be refined to reflect an individual's personal situation by clicking on the "Detailed Estimate" line just below the calculations. The page that appears then gives the user the opportunity to select his or her state and county, as well as marital status and number of dependents. It is followed by a page to indicate the length of the mortgage desired, the interest rate anticipated, the cash available for down payment and closing costs, and the maximum monthly note. By clicking on the "Get Estimate" line at the end of that page, the user will get the same type of information as before, but specifically for the party requesting it.

One of the biggest advantages of FHA loans is that borrowers can pay as little as 3% down when purchasing a primary residence and borrow the rest. Borrowers can even add most of the closing costs that are associated with the property and finance 97% of the total of those costs plus the price of the property. Since the federal government insures FHA loans against default by agreeing to pay off the loan in the event that the borrower fails to repay the loan, interest rates on FHA loans are relatively low. This is despite the fact that borrowers often owe more on the residences that they purchase with FHA loans than they pay for the properties, since they are allowed to borrow against both the purchase price and closing costs of the properties that they buy.

Example: *Benito bought a house for $100,000. His closing costs that were eligible to be financed as part of his FHA loan totaled $6,000. At the closing of the transaction, Benito was required to pay 3% of the total of the $100,000 purchase price plus $6,000 in closing costs (.03 x $106,000 = $3,180). Therefore, upon closing the sale, Benito owed $102,820 ($106,000 - $3,180) on the house that he had just bought for $100,000.*

Disadvantages of FHA Loans

As with most things, FHA loans have their unappealing aspects, too. There are limits on the amount for which FHA loans will be made, regardless of the fact that the borrower's credit history and income would qualify him or her for a loan in a much higher amount. The limits are based on median housing costs in the U.S., with larger limits in place in locations where housing costs are substantially higher than the national average. The limits are adjusted as housing costs rise, but they are relatively modest. By working through the "How Much Home Can I Afford?" calculations on the HUD website, a prospective borrower can determine the maximum FHA loan amount available in his or her location by using the "Detailed Estimate" option.

When borrowers who have gotten FHA loans to buy homes default on them, so HUD must pay off the balance on those loans to the private lender and foreclose on the property, the properties commonly sell for less than is owed on them. In order to cover these losses, borrowers who get FHA loans are required to pay premiums to HUD for mortgage insurance. These *mortgage insurance premiums* (MIP) are usually divided into a lump sum payment, which is due at closing, and monthly payments that are added into the borrower's mortgage note payment. The amount of the MIP is determined by the size of the borrower's mortgage, and is usually large enough to be another significant drawback to getting an FHA loan.

VA Loans

The *U.S. Department of Veterans Affairs* (VA) has a home loan program for qualified military veterans. As in the case with FHA loans, rather than make actual home loans to veterans, the VA simply *guarantees* repayment of loans that were made to qualified veterans by private lenders under the VA loan program. In order to be eligible for a VA loan, an applicant must have served on active duty in the U.S. military, or in the military of certain U.S. allies, for some minimum amount of time, and if discharged, must have received other than a dishonorable discharge. As little as ninety days of continuous active duty is enough to be eligible for a VA loan for those who are considered to be veterans of World War II (served between September 16, 1940 and July 25, 1947), veterans of the Korean Conflict (served between June 27, 1950 and January 31, 1955), or veterans of the Vietnam Era (served between August 5, 1964 and May 7, 1975), but others must generally have served longer. The Veterans Affairs website at **www.homeloans.va.gov** offers comprehensive information on eligibility for VA guaranteed home mortgages.

One of the most attractive features of VA loans is that borrowers are permitted to buy homes and pay out only a very modest amount of money at closing. This is accomplished by requiring sellers to pay some of the closing costs that buyers would have been required to pay had they gotten most other types of loans, by allowing lenders to lend

100% of the purchase price of the property, and by negotiating with sellers to pay some of the buyer's closing costs that the sellers are not already required to pay.

Rather than using mortgage insurance to cover the costs of loan defaults, the VA program relies on a VA *funding fee* of 2% (2.75% for reservists) of the loan amount when the borrower makes a down payment of less than 5%. The VA funding fee is reduced to 1.5% (2.25% for reservists) when the borrower makes a down payment of 5–10%, and the fee is reduced to 1.25% (2% for reservists) when the borrower makes a down payment of 10% or more. The VA funding fee can be included in the borrower's loan, and, with enough help from the seller on paying costs, it is possible for a buyer to get a VA loan and pay nothing at the closing of the loan.

For most borrowers, the maximum of their loans that the VA will guarantee is $36,000. That does not mean that the maximum VA loan amount is $36,000. There is no maximum VA loan amount set by the VA, but the amount of each loan that is guaranteed will be 40%, up to the maximum of $36,000. Despite the fact that VA loans are not fully guaranteed, since a sizable portion of each is guaranteed, lenders are willing to make VA loans at competitive rates even though buyers often have nothing invested in the properties that they buy with those loans.

Borrowers can use VA loans to buy houses, condominiums, townhouses, mobile homes, and prefabricated homes. VA loans can also be used to build, repair, or improve a home, buy a home in need of repair and use some of the loan proceeds for repairs, or refinance a home. However, VA loans cannot be used to acquire rental property or other properties that the buyer/owner is not already using, or soon will use, as his or her primary residence.

Conventional Loans

Loans that are not guaranteed by a government agency are referred to as *conventional loans*. Since governmental agencies are not directly involved in the loans, lenders are free to set their own loan terms and conditions, loan amounts, and requirements to qualify for a loan. However, since lenders often transfer loans they have made to other parties, they will usually only make loans that are in conformity with loan guidelines set forth by governmental agencies that help stabilize the mortgage market by buying these *conforming loans.*

On the other hand, there are lenders who specialize in making *nonconforming loans* that do not meet the guidelines of U.S. federal agencies. Lenders make those loans, which are nonconforming due to such things as non-creditworthy borrowers, substandard property as collateral, or a loan amount in excess of the property's value, because they can usually charge higher fees and interest rates on the loans.

From the borrower's point of view, the availability of a nonconforming conventional loan can be a mixed blessing. If it were not for the availability of nonconforming loans, many buyers would not be able to get a home loan at all. However, because nonconforming loans often require additional fees that can easily equal 5–6% of the amount of the loan, and interest rates charged on these loans are routinely two or more percentage points higher than the rates charged on conforming loans, any appreciation that a buyer expected to realize on the property may end up being paid out to the lender in the form of fees and interest. However, in a truly booming market, real estate prices can escalate so quickly that the extra fees and interest associated with the nonconforming loan can readily be paid and leave the buyer with a sizable gain.

Down Payments

Borrowers who have good credit ratings can reduce their closing costs and monthly notes by getting conforming conventional loans. This is accomplished by making a down payment of 20% or more on the purchase of a primary residence. A down payment of 20% or more will eliminate the requirement of mortgage insurance, which is imposed on borrowers through private insurers when borrowers take out conforming conventional loans and pay less than 20% down on the properties that they purchase. As with the MIP imposed on borrowers who get FHA loans, regardless of the amount they pay down, the private mortgage insurance generally requires a substantial premium payment at the time of the closing of the loan, plus a significant amount of monthly premium payments that are added into the note. Once a buyer reaches the point where the debt against his or her property is 80% or less of its value, the owner can get the lender to drop the mortgage insurance requirement and realize a reduction in the monthly note by the amount of the private mortgage insurance premium. Therefore, even borrowers who cannot pay down 20% of the purchase price of the properties they buy can still eventually benefit from having chosen a conventional loan.

Chapter 13:

Financing Investment Properties

Most of the federal programs in the U.S. that are designed to make mortgage loans more readily available are designed to benefit individuals who are trying to purchase a primary residence. For example, the VA loan program was designed exclusively for the benefit of those who need a loan to acquire, build, improve, or refinance housing that they live in or will soon occupy as a primary residence. However, it is permissible for an owner who has financed his or her primary residence with a VA loan, and lived in the property for a substantial period of time, to move to another residence and keep the VA-financed property for rental purposes.

For the most part, financing for the acquisition of investment properties will have to come in the form of a loan that is not part of a program that receives direct government guarantees of loan repayments.

Owner Financing
There are a number of heavily advertised, popular programs that tout rapid accumulation of wealth by means of acquiring real estate

through owner financing. Certainly, owner financing should be explored as an option, since many of the closing costs that are associated with obtaining mortgage loans can be avoided when purchasing properties by paying the owners for them on installments. If the properties that are under consideration are rental properties that the landlord has decided to sell, and the owner does not have a mortgage on them that must be paid off, the likelihood that the seller would carry owner financing on the properties is much greater than it would be than if the seller were trying to sell his or her primary residence and would likely need the proceeds to buy a replacement home. Even if a landlord does owe some money on the rental properties that he or she has decided to sell, the buyer may find it beneficial to work out an arrangement to pay the seller enough money to pay off the mortgages and have the seller carry financing on the balance.

Still another option involving owner financing may be to persuade the owner to carry a sizable second mortgage and then find a lender who is willing to give a first mortgage on the property for the bulk of the funds that are needed in order to make the purchase. Some lenders are willing to make first mortgage loans for 80% or more of the purchase price, regardless of where the borrower gets the rest of the money that is needed for the purchase of a property.

When buyers enter into transactions in which owner financing is involved, it is important that they take an especially cautious approach. When lenders are involved in transactions, they will almost always insist on appraisals of all properties used as collateral for loans, as well as termite clearance letters, flood determinations, surveys, and perhaps even EPA tests and other examinations of those properties. The primary reason that lenders impose these requirements is to promote their own self-interest by ensuring that the properties that they lend money on are of sufficient value and marketability. This way, in the event of foreclosure, they would sell for enough to cover most, if not all, of what the borrower owes on them. A by-product of the lender's requirements is that the borrowers are also prevented from buying properties that are overpriced or that have serious problems that affect their value. It is not uncommon for buyers of properties, even those that they are not going to personally live in, to become so excited about their purchases that they do not want to have to wait for appraisals and inspections before entering into a contract and closing the transaction. Without a lender imposing these requirements, buyers are free to make the mistake of buying properties without investigating them as they should. Smart investors will resist the urge to buy properties without first subjecting them to the kinds of evaluations and tests that lenders typically require.

Past Rental Properties

Buyers should also be especially cautious when they are offered rental properties that landlords have decided to sell. As with any commercial activity, there are times when good properties are offered for sale by landlords who have decided to retire or who have health problems that prevent their continuation of rental activities. Also, rental properties often become available due to the death of a landlord. However, some rental properties are offered for sale because they have proven to be problem properties for the landlord, and it would probably be best to avoid purchasing these. Requesting written rental records would be a good first step in determining whether or not a rental property is desirable. Spending some time in the area where the property is located, and perhaps even talking with neighbors and past or present tenants, may also prove helpful.

FHA Loans

The primary purpose behind creation of the Federal Housing Administration was to increase the availability of financing for buyers who are purchasing property as a personal residence, and that is still the purpose of FHA today. There are a few loan programs available to those who want to acquire low-income rental properties. Local lenders will have information on what, if any, programs are available in a given area for a specified property.

For most landlords, the only type of FHA loan available is one used to purchase a multi-family property that has two, three, or four dwelling units. However, this type of loan does not appeal to the typical landlord, because he or she must occupy one of the units as his or her principal residence. Buyers who are willing to live in one unit of a two-, three-, or four-unit property will find that the FHA loan available to them offers the advantages of a low down payment and the option of financing many of their closing costs along with the purchase price of the property, just as FHA loans that are available for single-family properties do. As a reflection of the fact that multi-family properties are usually more costly than single-family ones, there are higher loan limits for two-unit properties than there are for single-family properties, still higher loan limits for three-unit properties, and even higher loan limits for four-unit properties.

The availability of an FHA loan for a multi-family property may be appealing, but buyers must be cautioned that they should not apply for such a loan unless they are actually going to live in one of the units as a primary residence. Borrowers who obtain FHA loans in order to buy multi-family properties will be required to sign affidavits to the effect that they are going to occupy one of the units as a primary residence. Parties who misrepresent their intention to occupy a unit of a multi-family property in order to qualify for an FHA loan are committing loan fraud that is punishable by severe fines and imprisonment.

Conventional Loans

Most buyers of rental properties or other properties that are acquired for investment purposes will have to rely on a conventional loan from a lending institution to make their purchases. Since conventional loans are those whose repayment is not guaranteed by a federal agency, most lenders are going to be more selective in making these loans than they are in making FHA and VA loans. Lenders are also more wary of making loans to borrowers who are buying real estate they are not going to live in, because the lenders realize that borrowers are less likely to make extreme sacrifices to keep from defaulting on rental property or investment property than they are to keep from defaulting on their own homes. Also, most landlords are dependent on the rents that they collect in order to be able to service the debts on their rental properties. This leaves them vulnerable to default when they have trouble renting out their properties or collecting their rents. As a result of these concerns, lenders who are making loans to borrowers so that they can acquire rental or investment properties will often loan those borrowers no more than 75% to 80% of the value of the properties that they are pledging as collateral for their loans. Furthermore, when the most reputable lenders make loans to borrowers with good credit ratings and charge them favorable rates, the borrowers will usually be required to pay their down payments from their own assets in order to qualify for such loans, which are referred to as *A-grade loans*.

For many landlords and investors, the biggest obstacle to getting the financing they need is meeting the lender's down payment requirement. Even though investors and landlords will not be able to get second mortgage financing from the seller to cover the difference between the purchase price of the properties that they want and the amount of the available A-grade loans on the properties, the borrowers merely have to cover their down payments from their own assets, rather than the down payment having to come from an accumulated cash pool.

Borrowing against Equity

Investors and landlords who own their own homes may be able to get the down payment money they need to acquire investment properties by taking out home equity loans on their personal residences. However, the borrowers who take this approach must bear in mind that taking out a home equity loan requires that they give an additional mortgage on that property, which could result in it being lost by a foreclosure sale in the event of default. Rather than risk losing their homes, some borrowers prefer to get a *B-grade* or even lower grade loan. Such a loan requires them to make a much smaller down payment, if any, but typically requires them to pay considerably higher fees to obtain the loan and substantially higher interest over the life of the loan. Although lower grade loans are a relatively costly alternative, some of them are available for amounts that are sufficient to cover both the acquisition of a property and the costs necessary to repair it and make it ready for resale or rental. When properties are available at prices that offer substantial opportunity for gain, the added costs associated with financing them with lower grade loans may prove to be relatively insignificant. Borrowers who take out loans at relatively high interest rates in order to buy houses to fix up and resell should be able to avoid having to pay that interest for too long, since the loans will be paid off when the properties are sold. In fact, if they are given a choice, buyers who are acquiring investment properties should choose higher interest rates over larger loan origination fees and other loan costs, since those costs will be lost even if the loan is paid off soon, but the interest will be eliminated by an early payoff.

A relatively common technique that landlords and investors who already own properties use in order to raise capital to acquire more properties is to refinance the properties they already own and borrow out some of their equity in those properties. After some time has gone by since an owner has acquired a rental or investment property and has done any necessary improvements, if the owner has a good credit rating, he or she should be able to get an A-grade loan against the property for as much as 80% of its value. When properties are bought substantially below their market values, and those values are enhanced by improvements and market appreciation, it is not uncommon for owners to be able to pay off their existing mortgages and have a substantial amount of their loan proceeds remaining, even with loans that are limited to 80% of the value of their properties.

The major disadvantage of refinancing rental properties and investment properties in order to borrow out equity in them is that the owner will not be able to attain the ideal goal of owning several properties that are paid for that can either generate large net rental income or provide a source of substantial net proceeds upon sale. Refinancing not only adds years to the borrower's mortgage, but it also adversely impacts equity accumulation. Payments in the earliest years of a mortgage are mostly interest, with only a small amount of debt retirement, whereas the ratio of interest to principal payments shifts in favor of principal payments as more mortgage payments are made. Therefore, a borrower who replaces a loan with one of similar duration and at a similar interest rate will also be replacing payments that have begun to retire more of the indebtedness than earlier payments on the mortgage. Initial payments on a new loan retire almost none of the principal of the debt.

If the new loan is available at a significantly lower interest rate than the loan it replaces, refinancing would be more appealing. If the rates are significantly lower, and the borrower does not borrow a great deal more than the original amount of the loan that is being paid off with the new loan, it may be feasible for the borrower to take out a shorter term mortgage and actually pay the property off more quickly.

The biggest danger in refinancing rental properties and investment properties in order to borrow out the equity in those properties is that the borrowers may be tempted to use some of those funds to cover living expenses, take vacations, or buy luxury goods. Some of the real estate programs that are offered for sale even advocate using funds from refinancing for these purposes. Owners who succumb to those temptations will end up with a collection of properties that are so heavily mortgaged that they may be difficult to sell for enough to even pay them off.

Lines of Credit

If used wisely, refinancing rental and investment properties to raise investment capital can be invaluable to real estate dealers and landlords. One of the smartest approaches is to pledge investment properties and rental properties as collateral for a line of credit, and then draw against that credit line to buy additional properties and cover the costs of repairs and improvements of them. This gives the buyer the flexibility to move quickly and buy properties, such as those sold at auction, when there is not enough time to go through the typical loan process. If lenders are unwilling to give a borrower a line of credit against his or her properties, an alternative approach would be to borrow against them, put the loan proceeds in an account that pays as much interest as there is available, and then draw against that credit line to buy additional properties and cover the costs of repairs and improvements of them. This approach also gives the buyer the flexibility to move quickly and buy properties when there is not enough time for buyers to go through the typical loan process. Once again, it is imperative that the borrower be disciplined enough to use the loan proceeds only for business purposes.

Balloons

Most loans that are available to landlords and real estate investors on the properties they own for commercial purposes have a *balloon* provision in them that requires full payment of the remaining balance of the loan at the end of some period of time. This period is usually somewhere between five and ten years, despite the fact that the payments may have been set up as if the loan were to run for thirty years. Therefore, owners of such properties need to be prepared to refinance their loans when the balloon payments come due. This will require them to diligently make all of their mortgage payments on time, to maintain their properties well enough to get good appraisals on them, and to periodically increase their rental rates so that the income streams from the properties will justify higher appraisals and will show lenders a source of revenue available to service debt.

Chapter 14:

Tax Law Affecting Owner-Occupied Realty

There are a number of provisions in the U.S. Tax Code that allow for deductions of expenses associated with ownership of real estate and address taxation of income derived from either the rental or sale of real estate. The Internal Revenue Code (I.R.C.) applies different provisions to owner-occupied residential real estate than it does to rental property, or to property bought as a speculation and resold. Therefore, it is necessary to separate realty by how the owner uses it when discussing U.S. tax laws as they apply to real estate.

One of the most appealing incentives to owning one's residence is that owners are allowed to take a tax deduction for the *home mortgage interest* and *property taxes* that they pay on their residences, as long as they meet certain requirements. In fact, taxpayers can even take a home mortgage interest deduction for the interest they pay on the mortgage of a second home that they own for personal use.

The Home Mortgage Interest Deduction

For purposes of establishing that interest paid constitutes deductible home mortgage interest, it must be shown that the loan on which the interest was paid had been obtained to buy a main home or second home, or the loan must have been a second mortgage, line of credit, or home equity loan on a main or second home. Additionally, the taxpayer must be legally liable on a valid, bona fide debt that is secured by a legitimate mortgage.

In addition to payments that are specifically labeled as interest, those who itemize deductions are also allowed to deduct *discount points*, *origination fees*, *late payment fees*, and *prepayment penalties*, since all of these charges are generally considered to be part of the cost of using borrowed money. Generally, the deduction for discount points and origination fees cannot be taken in the year in which they were paid, but must be spread over the life of the loan, unless the following are true:

- the proceeds of the loan were used to buy or build the taxpayer's main home;
- paying points or origination fees of the amount paid is an established business practice in the area where the loan was made;
- the points are fees that are computed as a percentage of the amount of the mortgage;
- the charges are clearly shown on the settlement statement; and,
- the funds for the points or origination fees were not borrowed as part of the mortgage.

Fees for services connected with obtaining a home mortgage (such as appraisal fees, mortgage insurance premiums, and the cost to record a deed or mortgage) are not deductible as interest.

All of the interest on any mortgages originated on or before October 13, 1987, is deductible on Schedule A as home mortgage interest, since that was the last date virtually all interest payments qualified as itemized deductions. Such obligations are referred to as *grandfathered debt*. Mortgages that originated after October 13, 1987, in order to buy, build, or improve a main home or a second home, are referred to as *home acquisition debt*. Interest on such debts is fully deductible on Schedule A as long as the total of the home acquisition debt and the grandfathered debt on all of the mortgages on the individual's main home and second home combined does not exceed $1 million ($500,000 if the taxpayer's filing status is married, filing separately). Otherwise, the interest deduction will have to be reduced to reflect the interest charged on the maximum allowable indebtedness.

Mortgages originated after October 13, 1987, for purposes other than to purchase, build, or improve a main home or second home, are known as *home equity debt*. Interest on home equity debt is deductible on Schedule A as long as the total home equity debt on an individual's main home and second home combined does not exceed $100,000 ($50,000 for married couples choosing to file as married, filing separately), and the total of grandfathered debt, home acquisition debt, and home equity debt do not exceed the fair market value of the property that is mortgaged. If the total indebtedness exceeds the fair market value of the property mortgaged, the interest deduction must be reduced to the level that would be paid if the total indebtedness equaled the fair market value of the property mortgaged.

Example: *Linda owns a home worth $500,000, which she obtained with a mortgage that has a $375,000 balance. She just bought a home at a nearby lake for $175,000. She paid her closing costs, which included a $3,000 loan origination fee, in full and obtained a mortgage for $150,000 against the lake property to pay for it. Linda will be allowed to fully deduct the interest on both of her mortgages on Schedule A, since they are both home acquisition debt, neither of which exceeds the value of the property on which each mortgage is placed, and the combined total of the two mortgages does not exceed $1 million. The $3,000 loan origination fee* *is deductible as interest expense on Schedule A, but it must be spread out over the life of the loan for purposes of calculating the interest deduction. If Linda had not already owned a home and the lake home had been purchased as her main home, she would have been allowed to claim an interest deduction for the full origination fee for the year in which it was paid. (As long as she had not used proceeds of her loan to pay it, such fees are customary at the place where she got the loan, and it was shown on her settlement sheet.)*

The Property Tax Deduction

Taxpayers are allowed to take an itemized deduction for qualified taxes paid on real estate that they own and that is not used for business. It does not matter whether the taxes were paid to a state or local government, or even a foreign government, and all of the taxes paid to each governmental entity are added together to determine the amount of the deduction. The deduction is available for all qualified real estate taxes paid on nonbusiness realty, and is not limited just to *real estate taxes* that are paid on a primary residence or secondary home, as is the deduction for mortgage interest payments.

In order for real estate taxes to qualify for the deduction, the person who paid the taxes and is taking the deduction must own the property. Also, the property taxes that were paid must be based on the assessed value of the property, and the assessment must be based on criteria that are uniformly applied across the community. Therefore, if a taxpayer were charged a property tax, but it was actually a bill for the utilities that the party had used and was based on the amounts of those utilities that were consumed, the payments of the so-called tax would not be deductible as a property tax on the taxpayer's federal income tax return, despite the fact that the governmental agency that had levied the charge had labeled it as a property tax.

Another requirement that must be met in order for a property tax payment to qualify for deduction on U.S. federal tax returns is that the tax revenue collected by the taxing authority must be used to finance general governmental activity. Charges levied against a property owner for the cost of things such as government employees having to clean up neglected property, or charges levied against property for improvements that specifically benefit that property, such as special assessments to run utilities to it or put sidewalks around it, do not qualify as deductible property taxes on U.S. federal tax returns. This is true even if the charges are labeled as property taxes and levied by the same agency that collects property taxes and are included on the owner's property tax bill.

The Benefit of the Itemized Nonbusiness Deductions

Being allowed to take a personal itemized deduction for home mortgage interest and property taxes that taxpayers pay on the real estate that they own and do not use in business may or may not actually reduce their federal income tax liability. This is primarily due to the fact that most taxpayers are allowed to take a relatively sizable *standard deduction* in lieu of itemizing deductions. No benefit is realized from itemizing deductions until their total exceeds the allowable standard deduction for a given taxpayer. Even if a taxpayer's itemized deductions exceed his or her allowable standard deduction, his or her will benefit from itemizing only to the extent that the itemized deductions exceed the available standard deduction. The benefit derived from having itemized deductions in excess of the standard deduction will be only the amount of the excess multiplied by the marginal tax rate that the taxpayer would have to pay on the income, had it not been excluded by itemizing deductions.

Example: *In March of 2005, Mildred and Wally filed their 2004 tax return. In calculating their itemized deductions, they had $5,000 in charitable contributions that qualified for deduction, $4,600 in home mortgage interest, and $2,000 in property* *taxes that qualified for deduction. As a married couple filing jointly, they would have been allowed to take a standard deduction of $9,700 had they not itemized their deductions. Therefore, their total of $11,600 in itemized deductions gave them only $1,900 more than they would have had if they merely used the standard deduction of $9,700. If the $1,900 in additional deductions would have been taxed at 25% had the couple not had itemized deductions in excess of their standard deduction, their net tax savings from itemizing deductions would be $475. If Mildred and Wally had made only $2,500 in charitable contributions, their standard deduction of $9,700 would have exceeded their total itemized deductions of $9,100. They would have received absolutely no reduction in their federal income tax liability from being entitled to deduct the home mortgage interest and property taxes that they had paid.*

On the other hand, if their deductible charitable contributions had been $10,000, since that deduction alone would have exceeded the standard deduction, their deductible home mortgage interest and property taxes would have reduced their taxable income dollar for dollar. If that income would have been taxed in the 25% marginal tax bracket had it not been excluded from taxation due to the interest and property tax deductions, those deductions, which total $6,600, would save the couple $1,650. This could easily be the equivalent of a couple of their monthly mortgage payments.

The U.S. has a *progressive* federal income tax system. This means that the lowest income earners are taxed at the lowest marginal rates, with gradual increases in tax rates that apply to higher segments of income, which are referred to as *tax brackets*. The household income of most U.S. taxpayers puts them in a tax bracket that is at or below the 25% marginal tax bracket. This does not mean that their entire incomes are taxed at the rate for the highest bracket that they have reached. There is a *zero bracket amount,* which is an amount of income that individual U.S. taxpayers are allowed to earn without having to pay any federal income tax on it, followed by a 10% bracket, and then a 15% bracket, before the 25% bracket is reached. There are also subsequent brackets of 28%, 33%, and 35%. The amount of tax savings that a taxpayer will realize from being allowed to take a tax deduction for home mortgage interest and property taxes will depend heavily on the tax bracket that he or she has reached.

Example: *James and Maxine are retired and have a relatively low earned income, which they supplement with Social Security income and money from their savings. Their itemized deductions totaled $16,200, of which $6,500 was expenditures for home mortgage interest and deductible property taxes. Their income that was subject to federal income taxation before subtracting their itemized deductions was $18,000. The couple's zero bracket amount was $15,900. Even though the amount of the taxpayers' itemized deductions exceeded their standard deduction by the full amount of their expenditures for home mortgage interest and deductible property taxes, most of their income would have been spared from federal income taxation due to the $15,900 zero bracket. The $16,200 in itemized deductions will actually only reduce their taxable income by the amount that those deductions exceed the zero bracket amount, which is only $300. Since the couple's taxable income is so low, what little of it is subjected to federal income taxes will be taxed at only 10%. Therefore, the net tax savings that James and Maxine will realize due to their deductions for home mortgage interest and property taxes will be a mere $30 (10% of $300).*

Taxpayers with above-average incomes will be the ones likely to benefit the most from taking an itemized deduction for home mortgage interest and property taxes, since they are more likely to have purchased expensive homes with sizeable mortgages that generate large interest charges and bigger property tax levies that are based on property values. However, taxpayers with exceptionally high incomes are subject to provisions that directly reduce their itemized deductions. The instructions for completing Schedule A of Form 1040, which is the schedule used for determining itemized deductions for federal income tax purposes, provides a worksheet for determining the amount by which taxpayer's itemized deductions are reduced due to their having made exceptionally high amounts of income. The reduction provisions apply to taxpayers with *adjusted gross income*, which is income before taking deductions for exemptions and the standard or itemized deductions, in excess of $142,700 ($71,350 for married taxpayers who file separately). The reduction in the itemized deductions on Schedule A of Form 1040 was calculated by subtracting $142,700 ($71,350 if married filing separately) from the taxpayer's adjusted gross income and multiplying the remainder by 3%. However, the reduction is limited to a maximum of 80% of the party's itemized deductions.

Example: *Sebastian and his wife, Moonglow, are artists. Last year, they had an adjusted gross income of $140,000. Their itemized deductions were $27,400, of which $17,400 consisted of home mortgage interest and deductible property taxes. Since their adjusted gross income did not exceed $142,700, if Sebastian and Moonglow file a joint return, their itemized deductions will not be subject to reduction. Also, they will be able to reduce their adjusted gross income by the full amount of the home mortgage interest and property taxes that they paid for the year, since their other itemized deductions were already larger than their standard deduction. If they did not have the $17,400 deduction for home mortgage interest and property taxes, they would have an additional*

$17,400 taxed in the 28% bracket. Therefore, the tax deductions associated with owning their residence saved them $4,872 ($17,400 x 28%).

Just before the end of the year, an art dealer had tried to acquire the couple's entire group of their completed works, but had been unable to get the loan that he would have needed. If the dealer had completed the purchase, Sebastian and Moonglow would have had a joint adjusted gross income of $510,000. If that had been the case, their itemized deductions on their joint return would have been reduced by an amount equal to their adjusted gross income, less $142,700, times 3% ($510,000 - $142,700 = $367,300 x .03 = $11,019). This $11,019 reduction would have left the couple with itemized deductions of only $16,081, but the $6,381 by which their allowable itemized deductions exceed their standard deduction would have been taxed at 35% if they did not have the deduction. Therefore, they would still have a net tax savings of $2,233 that is attributable to the tax deductions that are associated with the home that they own.

U.S. tax laws have built-in adjustments for inflation that annually adjust the various tax brackets and the maximum amount of income that a taxpayer can earn without having to reduce his or her itemized deductions. Despite these adjustments, the basic requirement for adjusting itemized deductions has remained the same for a number of years. Also, although some taxpayers realize little or no benefit from being allowed to take a tax deduction for the home mortgage interest and property taxes they pay, many homeowners save thousands of dollars in federal income taxes each year as a result of those deductions.

Taxation of the Gains from the Sale of a Primary Residence

One of the most beneficial provisions for taxpayers in the entire U.S. Tax Code is I.R.C. §121, which deals with the tax treatment of gains from the sale of a principal residence. If they meet certain requirements, married taxpayers are allowed to realize a gain of up to $500,000 from the sale of their primary residence without having to pay any U.S. federal income taxes on that gain. Taxpayers who file under any status other than married, filing jointly, are allowed to exclude up to $250,000 in gain from the sale of their primary residence when they meet the requirements for eligibility. Unlike previous laws that included special provisions for avoiding taxation on gains from the sale of a principal residence, the current law does not require taxpayers to reinvest the proceeds from the sale of their residence in another principal residence in order to qualify for the exclusion, and it does not require the taxpayers to have attained some minimum age. Also, the exclusion can be taken on numerous properties over a taxpayer's lifetime, as long as the requirements for the exclusion are met on each property. (Previous laws allowed for only one such exclusion in a taxpayer's lifetime.)

Qualifying Residence

The place where a taxpayer lives most of the time is considered to be his or her *principal residence*. In addition to the more traditional housing, mobile homes, houseboats, camper trailers, and motor homes can qualify as a principal residence as long as the taxpayer actually resides there more than anywhere else.

Example: *Rob, a professor at a small college, lives in a motor home that he is allowed to park on campus. He acquired a cabin at a lake where he has gone for spring break and the entire summer for the past few years. Rob accepted an administrative position at the college, and since he would no longer be off for summers, sold his cabin at a gain of $32,000. Rob will not be eligible to exclude the gain on the sale of his cabin, since his motor home, rather than the cabin, was his primary residence.*

One of the most troublesome questions that arises in determining whether a property is considered to be a primary residence is whether renting out a vacated primary residence while the owners attempt to sell it will cause the property to be regarded as rental property, which does not qualify for the exclusion. If it can be shown that the owners are merely temporarily renting out their former principal residence, while awaiting its sale, the period of rental should not cause the property to be reclassified as rental property. This can be demonstrated by showing that the owners rented the property merely on a month-to-month basis, continued to attempt to sell the property, and reserved the right to show the property to potential buyers. However, if the owners' renting out of a former residence goes beyond temporary rental, such as when the property is leased for a long time, the property will no longer qualify as the owners' primary residence.

If a principal residence that is situated on acreage is sold at a gain, and the owners qualify for exclusion of gain on their primary residence, the gains from both the structure and the acreage are excludable, as long as the acreage was acquired along with the structure, or was acquired in a single purchase and the structure was later added. However, if additional acreage was acquired after acquisition of the property that a taxpayer's principal residence is situated on, any gain from the sale of the additional acreage will not qualify for the exclusion.

Example: *John bought fifty acres in Happy Valley with the intent of building a home on the property. Before building his home, an adjacent landowner offered to sell a hundred-acre parcel that adjoined John's fifty acres and he bought it. John paid $100,000 for his fifty-acre parcel, $75,000 for the hundred-acre parcel, and spent $150,000 constructing a house on the fifty-acre parcel. Five years later he sold the house, which was his principal residence, and all 150 acres of the land for $550,000.*

*The contract for the sale of the land broke down the
price and allocated $3,000 per acre for the 150 acres
of land and $100,000 for the house. Even if John
qualifies for exclusion of up to $250,000 of his gain
from the sale of his principal residence, he will not be
entitled to exclude any of his gain from the sale of his
property. Only the original fifty acres, which cost
$100,000, and the $150,000 cost to build his house
will qualify as principal residence. The sale price of
$3,000 per acre for the fifty acres, which is $150,000
and $100,000 for the house on it, total up to exactly
equal what the fifty acres, and the house on it, cost
him. His gain of $225,000 from the transaction is
attributable entirely to the sale of the hundred-acre
parcel of land, which he bought for $75,000 and sold
for $300 an acre for a total of $300,000.*

*If John had chosen a site to build his house on the
hundred-acre parcel, he would have been able to
treat the hundred-acre parcel, instead of the fifty-
acre parcel, as part of his principal residence. If that
had been the case, he would have the cost of the
house ($150,000),.plus the cost of the hundred acres
($75,000), for a total of $225,000 invested in his
principal residence, which he would have sold for
$400,000 ($100,000 for the house and $300,000 for
the land), causing him to realize a gain of $175,000,
which would have fully qualified for exclusion.*

If, in the previous example, John's original fifty acres were more valuable per acre than the hundred acres that he subsequently bought, he
should have insisted on reflecting that fact in his contract for the sale
of the property, so that he could have properly allocated any of the
gain to the more valuable acres. Of course, in situations such as
John's, there is the potential for taxpayers to over-allocate value to the
acreage on which their residences are built in an attempt to qualify
more of their gain for exclusion. Therefore, in anticipation of a

challenge by the IRS, taxpayers should obtain an appraisal from a qualified appraiser, in order to substantiate their allocation of value, when they sell their principal residences along with acreage that does not qualify as part of their principal residences.

Still another provision that owners of primary residences with acreage must contend with is that any part of the acreage that is sold in a transaction that is separate from the sale of the actual residence does not qualify as a principal residence, even if the acreage would have qualified if it had been sold along with the actual residence. Therefore, if John, in the previous example, had sold thirty of the fifty acres that he had built his house on, but kept twenty acres and the house, none of the gain on the thirty acres that he sold would qualify for exclusion. Likewise, if he had sold the house and the twenty acres, the property would have been considered to be his primary residence, but if he later were to sell the remaining thirty acres, it could no longer be treated as part of his primary residence and would not qualify for exclusion.

Qualifying for the Section 121 Exclusion

In order to qualify for the exclusion of gain from the sale of one's primary residence, a taxpayer must have owned and occupied the property as his or her primary residence for an aggregate total of at least two years out of the last five years prior to the sale. The two years do not have to be continuous. A taxpayer who lived in a house for a year and relocated for six months for temporary employment, and then moved back into his or her house for another year, would have met the residency test.

Taxpayers are allowed to exclude the gain from the sale of a primary residence only once every two years. There are exceptions to the rule that a property owner cannot take an exclusion but once every two years. If a taxpayer must sell a primary residence due to change in employment, health, or unforeseen circumstances, the homeowner will still be allowed to take a prorated exclusion of the gain, even if the party had previously excluded gain from the sale of a primary residence within the last two years. The amount of the exclusion is calculated by dividing by 730 the smaller of either 1) the aggregate number of days in the last five years that the property was held as a principal residence or 2) the number of days since the most recent sale that qualified for exclusion. (The number of days in two years is 730.)

Example: *Janet's principal residence for a period of one year had been a small home on a lakeside lot. She then moved into a larger home that she bought as her principal residence, but kept the lake property for recreational use. After owning and residing in the larger residence for twenty-six months, she sold it at a gain of $80,000, which she was able to exclude from her taxable income, and moved back into her lake home. One year and three months (a total of 455 days) after moving back to her lake home, Janet had to sell it in order to move to her mother's home and take care of her after she suffered an unforeseen stroke. In the last five years, the lake house had been Janet's principal residence for a total of 820 days, but it had been only 455 days since she had sold her last home. Therefore, if she had sold her lake property at a gain of $100,000, she would still be allowed to exclude $62,328.76 (455/730 x $100,000) of her gain, provided that her sale of the lake property is considered to have been necessitated by unforeseen circumstances.*

Other Exclusion Regulations

There are other provisions that limit taxpayers' rights to exclude their gains from the sale of their principal residences. One of these provisions is that if only one spouse meets the ownership and use requirements in order to qualify for exclusion of the gain on a jointly owned principal residence, then the exclusion will be limited to only $250,000. Another limitation on the right to excluded gains from the sale of a principal residence is that any deductions taken for business use of a principal residence, and any depreciation taken on a principal residence while it was rented out, must be *recaptured* and shown as gain that is ineligible for an exclusion.

Chapter 15:

Tax Treatment of Rental Property

The Internal Revenue Code lists all the various sources of *gross income* for tax purposes, and among them is *rents*. The term *rents* refers to money received for letting someone else use the recipient's real estate or personal property. Only the *net* income from rental activities is included in a taxpayer's gross income, since deductions are allowed for expenses that are incurred by a property owner in connection with his or her rental enterprise.

Allowable Deductions

Individuals are required to report their rental incomes on Schedule E of Form 1040. In addition to showing their gross rental income on a Schedule E, taxpayers also list all of the deductible expenses that they incurred in connection with generating that income. The tax code does not enumerate every expense that is eligible for deduction, but instead takes the approach that any expense associated with a rental activity is deductible as long as it was an *ordinary and necessary* expense.

There is no clear-cut test to determine whether or not an expense is *ordinary* for the landlord who wants to deduct it. The requirement that an expense be ordinary and necessary in order to be deductible applies to businesses of all kinds—not just to the activity of renting out property. Therefore, disputes with the IRS over the deductibility of certain expenses have been common, and there have been numerous court cases in which the question of whether or not an expense was ordinary was raised.

In general, the courts have traditionally considered the issues of whether a business expense should be considered ordinary for a given taxpayer from two distinctly different points of view—the reasonableness of the purpose and the amount of the expenditure.

On the one hand, courts consider whether a given expense that a business deducted was appropriate for that business in light of the type of business that it does. Courts have not required that expenditures for which a deduction is sought be typical of businesses in their field or even that they were historically incurred by the company in question. The key determinant seems to be whether the expenditure was a *reasonable* one for that taxpayer at the time it was made. As long as there was a reasonable business purpose for the expenditure, it will likely be regarded as reasonable, and therefore, ordinary, even if it does not result in any improvement in the taxpayer's profitability.

Example: *Dagmar bought an apartment complex. She decided to have an open house and invite residents in nearby houses to come by for refreshments and a tour of the remodeled complex. She hoped that this would cause homeowners to tell their friends and relatives about her apartments and help her get new tenants. The invitations that she sent out and refreshments that she served cost $460, but she did not get a single new tenant as a result of her open house. Since there was a reasonable business purpose in having the open house, Dagmar should be allowed to deduct the expense of it from her rental income.*

The other aspect of ordinary that courts analyze in considering whether or not an expense should be deductible also focuses on the reasonableness of the expenditure. However, rather than involving the question of whether the purpose of the expenditure was reasonable, it deals with the issue of whether the *amount* of the expenditure was reasonable. Expenditures connected with rental activities that are clearly ordinary will likely still be considered nondeductible if they are considered to be extravagant.

In practice, the requirement that an expense must be *necessary* in order to be deductible is not much different than the requirement that it must be ordinary. As long as it can be shown that an expenditure was reasonable, both from the perspective that it would be beneficial to the business or landlord and that it was not lavish, it should qualify as a necessary expenditure for tax purposes.

Specific Deductions

A basic checklist of deductible expenses that are available to landlords is incorporated in the Schedule E of Form 1040 that recipients of rental income must use to report that income. Schedule E of Form 1040 has enough space to report the income and expenses associated with up to three separate properties. Landlords with more than three rental properties will have to use multiple Schedule Es.

Advertising

The deductible expenses listed on Schedule E of Form 1040 begin with *advertising*. Included in this category would be the cost of running advertisements in local newspapers and other publications in an effort to attract tenants. In the previous example, in which Dagmar held a reception in order to promote her apartment complex, the expense of the reception should qualify as an advertisement expense.

Auto and Travel Expense

Landlords are allowed to deduct the expense of *auto and travel* incurred in connection with their rental activities. Landlords are even allowed to deduct 50% of their meal expenses when they travel away from home in connection with their rental activities, as long as their meal expenses are ordinary and necessary. The primary component of the auto and travel expense category is the cost of operating an automobile in connection with acquiring, repairing, managing, or otherwise carrying out the duties involved in renting out real estate.

Taxpayers who are engaged in rental activities have the choice of taking a cents-per-mile deduction or a deduction for their actual expenses for the operation of their vehicles in carrying out their rental real estate enterprises. Regardless of which method is chosen, landlords who do not use their vehicles exclusively in their real estate rental activities will need to keep a logbook that shows the number of miles that they drive each year in connection with their rental activities, as well as the miles they have driven for other purposes. When a landlord takes an auto expense deduction, a breakdown of mileage driven in connection with rental activity and mileage driven for other purposes is required on Form 4562, which must be filed with the landlord's tax return in order to claim the auto expense deduction. The taxpayer's mileage logbook does not have to be any special book, but whatever form it takes, an entry should be made showing the beginning mileage, ending mileage, destination, and purpose of each trip made in connection with the party's rental activity.

Landlords who use more than four vehicles simultaneously in rental activities must use actual expenses to calculate their auto deduction, rather than the cents-per-mile method. Also, if landlords who own their vehicles take their actual expenses to calculate their auto expense deduction for the first year that it is used in rental activities, they must continue to use their actual auto expenses to calculate future deductions. Those who lease their vehicles can use the cents-per-mile method only if they use it throughout the term of the lease.

Taxpayers who use the cents-per-mile method, which is also known as the *standard mileage rate*, to calculate their expense, determine their deduction by multiplying the cents-per-mile rate, which is subject to change annually and is published in the Schedule E instructions, by the number of miles driven for rental activities. The result, plus deductible parking fees and tolls, is then entered in the space for auto and travel expenses on Schedule E.

Taxpayers who use their actual auto expenses to calculate the auto expense deduction must determine what percentage of the mileage put on their vehicles for the taxable year was for rental activity, and multiply that percentage times their total expenditures for gas, oil, repairs, insurance, tires, and other auto expenses. The information in the taxpayer's mileage logbook will enable him or her to calculate the percentage of rental activity use by dividing the rental activity miles by the total miles driven for the year. The auto-related expenditures will have to be determined from the taxpayer's records of those expenditures.

Cleaning, Maintenance, and Repairs

The costs of having rental properties cleaned and made ready for a new tenant are deductible expenses, as are the costs of repairs that are performed for tenants while they occupy the property or must be performed after a property is vacated. Even if a former tenant is legally liable for the cost to repair damages to property, if the landlord pays for the cost of the repairs, he or she will be allowed to take a deduction for that expense, and if costs are recovered from the tenant, the amount recovered will be reported as income.

Commissions, Management Fees, and Professional Fees

Schedule E of Form 1040 lists commissions as a deductible expense. Payments to rental agents who provide tenants and referral fees to both real estate professionals and individuals alike qualify as deductible commissions. *Management fees* are payments to real estate management companies to oversee rental properties on an ongoing basis. Legal and other professional fees include payments to attorneys to draft and review leases and evict tenants, as well as fees to other professionals, such as collection agencies and accountants.

Insurance

Property and casualty insurance, which covers damage to property from such perils as fire, storms, and frozen water pipes, is clearly an ordinary and necessary expense for landlords. Mortgage companies that have made loans on rental property will insist on the landlord taking out property and casualty coverage. Landlords who have fully paid for their rental properties and have voluntarily chosen to buy such coverage will be entitled to take a tax deduction for the expense of those polices, as can those who are required by a mortgage holder to buy such policies. A deduction is also permitted for the premiums that landlords pay for other coverage, such as liability insurance to protect them from claims from tenants and others who are injured on the landlord's property, flood insurance, and earthquake coverage.

Interest

Whether or not a taxpayer can take an interest expense deduction on Schedule E will depend on whether or not the proceeds of the loan on which the interest was paid are allocable to rental activities. Whether or not the loan on which the interest was paid is secured by rental property will have no bearing on whether or not the interest on the loan is deductible. If a landlord were to borrow money by pledging rental property as collateral and then used the proceeds partly in his or her rental activities and partly for other purposes, the landlord would have to allocate the interest expense between the uses in accordance with the amount used for each purpose.

Example: *Yogi owned a house free of any debt, and he rented it out. He bought a second property that needed repairs, but its condition was too poor to borrow against. He took out a $60,000 loan on the house* *that he has been renting, and used $20,000 of the proceeds to repair the newly acquired house and $40,000 to buy a new convertible truck for personal use. Since Yogi used only $20,000 of the proceeds from the loan on his rental house in his rental activity, and that constitutes one-third of the total of the proceeds (20,000/60,000 = ⅓), he will be allowed to deduct only one-third of his interest expense on the loan on Schedule E.*

If loans for use in rental activities were obtained from a source other than a financial institution, or the interest paid to a financial institution was not reported by the recipient on a Form 1098, landlords should report interest payments for those loans on the line "other interest" of Schedule E.

If a landlord must pay prepaid interest, which is often referred to as *origination fees* or *discount points*, in order to obtain a loan for use in his or her rental activity, the prepaid interest should not be deducted in the year in which it was paid. It must be allocated over the life of the loan, with a deduction taken each year for only the part allocated to that year.

Supplies

Landlords can deduct office supplies used in connection with rental activities, as well as such things as stamps to send notice to tenants or to mail in mortgage payments.

Taxes

Property taxes that landlords must pay on their rental properties are deductible. If a landlord's mortgage payments on rental property include payments into an escrow fund to cover those taxes, the landlord will not be allowed to take a deduction for those payments until the mortgage company actually pays them out of the escrow account. Therefore, if the mortgage company does not pay the property tax liability that it has been collecting for monthly installments, the landlord's actual deduction will be postponed until next year. Landlords will also be permitted to take a deduction for taxes (in addition to property taxes) that they must pay in connection with their rental activities, such as business taxes. No deduction is allowed for federal income taxes, which landlords must pay on their rental incomes.

Utilities

Landlords sometimes must incur utility expenses to light common areas or operate security systems. Some landlords even supply tenants with water or other utilities. Even landlords who do not provide utilities of any kind to tenants and do not have complexes of property with common areas will usually have to turn on the utilities at their properties when they become vacant in order to clean, repair, maintain, and show them. These utility expenses are deductible.

Other Expenses

Schedule E provides for the deduction of expenses that do not fit one of the previously discussed categories. Expenses that would qualify as *other expenses* that are related to rental activities are easily overlooked. Expenditures for such things as telephones used in rental activities, the cost of a security patrol service, trade journals, or publications such as this book, should all qualify as deductible expenses for a landlord. It is in this category that a diligent landlord can be sure to include all of the deductions to which he or she is entitled. All that must be shown in order to take a deduction for an expense is that it was ordinary and necessary for the landlord's rental activity.

Depreciation

In addition to the ordinary and necessary expenses that are incurred in connection with a rental activity, landlords are entitled to take *depreciation* on their rental properties. Depreciation is the allowance that landlords are required to allocate for the wear and tear of their rented properties. Since the land that rental buildings are constructed on does not wear out, it is not depreciable. However, buildings, parking lots, and other improvements that are constructed on the land are depreciable. In order to determine the allowable depreciation on a piece of rental property, the owner must start by allocating the cost between the non-depreciable land and the depreciable improvements. The part of the purchase price of a landlord's rental property that is allocated to improvements, plus expenditures for subsequent permanent improvements (such as erecting an additional bay on to a shopping center or adding a bathroom on to a rental house) will constitute what is known as the owner's *depreciable basis* in the property.

Once depreciable basis is determined, the next step in calculating the landlord's allowable depreciation deduction is to determine the classification of the property being depreciated. If 80% or more of the rental income derived from a building is from dwelling units, the rental real estate is classified as *residential rental property*. If less than 80% of the rental income derived from a building is from dwelling units, and the building is not a farm building or special use structure (such as a water distribution plant) designated in the Internal Revenue Code, it is classified as *nonresidential real property*.

Currently, residential rental property must be depreciated over a period of twenty-seven and a half years, and nonresidential real property must be depreciated over a period of thirty-nine years.

Other assets, such as automobiles and machinery, may be depreciated in even increments on a pro rata basis over their assigned recovery period, a method known as *straight-line depreciation*. These assets may also be depreciated using an *accelerated depreciation* method, which allows a larger amount of depreciation in their earliest years of acquisition, at the expense of lower depreciation in later years. However, landlords are permitted to use only the straight-line method of depreciation in depreciating either residential rental property or nonresidential real property.

Example: *Zaman owns an apartment building that is entirely residential, for which he paid $750,000. The assessor in the county where the property is located has appraised the land that the property is on at $200,000 and the building at $550,000. Using the assessor's evaluation, Zaman will calculate his depreciation by subtracting the value of the land ($200,000) from the value of the entire property ($750,000) and dividing the remainder by 27.5, which is the recovery period for the property ($550,000/27.5 = $20,000). In the first year in which Zaman acquired the property, if he did not own it and use it for rental property for the entire year, he must prorate his depreciation deduction. For example, if he owned it and held it out for rent for only six months, his allowable depreciation would be only $10,000 (6 mo./12 mo. x $20,000).*

Recent changes in the tax law permit landlords to depreciate the cost of most leasehold improvements (such as the expense of finishing out rental space for a tenant in a shopping center) over a period of fifteen years, rather than the thirty-nine years assigned to the actual commercial realty. Therefore, landlords who want to maximize their depreciation deductions should not incorporate the finishing off of space in the construction of their buildings, but should perform as much of the completion as possible as a leasehold improvement for a tenant.

Owners of rental real estate and other depreciable assets are required to take depreciation on those assets. They are not allowed to save depreciation for use in later years, even if their taxable incomes are so low that they will receive little or no benefit from having taken the depreciation. As owners take depreciation on their properties, their *basis* in those properties will be reduced by an amount equal to the depreciation taken. Even if a taxpayer does not take an allowable depreciation deduction on his or her tax return, the party's basis in the depreciable asset will be reduced by the amount of depreciation that he or she would have been allowed to take. The consequence of reductions in the basis of depreciable assets is that when they are sold, since gain or loss on the sale is calculated by subtracting basis, rather than initial cost, from the net sale price of the asset, the reductions in basis will either increase the seller's gain or decrease his or her loss on the sale. This will have an impact on the party's taxable income.

Taxation of Gains and Losses from Rental Activity

Once a landlord adds up all of his or her rental activity expenses for each rental property, plus the allowable depreciation, the total should be deducted from the gross rental receipts for the property. This yields the net rental income or loss for each property. The net rental income or loss from all of the taxpayer's rental properties should then be combined for a net income or loss total for all of his or her rental activities. If a taxpayer has rental income and is not considered to be in the real property business, it should be entered on line 17 of Form 1040.

If the combined result from all of a taxpayer's rental activities is a loss, whether that loss can be used to offset other income in determining the individual's taxable income may also be affected by whether he or she is in the real property business. The determinants that will establish that a taxpayer is considered to be in the real property business are set forth in I.R.C. §46(c)(7)(B). Those requirements are that over half of the taxpayer's personal service performed in trades or businesses in which he or she materially participated must have been in real property trades or businesses, and the taxpayer must have performed 750 hours of services in real property trades or businesses during the tax year. Married couples who file joint returns are not allowed to add their hours of performance together in order to meet the test.

Individuals who are in the real property business should report their income on a Schedule C of Form 1040, which is the schedule for reporting income from virtually all proprietorships, since they are considered to have earned their income from a business that happens to involve real estate, rather than from rental activities. The income or loss generated from the real property business and calculated on Schedule C should be reported on line 12 of Form 1040, and the losses will be available to offset income from other sources in calculating the recipient's adjusted gross income. Taxpayers who are in the real property business have the advantage of using their losses from that business to offset income from other sources without limitation, for income tax purposes. However, they suffer the disadvantage that any net income they make from their businesses is subject to self-employment tax. Income from rental activities received by taxpayers who are not in the real property business are not subject to self-employment tax.

Passive Income and Losses

If a taxpayer is not in the real property business, the income and losses from his or her rental activities are categorized as *passive*, regardless of whether or not he or she materially participated in the rental activity that generated the income or loss. Passive losses can be used to offset passive income without limitation. Passive income and losses are those that are attributable to a *passive activity*, which the IRS defines as "any activity—(A) which involves the conduct of any trade or business, and (B) in which the taxpayer does not materially participate."

Wages, salaries, bonuses, or other types of income derived from active participation in a trade or business is regarded as *active income*, which cannot be offset by passive losses. Furthermore, income derived from interest, dividends, royalties, and annuities, although often earned with little or no active involvement on the part of the taxpayer, are categorized as *portfolio income* rather than passive activity income. Passive activity losses and credits cannot be used to offset that income or the tax levied on it. However, there is a special exception that may permit the use of some losses from real estate activities to offset both active income and portfolio income, even though those losses are passive losses.

Individuals who are not in the real property business, but who actively participate in management of rental property that they own, may offset ordinary income of up to $25,000 with net losses from their rental activity. However, the $25,000 amount must be reduced by 50% of the amount by which the taxpayer's adjusted gross income for the taxable year exceeds $100,000. Therefore, this exception is completely phased out for a taxpayer with an adjusted gross income of $150,000 or more for the tax year.

Passive activity losses from any passive activity that are not used in any tax year may be *carried forward* indefinitely and used to offset subsequent passive activity income. If a taxpayer disposes of his or her entire interest in a passive activity and has unused passive activity losses that he or she was carrying forward, the losses will no longer be considered attributable to a passive activity.

The fact that income is considered to be passive will have no impact on the taxability of that income. However, the fact that income is passive will make it eligible to be offset by passive losses that are either concurrently incurred with the passive income or that are being carried forward from prior years.

Gains and Losses from Sale of Rental Property

The gains that taxpayers realize from the sale of capital assets that they have held for over a year are known as *long-term capital gains*, and they are usually taxed at lower federal income tax rates than the tax rates on ordinary income. Gains from the sale of capital assets that were held for a year or less are known as *short-term capital gains*, and are taxed at the same rates as ordinary income. Taxpayers who suffer losses on the sale of their capital assets will face limitations on the deductibility of those losses on their U.S. federal income tax returns, regardless of how long they had held the assets.

Although real estate held as inventory by a taxpayer who is in the real property business will not qualify as a capital asset, realty held in a rental activity, which is a passive activity, rather than a trade or business, is considered to be a capital asset.

Determining the Amount of Capital Gain or Loss

When realty that was used in a rental activity is sold, even if the sale was an involuntary transfer due to a governmental entity exercising its right of eminent domain, and the sales price exceeds the seller's adjusted basis in the property, the amount received in excess of the asset's adjusted basis is a *capital gain*. If the sale price of a capital asset is less than the seller's adjusted basis in the property, the difference is a *capital loss*. Capital gains and losses can also result from transfers other than sales (such as when a taxpayer suffers a casualty or theft loss, and the insurance company's payment for the loss is either greater or less than the taxpayer's adjusted basis in the property that was stolen or destroyed).

Usually, the sale price of a capital asset is simply the amount of money that a seller was paid for the asset. However, if a seller receives non-cash property, or a combination of cash and noncash property, in exchange for property, the sale price will be equal to the fair market value of the noncash property received plus any cash received. When a combination of cash and noncash is exchanged for an asset, the noncash part of the payment is referred to as *boot*.

Most calculations of adjusted basis start with the cost of the asset to the taxpayer. Basis is then adjusted upward to reflect the amount of any expenditures for permanent improvements to the asset. It is reduced by the amount of any depreciation taken on the property or insurance payments for theft or casualty losses that are not used to replace the stolen or damaged part of the asset. When a party acquires a capital asset as an *intervivos gift*, which is one from a living donor, the recipient's basis in the property will be the same as the donor's. This is commonly referred to as *carryover basis*. However, if property is acquired by *testamentary gift* due to the death of the donor, such as by inheritance or having survived a joint owner, the donee's basis will be the fair market value of the property as of the date of the donor's death. This is referred to as *stepped-up basis*.

Tax Treatment of Long-Term Capital Gains and Capital Losses

With the passage of the *Jobs Growth Tax Relief and Reconciliation Act* (JGTRRA), the tax rate on most long-term capital gains for most taxpayers on transactions occurring on or after May 6, 2003, but before January 1, 2009, is reduced from 28% to 15%. For taxpayers whose net long-term capital gains would be taxed in either the 10% or 15% tax bracket if the gains had been ordinary income, JGTRRA imposes a tax rate of only 5%, and it is scheduled to drop to zero in 2008. The 28% rate remains in effect for collectibles, such as coins, stamps, artwork, and antiques that are held for over one year, and also for gains on sale of stock in small businesses.

There is a special provision for taxing that portion of the long-term capital gain realized from the sale of real estate that was used in rental activities, known as *§1250 property*. To the extent that gain on §1250 property is attributable to depreciation taken on the property in excess of straight-line, it is taxed as ordinary income, and to the degree that the gain on §1250 property is attributable to actual increase in the value of the property or recapture of straight-line depreciation, it is taxed at the 15% rate.

Since landlords are no longer allowed to take accelerated depreciation on their rental properties, only the sale of properties that have been held for a while will result in part of the gain from the sale being taxed as ordinary income. Most of the time, when landlords sell rental properties that they have owned for a few years, they will realize a gain from the sale due to the combination of increasing real estate values and reductions in the taxpayer's basis in his or her rental property due to the depreciation taken on it. Therefore, the typical landlord, who sells off part or all of his or her rental property holdings, will have been able to reduce his or her taxable income by taking depreciation on rental realty. Plus, he or she saves taxes on that reduced amount of income at a rate that could have been as high as 35%, and then pays taxes at the rate of only 15% when it is recaptured at the time that the property is sold.

Example: *Amanda, a karate instructor, acquired a house to rent out. After expenses that she paid out in association with owning the house, she cleared $300 a month, all of which was exactly offset by her $3,600 annual straight-line depreciation deduction. Had she not been allowed to take her depreciation deduction on the house, she would have had $3,600 in taxable rental income, which, on top of her other income, would have been taxed in the 33% bracket.*

Five years after acquiring the house for $125,000, Amanda sold it for $160,000. Since Amanda had taken five years of depreciation at $3,600 per year, her initial basis of $125,000 would be reduced by $18,000 (5 x $3,600) to $107,000. Therefore, her long-term capital gain from the sale of her property would be $53,000 ($160,000 - $107,000). If she had no capital losses to offset her gain, this would result in capital gains tax of $7,950 ($53,000 x .15).

If, over the course of the five years in which Amanda owned the house, her depreciation each year had reduced her taxable income by $3,600 that would have otherwise been taxed at 33%, her depreciation allowance would have saved her $5,940 ($3,600 x 5 = $18,000 x .33 = $5,940). The fact that Amanda's gain from the sale of the property was increased by $18,000, due to her reduction in basis attributable to the depreciation that she took on the property, would cause her to have to pay only $2,700 ($18,000 x .15) in additional capital gains tax on the sale.

Losses on the sale of capital assets must be netted against capital gains. If they are not fully used up to offset capital gains, up to $3,000 of capital losses may be used each year to offset ordinary income. Unused capital losses may be carried forward and used to offset any amount of capital gains and $3,000 in ordinary income per year in future years until used up.

Like-Kind Exchanges

There are provisions in the U.S. tax code that allow landlords who want to sell rental properties that they own and replace them with other rental properties to postpone having to pay federal income taxes on any gains that they realize from those sales. Section 1031 of the Internal Revenue Code provides for nonrecognition of gain or loss when property held for productive use in a trade or business, or for investment, is exchanged solely for property of like-kind that will also be held either for productive use in a trade or business or for investment. However, not all property qualifies. The provisions of §1031 do apply to holdings of real estate, both improved and unimproved, held for investment or for productive use in a trade or business. *Like-kind exchanges* involving such realty is quite common.

Finding someone who would like to trade like-kind properties in a situation in which each of the parties wants the property that the other party wishes to trade is often next to impossible. Section 1031(a)(3) offers a solution to the dilemma. It provides that a party wishing to make a like-kind exchange may qualify for nonrecognition of any gain as long as he or she identifies a *replacement property* within forty-five days of having relinquished the property that the party is trading, and acquires that replacement property within the earlier of 180 days of having relinquished the property or the due date, plus extensions, of the transferor's return for the year in which the property was relinquished. This provision creates the opportunity for parties desiring to defer gain under §1031 to utilize the services of a *qualified intermediary* to whom they can transfer their property, and then, within forty-five days, find a property for the intermediary to buy and transfer to them, within the allotted time period, in order to complete the exchange.

If the transferor of property, which qualifies for tax treatment under §1031, receives a combination of like-kind property and some that is not like-kind in exchange, the party may still defer gain to the extent that he or she received like-kind property, but must recognize gain to the extent that the property received was not like-kind property. To the degree that a party defers gain on property received in a like-kind exchange, the deferred gain must be subtracted from the basis of the property received.

Chapter 16:

Taxation of Real Estate Professionals

Earnings from real estate by real estate dealers, or those who are otherwise involved in the real property business, will be taxed much differently than the earnings from real estate realized by investors or the passive income of taxpayers engaged in rental activities. The fact that a person's trade or business happens to involve real estate in some way will not alter the fact that his or her income from that trade or business will be classified as *net earnings from self-employment* for federal income tax purposes. Income that is realized from investing in real estate and income from the rental of real estate and personal property leased with the real estate are excluded from the definition of net earnings from self-employment. However, the exclusion does not apply if the income is received in the course of a trade or business as a real estate dealer.

In determining whether or not a taxpayer is a dealer in real estate, Treasury Regulation §1.1402(a)-4(a) provides the definition. It states:

> *In general, an individual who is engaged in the business of selling real estate to customers with a view to the gains and profits that may be derived from such sales is a real estate dealer. On the*

other hand, an individual who merely holds real estate for investment or speculation and received rentals therefrom is not considered a real estate dealer.

The fact that a taxpayer has been determined to be a real estate dealer will not prevent that person from being eligible to realize rental income. Following the definition of a real estate dealer, the Regulation states that when a real estate dealer receives rental payments on property that is being held as inventory for sale to customers, as well as rental payments on property that is being held for investment or speculation:

Only the rentals from the real estate held for sale to customers in the ordinary course of his trade or business as a real estate dealer, and the deductions attributed thereto, are included in determining net earnings from self-employment; the rentals from the real estate held for investment or speculation, and the deductions attributable thereto, are excluded.

Also, if certain services are provided to the occupant of rooms or other space that has been rented out, the income derived from the arrangement will not qualify as rental income and will be taxed as self-employment income. Treasury Regulation $1.1402(a)-4(c)(2)$ prohibits inclusion of payments received for use or occupancy of rooms or other spaces within the definition of rentals from real estate if services are provided to the occupant. The rendering of some services to occupants of rental rooms or spaces is permitted without jeopardizing the classification of the receipts from the activity as rental income. The Regulation provides that, "generally services are considered rendered to the occupant if they are primarily for his convenience and are other than those usually or customarily rendered in connection with the rental of rooms or other space for occupancy only." It goes on to state that the providing of maid service to an occupant of a rented space would be an example of a service rendered primarily for the occupant's benefit, whereas providing utilities, trash collection, or cleaning of common areas, such as stairways or lobbies, would not. Whether services are provided to occupants is determinative of whether payments received for the use or occupancy of space will be taxed as rental income or self-employment income, not only for rooms in hotels, boarding houses, apartment houses, or single family houses, but also for the use or occupancy of tourist camps, warehouses, parking lots, and storage garages.

Taxation of Income Earned as a Real Estate Dealer

The income earned by an individual taxpayer from activities as a real estate dealer will constitute self-employment income that must be reported on Schedule C of Form 1040. The schedule is a basic profit and loss statement, which shows the taxpayer's gross income from self-employment activities, and all of the allowable business expense deductions. These are then netted against the taxpayer's gross income to yield his or her net profit or loss from the business conducted as a self-employed individual. From the perspective of the tax consequences of being considered to be a real estate dealer, there are both pros and cons.

Deductible Business Expenses

One of the biggest advantages to being considered to be a real estate dealer is that the dealer will be entitled to take a deduction for a wide variety of business expenses, even if the deduction results in a loss. Furthermore, losses from a trade or business, unlike losses from passive rental activities, can be fully used to offset income from virtually any other source. As a result, there are actually times when taxpayers argue that they are real estate dealers and the IRS argues that they are not, although disputes on that issue are usually the other way around.

The key issue in determining whether or not a taxpayer is eligible to take a deduction for business expenses is whether the person wanting to take the deduction is engaged in a trade or business. Most of the cases in which there is a question as to whether a person or organization is actually engaged in a trade or business arise when the participant is involved only part-time or sporadically. In order to be considered to be carrying on a trade or business, a taxpayer must have begun the endeavor with the intent to make a profit, must consistently and significantly participate in the venture, must demonstrate a commitment to the enterprise, and must conduct the operation in a businesslike manner. The fact that an activity actually generates a loss rather than a profit will not be fatal to its being considered a trade or business, as long as it was started with the intent to make a profit. Commitment to an enterprise may be demonstrated by such things as attending seminars or trade shows, taking formal courses to gain expertise in operation of the business, or engaging in any other activity aimed at improving the person's ability to operate the enterprise profitably.

If a purported business activity is determined not to be a trade or business, it will likely be classified as a hobby. Since deductions for expenses are allowed only to the degree necessary to offset gross income from the activity, the deductibility of any loss generated by the venture (hobby) is eliminated.

Taxpayers who are sufficiently involved as real estate dealers to be regarded as being engaged in a trade or business will be allowed to deduct all of the expenses they incur in connection with their real estate activities, as long as they are *ordinary and necessary*. Whether expenses incurred in a trade or business are ordinary and necessary is based on whether they were appropriate for the activity involved, and reasonable in terms of the amount of the expenditures, rather than extravagant.

Unlike landlords who are involved in generating passive rental income, taxpayers who are involved in real estate to the degree that it has become a trade or business do not have to limit their deductions to expenses that are related to generating rental income. As a result of the broader scope of business activities of taxpayers who are engaged in a trade or business that involves real estate, they are usually able to show that a wider array of business expenses are ordinary and necessary, and therefore, deductible on Schedule C of Form 1040.

Example: *Stan is a real estate broker who lists and sells properties for sellers, represents buyers looking for properties, buys houses himself for resale after repairing them, rents out houses while attempting to resell them, and acquires houses to hold as rental property. Stan has decided to offer home inspection services to homebuyers and has run advertisements, attended workshops, acquired some tools, and hired an inspector. Since offering home inspection services is a logical extension of his business as a real estate dealer, and the expenses that he has incurred in connection with this new activity appear to be ordinary and necessary, he should be allowed to deduct them on the same Schedule C that he calculates his income on for the other aspects of his real estate business.*

If a landlord who received passive income from a rental activity were to decide to start a home inspection business, he or she would not be allowed to combine the activities for tax purposes. This would prevent him or her from using any losses that he or she generated from his or her rental activity to offset income from his or her inspection business by absorbing rental related expenses into his or her inspection business expenses.

As with Schedule E, a number of specific deductible expenses are listed on Schedule C. However, the checklist of deductible expenses on Schedule C is substantially longer than the checklist of deductible expenses shown on Schedule E. Several sources of deductible expenses available to taxpayers involved in a trade or business that are not typically available to landlords earning passive income are those associated with the costs of hiring employees. Both Schedule E and Schedule C provide a line for deducting commissions and payments for professional services. However, Schedule C also provides for deductions for wages, as well as for employee benefit programs and pension and profit-sharing plans, and no such items are listed on Schedule E, since landlords are unlikely to hire employees in connection with generating passive rental income.

The depreciation deduction that is available to taxpayers involved in a real estate trade or business will be quite different from that available to landlords earning passive rental income. Properties that real estate dealers have acquired to resell are considered to be their stock in trade or inventory. Therefore, the dealer will not be allowed to take a depreciation deduction on those properties, whereas taxpayers earning passive income from rental activities *must* depreciate the properties that they hold for rental.

On the other hand, real estate dealers will be much more likely to have furniture, vehicles, and equipment that are eligible for depreciation than are landlords with passive income from rental activities. Unlike real estate, these types of assets are eligible for accelerated depreciation. In fact, taxpayers who are operating a trade or business have the right, under I.R.C. §179, to fully deduct (a practice known as *expensing*) a certain amount of their depreciable assets, which are those expected to have a useful life in excess of one year, in the year in which they were placed in service as business property, rather than depreciating them.

A specific line is devoted to *repairs* on both Schedules C and E of Form 1040, but what qualifies to be taken as a deduction for repairs by someone who is a real estate dealer is quite different from the deduction for repairs available to a party who earns passive income from a rental activity. To the degree that a real estate dealer spends money to repair property that was acquired for resale, those expenditures will not be deductible. Unlike expenditures by landlords for repairs, which are intended to keep their properties in rentable condition, expenditures by real estate dealers for repairs to property that are being held for resale are actually a form of inventory acquisition, since the expenditures enhance the value of their inventoried properties. Therefore, rather than taking an expense deduction for such repairs, as landlords do on Schedule E, real estate dealers must show those expenditures as a purchase of inventory on Schedule C. The net result should be the same, since real estate dealers will deduct their investment in inventory that they sell as a cost of goods sold. However, since the deduction for the cost of a good that was sold cannot be taken until the item is actually sold, but landlords can take a deduction for repair expenses in the year in which they were paid, the inability to take a deduction for repairs to properties that are held for resale at the time that those expenses are paid may affect the timing of the real estate dealer's income.

Real estate dealers who also hold properties for rental will be considered to be engaged in a rental activity regarding those properties, as well as being a real estate dealer in regard to properties acquired for resale. Such taxpayers will be required to show income from rental activities on Schedule E, and income derived from being a real estate dealer on Schedule C. Speculators who buy properties to fix up and resell will be considered dealers, and the properties that they purchase will constitute their inventory, even though they may not have regarded their activities in that way.

The Tax Impact of Business Deductions

Most U.S. taxpayers are allowed to take itemized deductions on their individual federal income tax returns, but those deductions are limited to particular expenditures, such as home mortgage interest, property taxes, and charitable contributions. These provide tax savings to taxpayers only when their itemized deductions exceed the standard deductions that are available to them as an alternative. By contrast, real estate dealers and other taxpayers who are considered to be self-employed are permitted to take a tax deduction for any expenditures for business expenses whatsoever, as long as they are ordinary and necessary. They will also be permitted to take the larger of the standard deduction or individual itemized deductions to which they are entitled. Another advantage that self-employment taxpayers realize by being allowed to write off deductions for business expenses separately from personal itemized deductions is that, unlike individual taxpayers' itemized deductions, which are subject to reduction at a certain level of income, business expenses that qualify for deduction are fully deductible regardless of the self-employed person's income.

Since business deductions are not subject to the same types of limitations that itemized deductions available to individuals are, they will certainly reduce the self-employed taxpayer's taxable income. If a self-employed taxpayer's overall income is so low that his or her business deductions merely offset income that would have otherwise been in his or her zero bracket amount and gone untaxed, the taxpayer's business deductions will not reduce his or her federal income tax liability. Otherwise, even taxpayers who lose money from businesses in which they are self-employed will still benefit from their business expense deductions, since those losses can be used to offset other income that they have received in the form of wages, interest, and investment income. If they have no income to offset with losses from self-employment, they can carry those losses to other years to offset income.

Even taxpayers whose incomes are so low that their business deductions save them little or no federal income tax can still benefit from those deductions. Earnings from self-employment are subject to self-employment taxes, which are levied against taxpayers starting with the first dollar of self-employment income that they earn. Therefore, taxpayers with any amount of self-employment income who would have incurred self-employment taxes had it not been for their business deductions, will still have some tax savings to show for those deductions.

Self-Employment Taxes

One of the least appealing aspects of being classified as a real estate dealer for federal tax purposes is the fact that the taxpayer's income from his or her real estate business will be subject to self-employment taxes, whereas passive income from rental activities is not. Self-employment taxes are the self-employed person's equivalent of *Federal Insurance Contributions Act* (FICA) taxes. These taxes are comprised of *old-age, survivors, and disability insurance* (OASDI, generally referred to as Social Security tax), which is 6.2% of the income subject to the tax, and *hospital insurance* (Medicare), which is 1.45% of the income that is subject to the tax. This combined 7.65% rate must be withheld by employers from their employee's earnings, and the employers must pay a matching amount of FICA taxes to the U.S. Treasury on behalf of their employees. The OASDI portion of FICA taxes is imposed on just a specified amount ($94,200 in 2006) of each employee's earnings, but there is no limit on the amount of an employee's earnings that is subject to the Medicare portion of FICA taxes. The nominal self-employment tax rate is 15.3%, which is exactly twice the FICA tax rate that employees pay, since self-employed taxpayers do not have employers to pay any self-employment taxes in their behalf. Because employees do not have to pay taxes on the FICA taxes that are paid for them by their employers, Congress passed legislation allowing self-employed taxpayers to reduce their self-employment income by 7.65%, which is the FICA rate that employers pay on their employee's wages, before applying the self-employment tax rate. However, this still can result in a sizable tax liability.

Self-employment taxes are made particularly burdensome due to the lack of nonbusiness deductions, such as the itemized or standard deduction allowed in calculating taxable income for income tax purposes, and the lack of any allowance for exemptions for dependents, to reduce the amount of earnings to which the tax rate is applied. This lack of deductions and exemptions, coupled with the fact that the self-employment tax rate starts out at 15.3%, rather than starting out at low levels and progressing to higher ones as the federal income tax rates do, causes many self-employed individuals to pay more self-employment taxes than income taxes.

For some real estate dealers, the self-employment tax is not terribly burdensome, despite the fact that they make substantial self-employment income. Since real estate dealers often work as employees in addition to earning self-employment income from their real estate businesses, some of them benefit from the fact that the tax laws regard FICA taxes and self-employment taxes as components of a single program. Therefore, rather than impose self-employment taxes on a taxpayer's self-employment income independent of income that the party also earns as an employee, the specified base amount of earned income from all sources combined for the tax year is all that will be subject to the full FICA tax rates. If a taxpayer has salary or wages from a source that was not self-employment income and that had already been subjected to FICA taxes, half of which were paid by the employer, then the amount of those earnings will be deducted from the base amount of earnings subject to the Social Security part of FICA taxes. Only the balance will be subject to the full self-employment tax.

Example: *Matt works the night shift at a brewery. Last year, his earnings from that company were $70,000, which was subject to FICA taxes. His part of FICA taxes was withheld from his paycheck and his employer paid a matching share. During the day and on the weekends, Matt worked as a self-employed real estate dealer. He earned $40,000 in self-employment income from that work. The amount of self-employment income subject to Social Security tax was $94,200. However, since Matt also had earnings of $70,000 as an employee, which had been subject to Social Security tax, he is allowed to subtract the $70,000 from the earnings limit for self-employment income subject to Social Security tax, leaving only $24,200 that will be taxed at the full self-employment tax rate. The remaining part of his self-employment income that is subject to self-employment taxes will be subject only to the Medicare portion of self-employment taxes.*

Nonbusiness Deductions Available to the Self-Employed

In addition to the deduction for their business expenses, self-employed taxpayers are also permitted to take some specific nonbusiness deductions that are available only to the self-employed. These deductions cannot be used to reduce self-employment income in calculating self-employment taxes, but those who are eligible to take the deductions will be able to use them to reduce their incomes that are subject to federal income taxes. Furthermore, these nonbusiness deductions are not part of the itemized deductions that individual taxpayers report on Schedule A of Form 1040, but are separate, additional deductions, which self-employed taxpayers take on the front of Form 1040 in the section labeled *adjusted gross income*. This section actually lists about a dozen deductible items, referred to in tax parlance as *adjustments*, which when totaled up and subtracted from a taxpayer's total income, yield a balance that is known as *adjusted gross income*. Most of the adjustments listed in this section are not limited to self-employed taxpayers, but three of them are, and they can provide the self-employed with significant tax benefits.

Deduction for One-Half of Self-Employment Tax

The deduction for one-half of self-employment taxes paid is available only to taxpayers with self-employment income. The purpose of the deduction is to achieve a degree of equity between self-employed taxpayers, who must pay self-employment taxes at a nominal rate of 15.3%, and employees, whose share of FICA taxes are only 7.65%, since their employers are paying a matching share of FICA taxes. Although the deduction does not alter the fact that the nominal rate of self-employment taxes is twice that of an employee's share of FICA taxes, it does prevent taxation of the part of self-employment taxes that is the equivalent of the employer's share of FICA taxes, which, despite being paid on behalf of employees, is not considered to be taxable income to them.

The deduction for one-half of self-employment taxes is actually calculated on Schedule SE of Form 1040, which is used by self-employed taxpayers to calculate their self-employment tax liabilities. Once a party calculates his or her self-employment tax on Schedule SE, there is a line beneath the amount of the tax for the taxpayer to enter one-half of that liability, which is then transferred to Form 1040.

Self-Employed Health Insurance Deduction

One of the biggest disadvantages to being self-employed is the lack of employer-provided health care coverage. Employers commonly enroll in health insurance plans that offer group rates far lower than rates for individual policies, and the employers usually pay a substantial amount, if not all, of the premiums for the coverage. Furthermore, despite the fact that the insurance premiums paid by employers for their employees are clearly a form of compensation to those employees, the amount of the premium payment is not regarded as taxable income to the employees. Therefore, in order to give self-employed taxpayers similar tax treatment regarding health insurance premiums, Congress allows self-employed taxpayers to deduct their health insurance premiums as an adjustment for adjusted gross income. Prior to this provision, the only deduction for health insurance premiums allowed for self-employed taxpayers was a part of their itemized medical expense deductions on Schedule A of Form 1040. Therefore, since an itemized medical deduction on Schedule A is allowed only to the extent that it exceeds 7.5% of a taxpayer's adjusted gross income, hardly any self-employed taxpayers had enough medical expenses to take an itemized deduction, even though they generally paid out considerably more in health insurance premiums than did taxpayers who worked as employees.

Self-employed individuals are not eligible to take the deduction for self-employed health insurance premiums that they pay if they are eligible for coverage in a subsidized health plan offered by an employer or a spouse's employer. A subsidized plan is one in which an employer pays some or all of an employee's premium for the insurance coverage. Since this qualification is determined on a monthly basis, a self-employed party who is eligible for subsidized group coverage for only part of the year will still be entitled to take the deduction for the months when no subsidized coverage was available.

The self-employed health insurance deduction that is available to a self-employed taxpayer is further limited by the amount of self-employment income that he or she earns. No matter how much a self-employed taxpayer may pay in qualified health insurance premiums, the deduction on Form 1040 cannot exceed the individual's profits from self-employment.

Deductions for Payments to Retirement Accounts

Another major detriment to being self-employed, rather than working for others as an employee, is that the self-employed individual will not have an employer-financed retirement plan, which is often provided for employees. The conventional wisdom in today's retirement planning is that workers should develop a plan in which Social Security payments are combined with employer-provided pensions and personal savings in order to provide adequate retirement income. Since self-employed workers have no employer to provide them with a retirement plan, it is imperative that they develop a sufficiently large personal retirement plan to compensate for the lack of an employer-provided plan and avoid the prospects of having to live at or near the poverty level in their retirement years. In an effort to encourage self-employed workers to develop retirement plans of their own, Congress allows them to take a deduction for adjusted gross income for certain payments that they make into certain plans.

Payments Into Individual Retirement Accounts

For many years, Congress has allowed taxpayers who meet certain qualifications to take a deduction for payments made into a qualified Individual Retirement Account (IRA). The maximum amount of the deduction available for 2005 was $4,000, plus an extra $500 for those who are 50 years of age or older; for 2006 and 2007, it is $4,000, plus an extra $1,000 for those who are 50 years of age or older; and it is scheduled to increase to $5,000, with an extra $1,000 for those who are 50 years of age or older in the year 2008. A deduction for a payment into an IRA is not restricted to only self-employed taxpayers. However, since those who are covered by a retirement plan that is provided by an employer may be partially or even totally ineligible for the IRA deduction, workers who depend solely on self-employment activities for their incomes will not only be more likely to need to establish an IRA, but will also be more likely to qualify for the deduction.

Payments into Self-Employed SEP, SIMPLE, and Qualified Plans

Due to the relatively modest limits on the available IRA deduction, some self-employed taxpayers opt for a retirement plan with larger limits. Although these plans are commonly used by corporations to provide retirement benefits for employees, self-employed taxpayers are also eligible for them.

The *Simplified Employee Pension* (SEP) allows employees to establish either an individual retirement account or individual retirement annuity for each of their employees and contribute to it the lesser of 25% of an amount equal to an employee's compensation for the year or $40,000. Since self-employed taxpayers are considered to be their own employers, they qualify to establish a SEP IRA and take a deduction for eligible contributions.

Another type of plan that qualifies for a deduction for adjusted gross income for the contributions made to it is the *Savings Incentive Match Plan for Employees* (SIMPLE IRA). This plan allows employers with one hundred or fewer employees whose earnings for the previous calendar year were at least $5,000 to establish a retirement account for each employee, and either match each employee's contribution up to 3% of the worker's earnings or make a contribution equal to 2% of each worker's earnings without regard to the amount of the worker's contribution. As with the SEP, since self-employed workers are considered to be their own employers, they are allowed to establish SIMPLE IRAs of their own and take deductions for qualified contributions.

There are several other types of retirement plans available to employers, such as profit-sharing plans and 401(k) plans, that self-employed tax-payers may also participate in and qualify for a deduction for adjusted gross income, since they are considered to be their own employer for purposes of qualifying for the deduction. Such plans are generally more complex than the SEP IRA or the SIMPLE IRA, but may be worth the extra effort since they may offer greater flexibility and larger contribution limits.

It is generally advisable for self-employed parties who wish to take advantage of the SEP IRA, SIMPLE IRA, or any of the other qualified plans, to seek professional guidance in establishing and administering the plan in order to be sure that contributions qualify for the deduction. Banks, brokerage houses, and other organizations that market investment choices that qualify for such plans will often gratuitously provide clients with the services they need to ensure the compliance necessary to qualify for the deductions. Also, there are professional plan administrators who, for a fee, will manage retirement plans so that they qualify for the deduction.

Taxation of Gains on Sale of Property by Real Estate Dealers

One of the biggest drawbacks to being a real estate dealer, rather than being a non-dealer engaged in a rental real estate activity, is that the properties that a dealer sells in the ordinary course of his or her business are not capital assets. Instead, they are *inventory*. As a result, the gains realized by a real estate dealer from properties that were bought, repaired, and sold will be self-employment income that is subject to both self-employment taxes and federal income tax. By contrast, gains realized by landlords from the sale of real estate that they had acquired to generate passive rental income will not be subject to self-employment taxes at all. If a landlord has owned a rental property for over a year before selling it, the gain will be long-term capital gain and the federal income tax on that gain will be no more than 15%, and perhaps as little as 5%, depending on the federal income tax bracket that the landlord is in.

In addition to the more favorable tax treatment of their gains, landlords have the option of postponing taxation of the gains from the sale of their rental properties through a §1031 like-kind exchange. Real estate dealers do not have such an option when they sell properties from their inventories, since only capital assets qualify for like-kind exchanges.

Conclusion

Everybody wants to make money and provide themselves with a more financially secure future. Real estate is the number one way to make that happen. With very little effort you can add a sizeable amount to your bottom line. With just a little more effort, those gains can be significant.

If you follow the advice and guidance found in these pages, you can be well on your way to seeing those riches for yourself. Good luck in taking your first step to fulfilling your dreams.

Glossary

A

abatement. A reduction in amount or a cessation.

acceptance. A basic part of forming a contract that occurs if, once an offer is made, the other party agrees to all the contract terms.

adjustable-rate mortgage. A loan with lower interest rates in the initial years that has rate adjustments periodically in the future. The right to adjust interest rates on mortgages protects lenders from the risk of holding mortgages at low fixed interest rates, and then facing subsequent increases in the market rate of interest that they must pay in order to attract funds.

adjusted gross income. Income before taking deductions for exemptions and the standard or itemized deductions.

agent. Another that works on your behalf.

allowances. Concessions, either in money or some other form, that are often given to induce a party to enter into a contract, carry out a contract, or accept a modification of some agreement.

amortization. The gradual paying off of a debt.

appraisal. An estimate of the value of something. When used in regards to real estate, the term usually refers to such an estimate done by someone who is a certified expert in determining property values.

appreciation. Increase in market value.

B

balloon note. Loan with payment terms set as if it were to be paid off over an extended period of time, such as thirty years, but with a provision that the unpaid balance will be fully due and payable at the end of some short period of time, such as two years.

breach. When one of the parties to a real estate contract refuses to carry out the agreement.

buy-down loans. A type of mortgage that provides the debtor with lower interest rates for some period of time in exchange for payment of a lump sum at the inception of the loan. Buy-down fees are often paid by sellers in order to enable the buyer to qualify for the loan needed, since initial mortgage payments will be lower than they would be otherwise.

C

capital gain. Income that a taxpayer realizes when a capital asset is sold or exchanged for more than the taxpayer's basis in the asset.

capital loss. The difference between the value that a taxpayer receives in the sale or exchange of a capital asset and the taxpayer's basis in that asset when the sale or exchange occurs at a value that is less than the taxpayer's basis in the asset.

chain of title. The record of ownership of a piece of real property.

closing costs. Expenses associated with obtaining a mortgage and completing the transfer of real estate.

commercial real property. Real estate that is used for business purposes, such as a shopping center or office building.

condition precedent. In contract law, a stipulated occurrence that must take place before a party is bound on an agreement.

conforming loans. Mortgages that meet the requirements of various federal agencies, so they can be negotiated by lenders to federal agencies who make a market for them. They are so named because they are said to conform to required guidelines.

consideration. A basic part of forming a contract that indicates what thing of value is being exchanged between the parties.

contingencies. Conditions that must be met or things that must occur before a contract can be completed.

contract. An agreement between two or more parties in which an offer by one party is accepted by another based on the consideration being given.

cooperative agreements. Contracts entered into between real estate listing agents, or property owners and real estate agents who represent buyers, that provide for a commission to the buyer's agent from the listing agents' commission or sellers' proceeds, if the party that he or she represents buys the property that was listed by the real estate agent or offered for sale by the owner.

counteroffer. A response to an offer that varies the terms of the original offer.

covenants of title. Promises concerning the validity of title made by a seller to a buyer in the instrument that conveys ownership.

curb appeal. The subjective value placed on a piece of property based on how it looks on the outside.

D

damages. Monetary compensation awarded by a court, from one party to another, due to a breach of contract or some other wrongful act.

deduction. A tax term used to refer to an amount of money that may be subtracted from a taxpayer's gross income in arriving at the party's taxable income.

deed. The legal title to a piece of real property.

deed of trust. A conditional deed given by an owner to a trustee that allows the trustee to foreclose and convey the property to the high bidder at auction, if the party who conveyed the deed fails to perform the conditions, especially repayment of a loan, set forth in the instrument. It is a type of mortgage instrument.

depreciation. An allowance for wear and tear that is allowed as a deduction for taxpayers on business property in calculating their tax liabilities.

distress sale. Liquidation of an asset under conditions that necessitate a rapid sale, which usually results in the asset bringing less than it would if marketed normally.

dual agency. A situation in which a single agent represents both the buyer and seller in a transaction.

due diligence. A level of investigation that is sufficient enough that the party conducting the investigation is not considered to have been negligent.

E

earned income. A taxpayer's total income from wages, salaries and tips; net earnings from self-employment; or, gross income received as a statutory employee.

earned income credit. A type of welfare payment for those taxpayers whose earned incomes are beneath certain statutorily prescribed amounts. The purpose of the credit is to keep moderate income earners working since they must have earned income in order to qualify for the credit.

eminent domain. The power of the government to take your land for the greater public good.

equity. In real estate, it is the difference between the value of a property and the indebtedness owed on it.

escrow fund. Money being held by one party on behalf of another. In real estate loans, lenders usually require homeowners to pay money into such a fund on a monthly basis to cover the owners' property taxes and insurance when they come due.

exemptions. Allowances that entitle a taxpayer to exclude some statutorily prescribed amount of income from taxation. The allowances are generally based on the number of parties that the taxpayer provides support to, including the taxpayer.

F

fair market value. The amount of money at which property or services would change hands in an arm's length transaction between unrelated parties.

federal income tax. A levy imposed by the federal government on earnings.

FICA taxes. Taxes paid to meet requirements of the Federal Insurance Contributions Act, half of which are paid by employers and half of which are paid by employees, to cover the employee for Social Security and Medicare benefits.

fixed-rate mortgage. Loans that have rates that do not adjust.

fixture. An item of personal property that has been attached to, or otherwise incorporated into, a structure on real property, such that it is then considered to be a part of the realty.

G

graduated payment mortgage. A type of financing in which interest rates are lower at the inception of the loan and increase in the future, usually at annual intervals.

gross income. A taxpayer's total income from all sources before any allowances for exemptions or deductions from adjusted gross income.

H

home mortgage interest. A term used to describe interest payments for which a taxpayer is allowed to take an itemized deduction on Schedule A of Form 1040. It consists of interest paid on a loan used to buy a main home or second home, or a loan that was a second mortgage, line of credit, or home equity loan on a main or second home.

I

incidental damages. Expenses incurred by a party to a contract due to some other party to the agreement having breached it. Included are costs such as having to run additional advertisements to sell property or having to pay for inspections of alternative properties.

income taxes. A levy imposed by a governmental entity upon what it defines as the income. Generally, such entities define income to include wages, salaries, profits, gains from the sale of assets, and returns from investments.

insurable interest. An interest in property to a degree that its destruction would cause the party with that interest to suffer a direct monetary loss. Owners generally have an insurable interest in the property that they own, as do creditors in the property that they have taken an interest in as collateral for loans.

interest. A form of income that is payment by one party to another for the use of money.

L

lease. A contract that allows a party to use real property, personal property, or both for some period of time, generally in exchange for monetary consideration.

leveraging. Using borrowed funds, which are obtained at an interest rate that is lower than what the borrower expects to earn on those funds, as well as non-borrowed funds, to make an investment in order to enhance the return on the non-borrowed funds.

liens of record. Claims against property by creditors, usually arising from loans, that have been recorded in a public record, such as records kept where deeds to property are recorded.

limited warranty deed. An instrument that conveys real estate without the usual covenants of title. *See warranty deed.*

liquidate. To turn an asset into cash by selling it.

listing agent. A real estate agent who enters into a contract to sell or lease property with a party who owns or controls real estate. Such contracts usually provide for the payment of a commission to the agent if the agent is successful, but no commission will be owed if the agent is unable to sell or lease the property.

listing contracts. The agreements in which those who own or control property agree to have real estate agents attempt to either sell or lease the property, generally in exchange for some form of compensation.

loan origination fee. A charge assessed by a lender for granting a new loan.

M

margin call. A demand by a securities broker to an investor who has purchased securities partially through the use of credit (a procedure known as buying on margin). The demand is usually made when the securities owned by the investor have dropped in value, so the investor no longer has the amount of equity in the investment that is required by federal law.

marketable title. Ownership of property that is sufficiently established by public records or otherwise, and that is free of liens, judgments, and other claims, such that a title company will issue a title policy to a buyer in the event the property is sold.

mortgage. A conditional conveyance of property by the owner to a creditor as security for a loan that gives the creditor the right to foreclose on the property in the event that the owner fails to live up to the terms of the loan.

mortgage insurance premium. Payments that a borrower must make to either a federal agency or private insurer to cover the cost of mortgage insurance, which is a type of insurance that will repay the lender in the event that the borrower defaults on the insured loan.

N

negative amortization. An increase in the balance of a loan over time as a result of initial payments being inadequate to cover the principal and interest payments necessary to prevent such a situation.

negative cash flow. The result of inadequate income from an investment to cover the costs, such as debt service, insurance, and taxes, that are associated with that investment.

near-cash assets. Items that can generally quickly be converted to cash at or near their fair market values.

non-qualifying loan. A loan that can be obtained or assumed without having to prove creditworthiness.

O

offer. A basic part of forming a contract in which one of the parties presents his or her demands to the other party.

opportunity cost. Choices that are forgone when a party chooses a different alternative.

option contract. An agreement that gives one or more parties the right to enter into still another agreement at some established terms if they choose to do so at a later time, but does not require them to enter into the later agreement.

owner financing. An arrangement whereby a seller allows a buyer to purchase realty or other items and pay for the purchase with credit that is extended by the seller.

P

preexisting conditions. Certain flaws that were present prior to purchase of a property.

profit. The gains that are realized when a venture generates returns in excess of the cost of conducting the venture.

property taxes. A levy imposed upon the realty or personal property that is owned, leased, or used by parties.

punitive damages. Awards given by courts against defendants that are designed to punish the plaintiffs for their conduct rather than reimbursing plaintiffs for their actual losses.

R

real rate of return. The nominal return generated on an investment less the rate of inflation.

reciprocity. In law, allowing similar remedies to all parties to a contract.

recourse financing. A loan with terms that allow the creditor to fully recover from the debtor in the event that there is a breach in the repayment of the loan and the sale of the collateral does not generate sufficient funds to pay the unpaid balance.

rejection. Refusal or nonacceptance.

rents. Payments made to the owner of rights in realty or personal property for the right to use that property.

reverse mortgage. An arrangement in which a lender makes monthly payments to a homeowner for a prescribed period of time, during which the owner continues to occupy the property, after which the lender then becomes the owner of the property.

right of rescission. The option to terminate a contract.

right to redeem. The option of reclaiming property that has been sold at a tax sale or through foreclosure by paying the buyer what was paid for the property along with interest and the cost of improvements.

S

security deposits. Money paid by tenants to landlords to ensure that the properties will be left in good condition when they are vacated.

selling agent. A real estate agent who provides a ready, willing, and able buyer for a property.

self-employment tax. A levy imposed upon those who earn income through self-employment, as a replacement for the Federal Insurance Contributions Act (FICA) tax that is paid by employees and their employers.

settlement agent. The party that closes a real estate transaction.

special warranty deed. An instrument that conveys ownership of real property without the usual covenants provided in warranty deeds. *See warranty deed.*

specific performance. A legal remedy wherein a court orders a breaching party to carry out what was agreed to.

stucco report. A written assessment from a certified inspector concerning the installation and condition of stucco and stucco-like compounds on structures, as well as an assessment of any moisture problems found in the structure.

subleasing. When tenants further lease out the properties that they have leased.

sweat equity. Value in real estate that was developed by means of improvements to the property that were actually performed by the owner.

T

tax credit. An allowance that can be used to offset tax liability on a dollar-for-dollar basis.

tax credits. The sum total of each tax credit that a taxpayer is allowed to take. Some tax credits are permitted to generate tax refunds (refundable credits) whereas others can be used only to the extent that they offset tax liability (nonrefundable credits). Some can be carried to other years and some cannot.

tax liability. The amount of money that a party owes as the result of the levy of some tax upon him or her.

termite letters. Written statements from licensed pest control experts concerning whether or not wood-damaging insects or damage from wood-damaging insects were found on a property as the result of an inspection.

title insurance. A policy that guarantees a buyer or lender that the covered real property was conveyed with marketable title.

title search. A compilation of documents from the public records that establish ownership of property and determine whether there are liens or other claims against it.

triple net lease. A lease arrangement in which the tenant is responsible for the taxes, insurance, and maintenance of the property in addition to paying the prescribed rent.

trustee's deed. A conveyance from a property owner to a trustee on behalf of a lender that provides, in the event of default on the terms of the loan, that the trustee may foreclose on the property and use the proceeds of the foreclosure sale to pay the lender.

U

unconscionable provisions. Terms in a contract that are so one-sided that they "shock the conscience of the court" to the degree that the court will not enforce those terms.

Uniform Residential Landlord Tenant Act. Model legislation, which has been adopted by a number of states, that governs the relationship between landlords and tenants of residential property.

V

VA loans. Mortgages that are insured by the Veterans Administration.

W

warranty deed. An instrument that conveys realty with the usual covenants that the seller has good title, has the right to convey the property, has not encumbered the property, and that the seller promises quiet enjoyment of the property and will defend the buyer against the claims of others.

wholesale buyers. Those who buy for resale and expect what they buy to be priced accordingly.

Z

zero, zero loans. Mortgages that are made without charging the borrower any discount points or origination fee.

Index

E

M

N

O

About the Author

After encountering an abundance of dubious pitches by various promoters touting their plans for getting rich quickly through real estate
investments, James Parker decided that is was time to offer investors
a compact, realistic, truthful, and informative guide to wealth accumulation through various forms of real estate investment. Unlike
most of those who are marketing various "programs" of real estate
investing, he has credentials that include thirty years as an educator at
Christian Brothers University teaching business courses, and over
twenty-six years as a practicing attorney with emphasis on taxation
and real estate matters. He is able to speak not only from his experience as an owner of numerous pieces of real estate, but also from the
perspective of an attorney who has been involved in hundreds of real
estate transactions on behalf of clients. Mr. Parker earned an LLM in
taxation from Emory University, an MA in Economics, and a JD from
the University of Memphis. He has authored two books on taxation,
Tax Smarts for Small Business and *Tax Power for the Self-Employed*. He
lives in Memphis, Tennessee.

SPHINX® PUBLISHING ORDER FORM

BILL TO:				SHIP TO:			

Phone #		Terms		F.O.B.	Chicago, IL		Ship Date

Charge my: ☐ VISA ☐ MasterCard ☐ American Express ☐ **Money Order or Personal Check**

Credit Card Number   Expiration Date

Qty	ISBN	Title	Retail	Qty	ISBN	Title	Retail
		SPHINX PUBLISHING NATIONAL TITLES			1-57248-164-1	How to Buy a Condominium or Townhome (2E)	$19.95
	1-57248-363-6	101 Complaint Letters That Get Results	$18.95		1-57248-384-9	How to Buy a Franchise	$19.95
	1-57248-361-X	The 529 College Savings Plan (2E)	$18.95		1-57248-497-7	How to Buy Your First Home (2E)	$14.95
	1-57248-483-7	The 529 College Savings Plan Made Simple	$7.95		1-57248-472-1	How to File Your Own Bankruptcy (6E)	$21.95
	1-57248-460-8	The Alternative Minimum Tax	$14.95		1-57248-390-3	How to Form a Nonprofit Corporation (3E)	$24.95
	1-57248-349-0	The Antique and Art Collector's Legal Guide	$24.95		1-57248-520-5	How to Make Money on Foreclosures	$16.95
	1-57248-347-4	Attorney Responsibilities & Client Rights	$19.95		1-57248-479-9	How to Parent with Your Ex	$12.95
	1-57248-482-9	The Childcare Answer Book	$12.95		1-57248-379-2	How to Register Your Own Copyright (5E)	$24.95
	1-57248-382-2	Child Support	$18.95		1-57248-394-6	How to Write Your Own Living Will (4E)	$18.95
	1-57248-487-X	Cómo Comprar su Primera Casa	$8.95		1-57248-156-0	How to Write Your Own	$24.95
	1-57248-488-8	Cómo Conseguir Trabajo en los Estado Unidos	$8.95			Premarital Agreement (3E)	
	1-57248-148-X	Cómo Hacer su Propio Testamento	$16.95		1-57248-504-3	HR for Small Business	$14.95
	1-57248-532-9	Cómo Iniciar su Propio Negocio	$8.95		1-57248-230-3	Incorporate in Delaware from Any State	$26.95
	1-57248-462-4	Cómo Negociar su Crédito	$8.95		1-57248-158-7	Incorporate in Nevada from Any State	$24.95
	1-57248-463-2	Cómo Organizar un Presupuesto	$8.95		1-572485-31-0	The Infertility Answer Book	$16.95
	1-57248-147-1	Cómo Solicitar su Propio Divorcio	$24.95		1-57248-474-8	Inmigración a los EE.UU. Paso a Paso (2E)	$24.95
	1-57248-507-8	The Complete Book of Corporate Forms (2E)	$29.95		1-57248-400-4	Inmigración y Ciudadanía en los EE. UU.	$16.95
	1-57248-383-0	The Complete Book of Insurance	$18.95			Preguntas y Respuestas	
	1-57248-499-3	The Complete Book of Personal Legal Forms	$24.95		1-57248-523-X	The Law (In Plain English)® for Restaurants	$16.95
	1-57248-528-0	The Complete Book of Real Estate Contracts	$18.95		1-57248-377-6	The Law (In Plain English)® for Small Business	$19.95
	1-57248-500-0	The Complete Credit Repair Kit	$19..95		1-57248-476-4	The Law (In Plain English)® for Writers	$14.95
	1-57248-458-6	The Complete Hiring and Firing Handbook	$19.95		1-57248-453-5	Law 101	$16.95
	1-57248-484-5	The Complete Home-Based Business Kit	$14.95		1-57248-374-1	Law School 101	$16.95
	1-57248-353-9	The Complete Kit to Selling Your Own Home	$18.95		1-57248-509-4	Legal Research Made Easy (4E)	$24.95
	1-57248-229-X	The Complete Legal Guide to Senior Care	$21.95		1-57248-449-7	The Living Trust Kit	$21.95
	1-57248-498-5	The Complete Limited Liability Company Kit	$24.95		1-57248-165-X	Living Trusts and Other Ways to	$24.95
	1-57248-391-1	The Complete Partnership Book	$24.95			Avoid Probate (3E)	
	1-57248-201-X	The Complete Patent Book	$26.95		1-57248-511-6	Make Your Own Simple Will (4E)	$26.95
	1-57248-514-0	The Complete Patent Kit	$39.95		1-57248-486-1	Making Music Your Business	$18.95
	1-57248-369-5	Credit Smart	$18.95		1-57248-186-2	Manual de Beneficios para el Seguro Social	$18.95
	1-57248-163-3	Crime Victim's Guide to Justice (2E)	$21.95		1-57248-220-6	Mastering the MBE	$16.95
	1-57248-251-6	The Entrepreneur's Internet Handbook	$21.95		1-57248-455-1	Minding Her Own Business, 4E	$14.95
	1-57248-235-4	The Entrepreneur's Legal Guide	$26.95		1-57248-480-2	The Mortgage Answer Book	$14.95
	1-57248-160-9	Essential Guide to Real Estate Leases	$18.95		1-57248-167-6	Most Val. Business Legal Forms	$21.95
	1-57248-375-X	Fathers' Rights	$19.95			You'll Ever Need (3E)	
	1-57248-517-5	File Your Own Divorce (6E)	$24.95		1-57248-388-1	The Power of Attorney Handbook (5E)	$22.95
	1-57248-553-1	Financing Your Small Business	$16.95		1-57248-332-6	Profit from Intellectual Property	$28.95
	1-57248-459-4	Fired, Laid-Off or Forced Out	$14.95		1-57248-329-6	Protect Your Patent	$24.95
	1-57248-516-7	Form Your Own Corporation (5E)	$29.95		1-57248-376-8	Nursing Homes and Assisted Living Facilities	$19.95
	1-57248-502-7	The Frequent Traveler's Guide	$14.95		1-57248-385-7	Quick Cash	$14.95
	1-57248-331-8	Gay & Lesbian Rights	$26.95		1-57248-350-4	El Seguro Social Preguntas y Respuestas	$16.95
	1-57248-526-4	Grandparents' Rights (4E)	$24.95		1-57248-386-5	Seniors' Rights	$19.95
	1-57248-475-6	Guía de Inmigración a Estados Unidos (4E)	$24.95		1-57248-527-2	Sexual Harassment in the Workplace	$18.95
	1-57248-187-0	Guía de Justicia para Víctimas del Crimen	$21.95		1-57248-217-6	Sexual Harassment: Your Guide to Legal Action	$18.95
	1-57248-253-2	Guía Esencial para los Contratos de	$22.95		1-57248-378-4	Sisters-in-Law	$16.95
		Arrendamiento de Bienes Raices			1-57248-219-2	The Small Business Owner's Guide to Bankruptcy	$21.95
	1-57248-334-2	Homeowner's Rights	$19.95			**Form Continued on Following Page**	**SubTotal____**

Qty	ISBN	Title	Retail
____	1-57248-529-9	Sell Your Home Without a Broker	$14.95
____	1-57248-395-4	The Social Security Benefits Handbook (4E)	$18.95
____	1-57248-216-8	Social Security Q&A	$12.95
____	1-57248-521-3	Start Your Own Law Practice	$16.95
____	1-57248-328-8	Starting Out or Starting Over	$14.95
____	1-57248-525-6	Teen Rights (and Responsibilities) (2E)	$14.95
____	1-57248-457-8	Tax Power for the Self-Employed	$17.95
____	1-57248-366-0	Tax Smarts for Small Business	$21.95
____	1-57248-530-2	Unmarried Parents' Rights (3E)	$16.95
____	1-57248-362-8	U.S. Immigration and Citizenship Q&A	$18.95
____	1-57248-387-3	U.S. Immigration Step by Step (2E)	$24.95
____	1-57248-392-X	U.S.A. Immigration Guide (5E)	$26.95
____	1-57248-478-0	¡Visas! ¡Visas! ¡Visas!	$9.95
____	1-57248-477-2	The Weekend Landlord	$16.95
____	1-57248-557-4	The Weekend Real Estate Investor	$14.95
____	1-57248-554-X	What They Don't Teach You in College	$12.95
____	1-57248-451-9	What to Do—Before "I DO"	$14.95
____	1-57248-518-3	The Wills and Trusts Kit (2E)	$29.95
____	1-57248-473-X	Winning Your Personal Injury Claim (3E)	$24.95
____	1-57248-225-7	Win Your Unemployment Compensation Claim (2E)	$21.95
____	1-57248-333-4	Working with Your Homeowners Association	$19.95
____	1-57248-380-6	Your Right to Child Custody, Visitation and Support (3E)	$24.95
____	1-57248-505-1	Your Rights at Work	$14.95

CALIFORNIA TITLES

Qty	ISBN	Title	Retail
____	1-57248-489-6	How to File for Divorce in CA (5E)	$26.95
____	1-57248-464-0	How to Settle and Probate an Estate in CA (2E)	$28.95
____	1-57248-336-9	How to Start a Business in CA (2E)	$21.95
____	1-57248-194-3	How to Win in Small Claims Court in CA (2E)	$18.95
____	1-57248-246-X	Make Your Own CA Will	$18.95
____	1-57248-397-0	Landlords' Legal Guide in CA (2E)	$24.95
____	1-57248-515-9	Tenants' Rights in CA (2E)	$24.95

FLORIDA TITLES

Qty	ISBN	Title	Retail
____	1-57248-396-2	How to File for Divorce in FL (8E)	$28.95
____	1-57248-490-X	How to Form a Limited Liability Co. in FL (3E)	$24.95
____	1-57071-401-0	How to Form a Partnership in FL	$22.95
____	1-57248-456-X	How to Make a FL Will (7E)	$16.95
____	1-57248-339-3	How to Start a Business in FL (7E)	$21.95
____	1-57248-204-4	How to Win in Small Claims Court in FL (7E)	$18.95
____	1-57248-540-X	Incorporate in FL (7E)	$29.95
____	1-57248-381-4	Land Trusts in Florida (7E)	$29.95
____	1-57248-491-8	Landlords' Rights and Duties in FL (10E)	$24.95
____	1-57248-558-2	Probate and Settle an Estate in FL (6E)	$29.95

GEORGIA TITLES

Qty	ISBN	Title	Retail
____	1-57248-340-7	How to File for Divorce in GA (5E)	$21.95
____	1-57248-493-4	How to Start a Business in GA (4E)	$21.95

ILLINOIS TITLES

Qty	ISBN	Title	Retail
____	1-57248-244-3	Child Custody, Visitation, and Support in IL	$24.95
____	1-57248-510-8	File for Divorce in IL (4E)	$26.95
____	1-57248-170-6	How to Make an IL Will (3E)	$16.95
____	1-57248-265-9	How to Start a Business in IL (4E)	$21.95
____	1-57248-252-4	Landlord's Legal Guide in IL	$24.95

MARYLAND, VIRGINIA AND THE DISTRICT OF COLUMBIA

Qty	ISBN	Title	Retail
____	1-57248-240-0	How to File for Divorce in MD, VA, and DC	$28.95
____	1-57248-359-8	How to Start a Business in MD, VA, or DC	$21.95

MASSACHUSETTS TITLES

Qty	ISBN	Title	Retail
____	1-57248-115-3	How to Form a Corporation in MA	$24.95
____	1-57248-466-7	How to Start a Business in MA (4E)	$21.95
____	1-57248-398-9	Landlords' Legal Guide in MA (2E)	$24.95

MICHIGAN TITLES

Qty	ISBN	Title	Retail
____	1-57248-467-5	How to File for Divorce in MI (4E)	$24.95
____	1-57248-182-X	How to Make a MI Will (3E)	$16.95
____	1-57248-468-3	How to Start a Business in MI (4E)	$21.95

MINNESOTA TITLES

Qty	ISBN	Title	Retail
____	1-57248-142-0	How to File for Divorce in MN	$21.95
____	1-57248-179-X	How to Form a Corporation in MN	$24.95
____	1-57248-178-1	How to Make a MN Will (2E)	$16.95

NEW JERSEY TITLES

Qty	ISBN	Title	Retail
____	1-57248-512-4	HFile for Divorce in NJ	$24.95
____	1-57248-448-9	How to Start a Business in NJ	$21.95

NEW YORK TITLES

Qty	ISBN	Title	Retail
____	1-57248-193-5	Child Custody, Visitation and Support in NY	$26.95
____	1-57248-351-2	File for Divorce in NY	$26.95
____	1-57248-249-4	How to Form a Corporation in NY (2E)	$24.95
____	1-57248-401-2	How to Make a NY Will (3E)	$16.95
____	1-57248-468-1	How to Start a Business in NY (3E)	$21.95
____	1-57248-198-6	How to Win in Small Claims Court in NY (2E)	$18.95
____	1-57248-122-6	Tenants' Rights in NY	$21.95

NORTH CAROLINA AND SOUTH CAROLINA TITLES

Qty	ISBN	Title	Retail
____	1-57248-508-6	How to File for Divorce in NC (4E)	$26.95
____	1-57248-371-7	How to Start a Business in NC or SC	$24.95
____	1-57248-091-2	Landlords' Rights & Duties in NC	$21.95

OHIO TITLES

Qty	ISBN	Title	Retail
____	1-57248-503-5	How to File for Divorce in OH (3E)	$24.95
____	1-57248-174-9	How to Form a Corporation in OH	$24.95
____	1-57248-173-0	How to Make an OH Will	$16.95

PENNSYLVANIA TITLES

Qty	ISBN	Title	Retail
____	1-57248-242-7	Child Custody, Visitation and Support in PA	$26.95
____	1-57248-495-0	How to File for Divorce in PA (4E)	$26.95
____	1-57248-358-X	How to Form a Corporation in PA	$24.95
____	1-57248-094-7	How to Make a PA Will (2E)	$16.95
____	1-57248-357-1	How to Start a Business in PA (3E)	$21.95
____	1-57248-245-1	Landlords' Legal Guide in PA	$24.95

TEXAS TITLES

Qty	ISBN	Title	Retail
____	1-57248-171-4	Child Custody, Visitation, and Support in TX	$22.95
____	1-57248-399-7	How to File for Divorce in TX (4E)	$24.95
____	1-57248-470-5	How to Form a Corporation in TX (3E)	$24.95
____	1-57248-496-9	How to Probate and Settle an Estate in TX (4E)	$26.95
____	1-57248-471-3	How to Start a Business in TX (4E)	$21.95
____	1-57248-111-0	How to Win in Small Claims Court in TX (2E)	$16.95
____	1-57248-355-5	Landlords' Legal Guide in TX	$24.95
____	1-57248-513-2	Write Your Own TX Will (4E)	$16.95

WASHINGTON TITLES

Qty	ISBN	Title	Retail
____	1-57248-522-1	File for Divorce in WA	$24.95

SubTotal This page _____

SubTotal previous page _____

Shipping — $5.00 for 1st book, $1.00 each additional _____

Illinois residents add 6.75% sales tax _____

Connecticut residents add 6.00% sales tax _____

Total _____